Endangered Wildlife and Plants of the World

Volume 3
CLA–DEE

Marshall Cavendish
New York • London • Toronto • Sydney

Marshall Cavendish Corporation
99 White Plains Road
Tarrytown, NY 10591-9001

Created by Brown Partworks Ltd.
Project Editor: Anne Hildyard
Associate Editors: Paul Thompson, Amy Prior
Managing Editor: Tim Cooke
Design: Whitelight
Picture Research: Helen Simm
Index Editor: Kay Ollerenshaw
Production Editor: Matt Weyland
Illustrations: Barbara Emmons, Jackie Harland, Tracy Williamson

Library of Congress Cataloging-in-Publication Data

Endangered wildlife and plants of the world
p.cm.
Includes bibliographical references (p.).
ISBN 0-7614-7194-4 (set)
ISBN 0-7614-7197-9 (vol. 3)
1. Endangered species--Encyclopedias. I. Marshall Cavendish Corporation.

QH75.E68 2001
333.95'22'03--dc21
99-086194

Printed in Malaysia
Bound in the United States of America
07 06 05 04 03 02   7 6 5 4 3 2

TABLE OF CONTENTS/VOLUME 3

ESA and IUCN

In this set of endangered animals and plants, each species, where appropriate, is given an ESA status and an IUCN status. The sources consulted to determine the status of each species are the Endangered Species List maintained by the U.S. Fish and Wildlife Service and the Red Lists compiled by IUCN–The World Conservation Union, which is a worldwide organization based in Switzerland.

ENDANGERED SPECIES ACT

The Endangered Species Act (ESA) was initially passed by the U.S. Congress in 1973, and reauthorized in 1988. The aim of the ESA is to rescue species that are in danger of extinction due to human action and to conserve the species and their ecosystems. Endangered plants and animals are listed by the U.S. Fish and Wildlife Service (USFWS), which is part of the Department of Interior. Once a species is listed, the USFWS is required to develop recovery plans, and ensure that the threatened species is not further harmed by any actions of the U.S. government or U.S. citizens. The act specifically forbids the buying, selling, transporting, importing, or exporting of any listed species. It also bans the taking of any listed species in the U.S. and its territories, on both private and public lands. Violators can face heavy fines or imprisonment. However, the ESA requires that the protection of the species is balanced with economic factors.

The ESA recognizes two categories of risk for species:

Endangered: A species that is in danger of extinction throughout all or a significant part of its range.

Threatened: A species that is likely to become endangered in the foreseeable future.

RECOVERY

Recovery takes place when the decline of the endangered or threatened species is halted or reversed, and the circumstances that caused the threat have been removed. The ultimate aim is the recovery of the species to the point where it no longer requires protection under the act.

Recovery can take a long time. Because the decline of the species may have occurred over centuries, the loss cannot be reversed overnight. There are many factors involved: the number of individuals of the species that remain in the wild, how long it takes the species to mature and reproduce, how much habitat is remaining, and whether the reasons for the decline are clear cut and understood. Recovery plans employ a wide range of strategies that involve the following: reintroduction of species into formerly occupied habitat, land aquisition and management, captive breeding, habitat protection, research, population counts, public education projects, and assistance for private landowners.

SUCCESS STORIES

Despite the difficulties, recovery programs do work, and the joint efforts of the USFWS, other federal and state agencies, tribal governments, and private landowners have not been in vain. Only seven species, less than 1 percent of all the species listed between 1968 and 1993, are now known to be extinct. The other 99 percent of listed species have not been lost to extinction, and this confirms the success of the act.

There are some good examples of successful recovery plans. In 1999, the peregrine falcon, the bald eagle, and the Aleutian goose were removed from the endangered species list. The falcon's numbers have risen dramatically. In 1970, there were only 39 pairs of falcons in the United States. By 1999, the number had risen to 1,650 pairs. The credit for the recovery goes to the late Rachel

Carson, who highlighted the dangers of DDT, and also to the Endangered Species Act, which enabled the federal government to breed falcons in captivity, and took steps to protect their habitat.

Young bald eagles were also successfully translocated into habitat that they formerly occupied, and the Aleutian Canada goose has improved due to restoration of its habitat and reintroduction into former habitat.

IUCN–THE WORLD CONSERVATION UNION

The IUCN (International Union for Conservation of Nature) was established in 1947. It is an alliance of governments, governmental agencies, and nongovernmental agencies. The aim of the IUCN is to help and encourage nations to conserve wildlife and natural resources. Organizations such as the Species Survival Commission is one of several IUCN commissions that assesses the conservation status of species and subspecies globally. Taxa that are threatened with extinction are noted and steps are taken for their conservation by programs designed to save, restore, and manage species and their habitats. The Survival Commission is committed to providing objective information on the status of globally threatened species, and produces two publications: the *IUCN Red List of Threatened Animals*, and the *IUCN Red List of Threatened Plants*. They are compiled from scientific data and provide the status of threatened species, depending on their existence in the wild and threats that undermine that existence. The lists for plants and animals differ slightly.

The categories from the *IUCN Red List of Threatened Animals* used in *Endangered Wildlife and Plants of the World* are as follows:

Extinct: A species is extinct when there is no reasonable doubt that the last individual has died.

Extinct in the wild: A species that is known only to survive in captivity, well outside its natural range.

Critically endangered: A species that is facing an extremely high risk of extinction in the wild in the immediate future.

Endangered: A species that is facing a very high risk of extinction in the wild in the near future.

Vulnerable: A species that is facing a high risk of extinction in the wild in the medium-term future.

Lower risk: A species that does not satisfy the criteria for designation as critically endangered, endangered, or vulnerable. Species included in the lower risk category can be separated into three subcategories:

Conservation dependent: A species that is part of a conservation program. Without the program, the species would qualify for one of the threatened categories within five years.

Near threatened: A species that does not qualify for conservation dependent, but is close to qualifying as vulnerable.

Least concern: A species that does not qualify for conservation dependent or near threatened.

Data deficient: A species on which there is inadequate information to make an asssessment of risk of extinction. Because there is a possibility that future research will show that the species is threatened, more information is required.

The categories from the *IUCN Red List of Threatened Plants*, used in *Endangered Wildlife and Plants of the World*, are as follows:

Extinct: A species that has not definitely been located in the wild during the last 50 years.

Endangered: A species whose survival is unlikely if the factors that threaten it continue. Included are species whose numbers have been reduced to a critical level, or whose habitats have been so drastically reduced that they are deemed to be in immediate danger of extinction. Also included in this category are species that may be extinct but have definitely been seen in the wild in the past 50 years.

Vulnerable: A species that is thought likely to move into the endangered category in the near future if the factors that threaten it remain.

Rare: A species with small world populations that are not at present endangered or vulnerable, but are at risk. These species are usually in restricted areas or are thinly spread over a larger range.

Giant Clam
(Tridacna gigas)

IUCN: Vulnerable

Class: Bivalvia
Order: Veneroida
Family: Tridacnidae
Length: 4½ ft. (1.4 m)
Weight: 506 lb. (230 kg)
Habitat: Shallow corals
Range: Tropical and subtropical waters of the western Pacific and Indian Oceans

Southern Giant Clam
(Tridacna derasa)

IUCN: Vulnerable

Class: Bivalvia
Order: Veneroida
Family: Tridacnidae
Length: 2 ft. (0.5 m)
Weight: Unknown
Habitat: Shallow corals
Range: Tropical and subtropical waters of the western Pacific and southern Indian Oceans

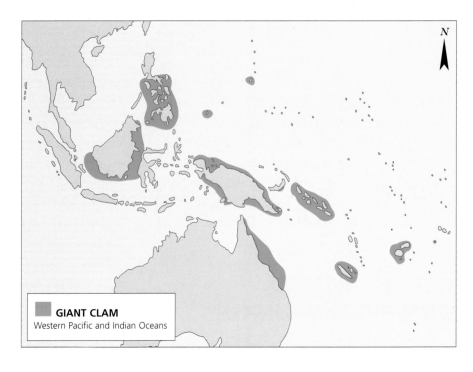

GIANT CLAM
Western Pacific and Indian Oceans

GIANT CLAMS ARE among the most fascinating shallow reef inhabitants due to their richly colored mantle tissue inside the large, solid, wavy shells. The mantle—a fold of flesh that secretes the shell—is embedded with millions of symbiotic microalgae, zooxanthellae, that provide the clams with nutrients through photosynthesis. The zooxanthellae gain nutrients from the waste products of the clam, and the clam digests surplus zooxanthellae.

The giant clam, *Tridacna gigas*, is the largest bivalve mollusk in the world, reaching around 4½ feet (1.4 meters) in length and weighing 506 pounds (230 kilograms). Its natural range is the tropical and subtropical waters of the western Pacific and Indian Oceans, where it lives among shallow corals. The southern giant clam, *T. derasa*, is confined to the southern Indian and western Pacific Oceans, where it also lives among shallow corals.

A southern giant clam, *Tridacna derasa*, clings to a coral reef in Papua New Guinea. This species suffers from overfishing in some areas.

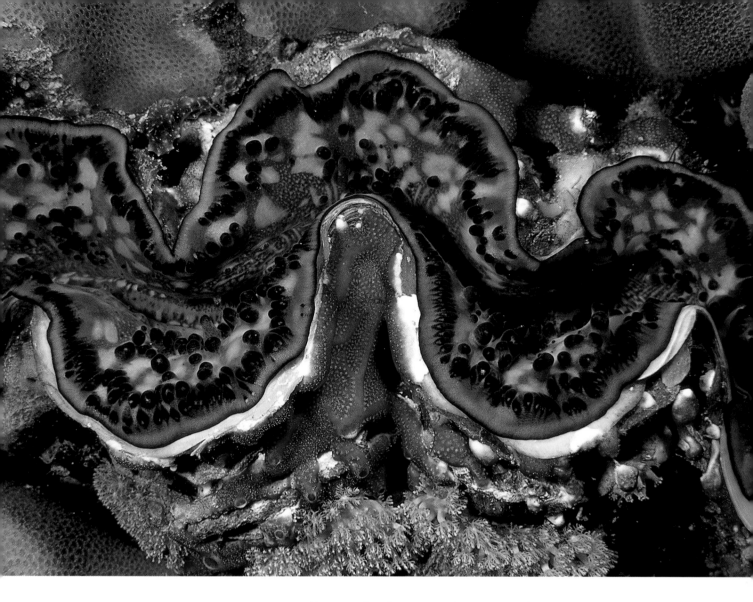

The giant clam, *Tridacna gigas*, has a red, wavy shell and blue mantle. It is still a taboo in many Pacific Islands to eat the giant clam, as a sign of respect to the most impressive animal on the reef.

Giant clams are hermaphrodites, and spawning occurs throughout the year on the equator, though may be seasonal elsewhere. Each animal produces about 500 million eggs in one spawning. Fertilized eggs hatch into tiny planktonic larvae that develop through a number of distinct stages, then settle and metamorphose into juveniles. Giant clams usually live together in groups. The population is characterized by fast-growing larval and juvenile stages with high mortality and slow-growing adults with low mortality. Reseeding of juvenile giant clams to the reef is slow, despite the high number of eggs produced.

Values and threats

In the South Pacific, shells of the giant clam are more valuable than the meat. The converse is true for the southern giant clam, which is intensively fished by local inhabitants mainly for the meat. Southern giant clams are widely considered the most desirable of the giant clams for food. Both of these clam species are vulnerable to intensive fishing pressures because they are relatively easy to see and take. Moreover, the young animals require many years to grow to maturity and survive in only moderate numbers.

The stocks of the giant clam are depleted in many areas of their range, and in recent decades they virtually disappeared from some areas, such as Guam, mainly due to over-exploitation of the reef resources. This led to interest in the introduction of cultured juveniles to restock and sustain all the depleted areas. There is also increasing legislation to protect the southern Indian and western Pacific Oceans from the poaching and smuggling of giant clams.

The International Centre for Living Aquatic Resources Management (ICLARM) has run a

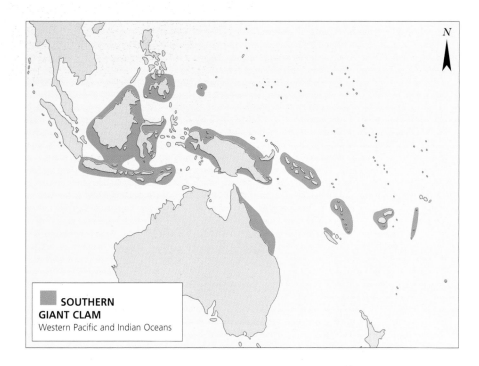

SOUTHERN
GIANT CLAM
Western Pacific and Indian Oceans

localities. The giant clam is also successfully farmed and has been reintroduced to the wild in the Solomon Islands, Guam, Australia, Fiji, and elsewhere.

Clam gardens are an old tradition in many South Pacific islands and have increased in recent years. The villagers collect clams and keep them in shallow water close to their homes. They store them for food consumption in bad weather, growing them to a bigger size before eating them. Many villagers believe that clam gardening also benefits the water quality around the clams as they circulate and filter the water. Cultivation and clam gardening can thus be beneficial to stocks of giant clams, but for now the giant clam and the southern giant clam remain overfished in many areas.

Salma Shalla

number of cultivation trials throughout the region. By the early 1980s, mass culture of the southern giant clam was a reality at the Micronesian Mariculture Centre in Palau. Since then, this clam has been successfully cultivated and reseeded on the coral reefs in the Solomon Islands, Indonesia, Fiji, Tonga, and other

Leafy Prairie-clover
(Dalea foliosa)

ESA: Endangered

IUCN: Vulnerable

Class: Magnoliopsida
Family: Leguminosae
Stem: Slender, up to 1½ ft. (0.5 m)
Leaves: Up to 1.8 in. (4.5 cm) long; compound, with pairs of narrow elliptical leaflets
Flowers: Small purple flowers borne in dense spikes, from late July through August
Habitat: Rocky glens and prairie fringes
Range: Southeastern United States

The prairie habitat of the leafy prairie-clover has come under intense pressure from agriculture and construction.

THE LEAFY PRAIRIE-CLOVER is a perennial plant that flowers in late July and August. Small purple flowers are borne in dense spikes at the end of the flower stems. Seeds ripen by early October and then the green parts of the plant die to the ground for

the winter. This species grows in the rocky cedar glades of Alabama and Tennessee, where the plants seem to prefer deeper soils of prairie-like areas.

In Illinois the species now grows only in prairie remnants on patches of thin soil over dolomite rock along the Des Plaines River. In general, limestone glades, like those where the leafy prairie-clover grows, form part of an unusual habitat type that occurs along the fringes of tall grass prairie in widely scattered parts of the American Midwest. Glades are nowhere abundant and in many states these habitats are under threat.

There are currently two populations of leafy prairie-clover in Alabama and the species has been lost from two other known locations within the state. In Illinois three remnant populations of the species are known in Will County. It is also very rare in Tennessee, where nine leafy prairie-clover populations are believed to occur. Most of the Tennessee populations are very small with fewer than fifty plants.

The leafy prairie-clover was listed as endangered under the U.S. Endangered Species Act in 1991. Reasons for the decline of

LEAFY PRAIRIE-CLOVER
North America

the species have been destruction and modification of the habitat, due, for example, to construction and use of the habitat to pasture livestock. The largest population in Tennessee grows on land acquired as part of the proposed Columbia Dam project in Maury County. Work on the project has been delayed while the Tennessee Valley Authority develops a conservation plan for the endangered

species of mussel found within the area. Various options are being considered with different possible outcomes for the leafy prairie-clover.

Listing under the U.S. Endangered Species Act now means that the leafy prairie-clover is protected and a recovery plan has been prepared for the species. There have already been some successes on its road to recovery. Two of the three remaining sites in Illinois are being managed to protect the species. In Tennessee two of the nine known sites are partially protected, one through acquisition by The Nature Conservancy. This species is also represented in the National Collection of Endangered Plants maintained by the U.S. Center for Plant Conservation.

Sara Oldfield

COCKATOOS

Class: Aves

Order: Psittaciformes

Family: Cacatuidae

Subfamily: Cacatuinae

Cockatoos make up a natural grouping of Old World parrots. Some ornithologists place them in a family of their own, the Cacatuidae. Other experts combine them into the larger parrot family, the Psittacidae. Depending on which characteristics are studied, the cockatoo group contains from 12 to 18 species. All of them live in Australia, Papua New Guinea, Indonesia, the Philippines, or on neighboring islands.

All cockatoos have crests on top of their heads. These crests may be quite large and elaborate or small, according to

the species. Typically cockatoos erect their crests immediately after alighting after a flight or when alarmed. The crests also serve in the courtship ritual and as a means for mates to recognize each other. Cockatoos all have powerful beaks, which they use to eat large fruits and hard, stony seeds. Many species seek insects in rotten wood.

Most cockatoos lead arboreal lives. Nests are made in tree hollows or other cavities, often quite high above ground. A few species descend to the ground to drink and find food.

Some 11 to 13 cockatoos belong to the genus *Cacatua*. Often called the white cockatoos, they have become very popular as cage birds. Because so many of these species are confined to small areas with naturally small populations, they are very vulnerable to excessive trapping and collecting.

Red-vented Cockatoo

(Cacatua haematuropygia)

IUCN: Critically endangered

Length: 12 in. (30 cm)
Weight: Unknown
Clutch size: Unknown
Incubation: Unknown
Diet: Fruits and seeds
Habitat: Forests near croplands
Range: Philippine Islands

THE RED-VENTED COCKATOO gets its name from the brightly colored patch between the tail and belly. The feathered area immediately surrounding this part of the body and extending back under the tail is called the crissum. The crissum has an opening, or vent, and this area is colored bright orange red, hence the name "red-vented" cockatoo.

The red-vented cockatoo is a striking bird. It is white overall with a faintly yellow or yellow-pink cheek. There is a small crest, and the base of the crest feathers are yellow and pink. The underside of this bird's flight feathers are pale yellow, while the underside of its tail feathers are bright yellow. This cockatoo has a bright orange-red patch underneath the base of the tail feathers. The bare

skin around the eyes is white or a very pale blue. The beak is pale gray. The feet and toes are gray, and males and immatures of the species have brown eyes, but the female's eyes are reddish brown.

Birds do not have the same anatomy as mammals. Their anus and urethra empty into an organ called the cloaca. Body wastes are eliminated from the cloaca through the vent.

Once widespread over the Philippines, the red-vented cockatoo has declined dramatically and is now considered to be one

of the Philippines' most endangered birds. Today, it is absent from as much as 98 percent of its former range, with a total population estimated at only 4,000. There are around 20 red-vented cockatoos in zoos and an estimated 300 held by private aviculturists. The red-vented cockatoo has probably declined for reasons similar to those affecting other forest and woodland birds in that part of the world. The cutting and clearing of forests reduces the amount of habitat available to support forest birds. The red-vented cockatoo is known to raid crops and is particularly fond of corn. As an agricultural nuisance, the red-vented cockatoo may be subject to shooting, trapping, or poisoning by farmers protecting their crops from damage.

The red-vented cockatoo probably figures in the pet trade, too. The international market for parrots—both legal and illegal—encourages local residents to capture wild birds for sale. Although CITES (Convention on International Trade in Endangered Species of Wild Fauna and Flora) extends some protection to many species, enforcing the treaty can be very difficult. Further, not all pet trade is international. Many local citizens enjoy cockatoos as pets.

As the demand increases for human living space, agricultural productivity, forest lumber products, and pets, birds such as the red-vented cockatoo will continue to decline.

The rich pink color of the salmon-crested cockatoo makes it a striking and unusual bird. Its plumage makes it a favorite among bird watchers.

Salmon-crested Cockatoo
(Cacatua moluccensis)

IUCN: Vulnerable

Length: 20 in. (51 cm)
Weight: Unknown
Clutch size: Unknown
Incubation: 30 days (one egg observed in captivity)
Diet: Fruits, seeds, possibly insects
Habitat: Forests, forest edges, and woodlands
Range: Seram, Saparua, and Haruku in the southern Molucca Islands of Indonesia

PEOPLE KNOW VERY little about the natural history of the salmon-crested cockatoo, but the bird is known for its beauty and its ability to peel young coconuts. Its softly hued, salmon-pink plumage makes this cockatoo a favorite among cage-bird fanciers, so the species commands good prices. Plantation managers are less impressed by the bird's beauty than by its appetite for coconuts and would consider it a pest. The cockatoo tears away the husks, then gnaws at the inner shell until it makes a hole. The bird then feeds on the coconut milk and pulp.

If wild salmon-crested cockatoos behave like other cockatoo species, they probably occur most often in pairs or small flocks. Concentrated food supplies such as coconut plantations may attract many small flocks. Together, they may inflict considerable damage.

The salmon-crested cockatoo is a rich pink or pinkish salmon color overall. The wings are paler, almost white. The undersides of the flight feathers are dark salmon pink at the base, while the undersides of the tail feathers are pale yellow orange or rich salmon pink. The bare skin around the bird's eyes is white or very pale blue. There is a large, prominent crest with very rich and dark salmon pink on the undersides. The feet and toes are gray, and the beak is dark gray.

The salmon-crested cockatoo lives primarily on three Indonesian islands. Seram, the largest, stretches around 220 miles (354 kilometers) east to west and is only about 50 miles (80 kilometers) wide. The other two islands are much smaller, and together they probably cover only 12,000 square miles (31,080 square kilometers). This limited area represents the salmon-crested cockatoo's range. Not all of it is suitable habitat, and much of the area that is suitable has been lost to human development. The world population of salmon-crested cockatoos is thought to be more than 8,000. This species is banned in international trade under CITES. However, with continued persecution by farmers and pet traders in a small area of declining habitat, this species cannot survive indefinitely.

Tanimbar Corella (Cockatoo)
(Cacatua goffini)

IUCN: Lower risk

Length: 12½ in. (32 cm)
Weight: Unknown
Clutch size: Possibly 3–4 eggs
Incubation: Unknown
Diet: Unknown (possibly fruits, seeds, and insects as in related species)
Habitat: Forests and woodlands
Range: Tanimbar Islands of Indonesia; introduced to Kai Islands of Indonesia

IF NOT THE LEAST known of all the cockatoos, the Tanimbar corella is certainly one of the least studied. Corella is an English name given to a few cockatoos in the genus *Cacatua*.

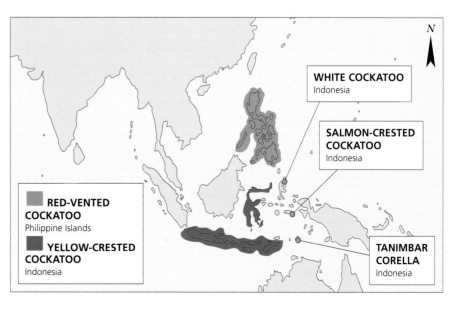

RED-VENTED COCKATOO
Philippine Islands

YELLOW-CRESTED COCKATOO
Indonesia

WHITE COCKATOO
Indonesia

SALMON-CRESTED COCKATOO
Indonesia

TANIMBAR CORELLA
Indonesia

Some bird books even use the name Tanimbar cockatoo for this species. The Tanimbar Islands are located halfway between the coast of northern Australia and the western end of New Guinea. They are among many islands that separate the Banda Sea from the Arafura Sea. The Tanimbar corella also occurs, or has occurred, on Tual in the Kai Islands almost 200 miles (322 kilometers) to the northeast, but it probably escaped or was released there.

This cockatoo is white overall with pale yellow cheeks. The crest is small, and the bases of the crest feathers are dark pink or salmon pink. The undersides of the tail and flight feathers are washed with yellow. The bare skin around the eyes is whitish, but the lore is salmon. The bird's feet and toes are dark gray, while the beak is pale gray. The male has brown eyes, while the females' eyes are a reddish brown.

The Tanimbar corella is very similar to the little corella (*Cacatua sanguinea*). Some ornithologists even consider them to be the same species. The little corella ranges in a great arc from western Australia through the north of the country and down through the interior east. A small population also exists in extreme southern New Guinea. The Tanimbar corella, then, is isolated from the little corella and occupies a vastly smaller range.

The Tanimbar corella is highly prized as a cage bird. Even if not sold into the international pet market, the bird is frequently kept by local people. The reasons for its population decline are not known for sure, but collecting for the pet trade undoubtedly plays a role. The Tanimbar corella is banned in international commercial trade under CITES and is estimated to number more than 200,000 birds.

White Cockatoo
(Cacatua alba)

IUCN: Vulnerable

Length: 18 in. (46 cm)
Weight: Unknown
Clutch size: 2 eggs in captivity
Incubation: 28–30 days in captivity
Diet: Fruits, seeds, possibly insects
Habitat: Forests
Range: Halmahera and nearby islands in the northern Molucca Islands of Indonesia

THE WHITE COCKATOO is white overall, including its large crest. The undersides of the tail feathers and flight feathers are washed with a very pale yellow. The bare skin around the eyes is pale yellow white. The feet and toes are gray, and the beak is a darker gray. The male white cockatoo has brown eyes; the female's eyes are a reddish brown.

Virtually nothing has been written of this bird's feeding or nesting habits. It is usually seen in pairs or small flocks, much the same as are other cockatoo species. The white cockatoo spends most of its time in forests, calling with a noisy screech.

The white cockatoo occupies several Moluccan islands that lie halfway between Mindanao (the large southern island of the Philippines) and the northwest tip of New Guinea. A valuable bird to parrot fanciers, the white cockatoo is trapped to satisfy their demand. Nestlings are particularly sought because when hand-reared by humans they are much tamer and easier to handle. The consequence is that few birds are left to sustain the wild population.

The peoples of the East Indies have a long tradition of keeping wild birds. Many trapped cockatoos travel no farther than the local village; others reach only Singapore or Jakarta. Protecting the white cockatoo requires more than regulating international trade—the bird needs local protection as well.

The world population of white cockatoos is unknown but is estimated to be 50,000 to 200,000 birds. Trade in this species is regulated under CITES.

Yellow-crested Cockatoo
(Cacatua sulphurea)

IUCN: Endangered

Length: 13 in. (33 cm)
Weight: Unknown
Clutch size: 3 eggs in captivity
Incubation: 24 days in captivity
Diet: Seeds, fruits, possibly flowers
Habitat: Open forests, forest edges, open farmland
Range: Indonesian islands in the eastern Java Sea and the Flores Sea

THIS COCKATOO IS white overall with yellow cheeks, crest, and bases to the neck, breast, and belly feathers. The bird has a pale yellow wash on the undersides of the flight feathers and tail. The bare skin around this cockatoo's eyes is ivory- or cream-colored, while the feet and toes are dark gray. The beak is also dark gray. Males have dark brown eyes, and females have red-brown eyes; immatures have gray eyes.

Called the "lesser sulphur-crested cockatoo" in many parrot books, the yellow-crested has six subspecies scattered across many islands. They differ in two ways from the four subspecies of the sulphur-crested cockatoo (*Cacatua galerita*) that they resemble. First, yellow-crested cockatoos are much smaller. Second, they have darker yellow on the cheeks but lighter yellow under the wings. The sulphur-crested cockatoo lives on New Guinea and in northern and eastern Australia, so the ranges of the two species do not overlap.

Travel in pairs

Adult yellow-crested cockatoos usually travel in pairs, but fledglings may remain dependent on their parents for several months. Immature birds may remain with their parents as well. Many parrots maintain a relationship with a single mate, but in many species bonds are easily broken and birds mate with other individuals. Whether this behavior applies to the yellow-crested cockatoo is not known for sure.

Larger flocks including more than one family group sometimes gather to feed. The yellow-crested cockatoo eats fruits, the seeds of fruits, and probably flowers. It also picks at the fruits of the kapok (*Ceiba pentandra*). Many cockatoo species also eat various insects, particularly larval insects, but it is not known for sure if the yellow-crested cockatoo does. Although they usually feed in treetops, they sometimes take food from the ground. Their taste for fruits has probably led them to feed on other crops besides kapok, making them unpopular with farmers.

Specific research to determine the causes for the species' decline has not been done. The pressures of limited and dwindling habitat, effects from the cage-bird trade, and killing to protect crops are certainly contributing to the yellow-crested cockatoo's decline. The total population is thought to be less than 40,000 individuals and shrinking.

Kevin Cook

COD

Class: Actinopterygii

Order: Perciformes

Family: Percichthyidae

The Australian freshwater fish known as cod are not related to the fish called cod that live in the cool oceans of the northern hemisphere. Some Australian cod are, however, in greater danger of extinction than their northern counterparts. Therefore this article focuses on these threatened freshwater species.

As a result of its geographic isolation since prehistoric times and the scarcity of fresh water there, Australia has relatively few native freshwater fish—only about 190 species, and many of these are derived from marine ancestors. The greatest number of these fish live in the warm waters of the tropical north in Queensland, the Northern Territory, and Western Australia. Fewer but significant numbers occupy the more southerly and temperate areas of New South Wales, Victoria, and South Australia. Most of the western half of the continent is desert and holds little or no freshwater.

Despite low human population density across the continent, people tend to live in the same places as many of these freshwater species, and an alarmingly high percentage of these fish (34 percent) are threatened by extinction to one degree or another. There are a number of reasons for this.

Dams play a significant role in the destruction of habitat and act as barriers to the free movement of fish in river systems. Favored breeding areas are destroyed.

Agricultural practices that lead to deforestation and overgrazing are particularly destructive because they cause erosion and siltation. Other water quality changes resulting from pollution are equally catastrophic.

Fishing pressure and competition for habitat and food from more aggressive, non-native species also threaten many of Australia's fish. Finally natural occurrences like disease outbreaks can contribute to the threat. Pollution and other human-caused factors can trigger these disease episodes.

Australia's government has introduced new laws to protect existing populations. For example, scheduled releases of water from dams during critical spawning and nursery periods should improve reproductive success. Efforts to collect more biological information about Australia's fish are increasing, and government hatcheries are attempting artificial methods to breed several species.

Clarence River Cod (Eastern Freshwater Cod)

(Maccullochella ikei)

IUCN: Endangered

Length: 28 in. (71 cm)
Reproduction: Egg layer
Habitat: Small, pristine streams
Range: New South Wales, Australia

BEFORE THE 1920s the Clarence River cod was an abundant species that spread across three large river systems. Today this species, which is also known as the eastern freshwater cod, is listed as endangered and can be found only in isolated tributaries of the Clarence River system in northern New South Wales in Australia. Unlike that of most endangered fish today, the cause of the decline of the Clarence River cod was due in large part to a very unusual natural catastrophe.

During the 1920s and 1930s enormous brushfires, triggered by lightning and followed by heavy rains and flooding, caused massive fish kills in the Clarence, Brisbane, and Richmond River systems. Many different kinds of fish perished, but human ignorance and apathy made the situation even worse. The fish's plight was increased as toxic cyanide released from nearby mining operations was washed into the rivers. In the years that followed these episodes, railroads were built across sensitive stretches of river, and construction included the use of dynamite that literally blew the Clarence River cod out of the water.

Scaly body

The Clarence River cod is closely related to the Murray cod (*Maccullochella peeli*) and the endangered trout-cod (*M. macquariensis*) and is prized as a food fish. The Clarence River cod has two dorsal fins: a spiny fin toward the front for protection from predators and a soft fin toward the tail. The fish's well-scaled body minimizes skin abrasion in the river environment. The Clarence River cod's colors are unspectacular—dark overall on the back and sides under a random pattern of small dark spots, and with a lighter belly.

Slow growth hurts

One trait that can make recovery harder for an endangered species is a slow growth and reproductive cycle. Clarence River cod have a long life span, slow growth, and relatively low production of eggs in the females. These factors help explain why other species recovered from the brushfires of the past but the Clarence River cod did not. Under ideal circumstances this species would grow normally and produce a sufficient number of eggs.

Unfortunately fisheries managers in Australia are forced to deal with a less-than-ideal situation. Techniques have recently been developed to artificially breed the Clarence River cod. These and similar efforts may be the species' best chance for continued survival.

Shrinking range

Overfishing, agricultural and urban development, predation by aggressive non-native fish, and disease have shrunk this fish's range to a fraction of its previous size. Another road block in the way of recovery for this valuable fish is the loss of a healthy genetic pool due to the cross-breeding with hatchery-raised Murray cod. Even assuming that these genetic problems can be overcome, the task of recovering and maintaining suitable habitat for the Clarence River cod is almost overwhelming.

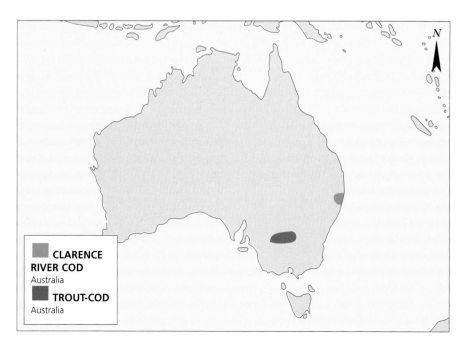

CLARENCE RIVER COD
Australia

TROUT-COD
Australia

Trout-cod

(Maccullochella macquariensis)

IUCN: Endangered

Length: 32 in. (81 cm)
Reproduction: Egg layer
Habitat: Cool streams
Range: New South Wales and Victoria, Australia

LONG SOUGHT AFTER as a game fish, the trout-cod now faces an uncertain future. The Murray-Darling river system is home to this endangered fish. Over the past 50 years, the distribution and numbers of the trout-cod have diminished significantly. The reasons for the decline of the trout-cod are numerous. Hydroelectric and flood-control dams play an important part in limiting the movement of the trout-cod and have changed temperature patterns in the entire Murray-Darling River system. Industrial and agricultural operations such as mining, farming, ranching, and logging have lowered the water quality.

In addition, the introduction of non-native fish species such as the brown trout and Eurasian perch have outcompeted the trout-cod for desirable river habitat and have preyed upon the species' eggs and young. Commercial and sport fishing have also contributed to the trout-cod's decline.

The trout-cod can grow up to seven pounds (3.2 kilogram). Its overall appearance is dark and spotted, with a blunt snout and a deep, bulbous body. The trout-cod has two dorsal fins on its back—a spiny fin for protection from predators toward the front, and a soft fin toward the tail. The fish's back, chin, throat, breast, and sides are brown, while its belly is lighter in color.

The trout-cod feeds on fish, crawfish, and other aquatic creatures, as well as mice. The reproductive habits of the trout-cod in the wild are unclear, but hatchery workers have successfully induced artificial spawning in this species with injections of steroid hormones.

Fortunately local government action may save the trout-cod from extinction.

Commercial fishing has been halted, and no fishing at all is allowed in the last stronghold of this fish—the Murray River.

William E. Manci

Coelacanth

(Latimeria chalumnae)

IUCN: Endangered

Class: Actinopterygii
Order: Coelacanthiformes
Family: Coelacanthidae
Length: 59 in. (150 cm)
Reproduction: Live bearer
Habitat: Steep, rocky bottom
Range: Off Comoros, a group of islands in the Mozambique Channel, possibly also Indonesia

BEFORE WORLD WAR II no one dreamed that such a creature from the past still existed, but in 1939 a fisherman off the coast of southeastern Africa, in an island group called Comoros, brought aboard a live specimen of a kind of fish that has endured almost unchanged for eons. The fish was a coelacanth (pronounced see-la-kanth). Truly the coelacanth is a living fossil—a creature that was thought to have become extinct over 60 million years ago.

Only the skin of the first coelacanth ever discovered was preserved for scientists to study, but after 14 years a second fish was finally found. A reward offered for other specimens led to the capture of about 100 additional coelacanths and gave researchers an incredible look back into the past.

Like people, this fish is classified as a vertebrate, or an animal that has an internal skeleton. Without a doubt the coelacanth is one of the oldest vertebrate species currently inhabiting the earth. Biologists believe that the ancestors of the coelacanth, a group called the crossopterygians that lived about 350 million years ago, gave rise to all air-breathing vertebrates, including human beings. The coelacanth is the closest link we have to a species that left the sea to walk on land. Ancestors of the coelacanth lived before the time of the dinosaurs. This is known from the fossil record.

Today's version of the coelacanth is surprisingly similar in size and structure to coelacanth fossils. The coelacanth is a large fish, and some individuals weigh as much as 160 pounds (73 kilograms). Because this fish has changed little since the time of its ancestors, the coelacanth has some peculiar physical features. Most noticeable are the lobed fins. Unlike the fins of more modern fish, the fingerlike fins of the coelacanth contain muscles and bones. This adaptation allows this fish to move quite freely in a number of positions and in unusual directions. For example, it can swim on its back and in a "headstand" position. This maneuver may aid the coelacanth to detect weak electric fields that are emitted by organisms on which it feeds, and the fish has an organ on the top of its head that is believed to be used for this purpose.

The first dorsal fin on the coelacanth's back is more typical of the fins of other fish. It is not lobed and contains spines for protection against predators. This steely blue fish has large scales and blotched skin with creamy

The fascinating coelacanth is a fish that was once known only from 60-million-year-old fossils.

coloration; the belly displays a soft shade of brown.

The structure that supports the coelacanth's body is called a notochord. It comprises nerve bundles and runs from the front of the head to the tailfin lobe. However, unlike the human spinal cord, the notochord is not sheathed in segmented bone (vertebrae). Instead, it is elastic, very flexible, and covered with a pliable protective coating.

Dweller of the deep

Because of the coelacanth's elusive nature and the lack of specimens to study, little is known about the reproductive and eating habits of this amazing creature. No coelacanth has lived longer than one day out of its natural environment, as a result of shock and decompression. It does eat other deep-water fish, and squid have been found in the

stomach. Based on the experience of fishermen in the fish's home range, it appears that this species has definite habitat preferences. It is a bottom-dweller found in steep, rocky areas in water as deep as 1,900 feet (580 meters). Coelacanths probably can be found in deeper water, but access to these fish is limited by the ruggedness of the terrain and the limitations of fishing gear.

Preserving this priceless relict of the past for future study must be a priority. More must be known about the coelacanth so that its habitat and food supply can be protected along with its population.

On July 30, 1998, American and Indonesian scientists discovered a population of coelacanths off the island of Sulawesi in Indonesia. This suggests that the coelacanth is far more widespread than was originally

thought. These Indonesia coela-canths differ from those found off southeastern Africa by being brown in color rather than steely blue. Early DNA analysis suggests that this is a new species of coelacanth and it has been named *Latimeria menadoensis*. More research is needed to verify this discovery and to ascertain whether this is definitely a new species of coelacanth.

There is great pressure and competition among prestigious aquariums around the world to be the first to successfully maintain a coelacanth. The Toba Aquarium in Japan mounted a massive $2 million effort to capture and display a pair of coelacanths. Its efforts failed but prompted a successful move to give this fish full protection under CITES. Nonetheless, an

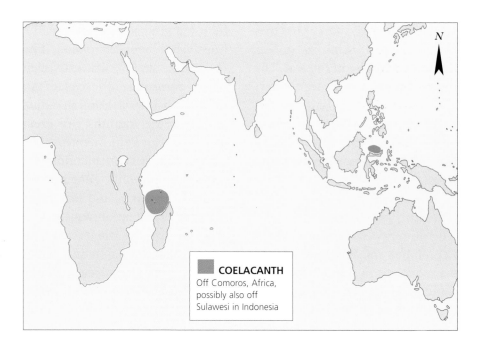

COELACANTH
Off Comoros, Africa, possibly also off Sulawesi in Indonesia

illegal market in this fish has emerged, particularly in the Orient where fluid from the fish is believed to promote longevity. Conservation initatives include research of distribution, popula-

tion numbers, and feeding behavior. Internationally coordinated studies are also under way on morphology, physiology, and growth rates.

William E. Manci

Coincya Wrightii

IUCN : Rare

Class: Magnoliopsida
Order: Capparales
Family: Brassicaceae
Life form: Herbaceous biennial to short-lived perennial
Height: Up to 3 ft. (1 m) tall
Flowering season: June to August
Habitat: Granite sea-cliffs
Range: Lundy Island, southwest Britain

THE SMALL GRANITE island of Lundy lies in the Bristol Channel 19 miles (30.5 kilometers) to the west of the British mainland. Home to less than a hundred people and several thousand sea-

birds, it is also the only place in the world where *Coincya wrightii* grows. Also known as the Lundy cabbage, this plant was first recognized as distinct in the 1930s. It occupies a somewhat isolated place in its genus, the six other species of which occur within the Mediterranean region, centered on the Iberian peninsula. One species, however, *C. monensis*, extends up the Atlantic coast of Europe as far as Scotland. The species that are most closely related to the Lundy cabbage mostly occur hundreds of miles to the southwest, in Spain.

The fact that the Lundy cabbage is the sole habitat of an endemic flea beetle, *Psylloides luridipennis*, and an endemic variety of the weevil, *Ceutorhynchus contractus*, is evidence that the species has been isolated for a

very long time. During this time a specific community of reliant animals may have co-evolved. The Lundy cabbage is thus thought to have survived here through the last cycle of glaciation in northern Europe more than 10,000 years ago.

Upright formation

This species is erect in form, branching from below and becoming woody at the base with age. It is a straggly, untidy plant up to 3 feet (1 meter) tall. When it grows in very dry soil, it can be smaller and less branched. The stem, which can be up to 5 millimeters in diameter, is covered in hairs. The leaves vary in shape up the flowering shoot. Leaves forming the initial rosette at the base of the stem are the largest, growing to a length of 6 inches

(15 centimeters). They are pinnately divided, with up to six lobes to each side of the leaf. The lower lobes are more widely spaced and distinct, with the leaf ending in a much bigger terminal lobe. Further up the stem the leaves have fewer, narrower, and more pointed lobes.

Landing platform

The flowers occur during June to September and have four petals, arranged in a crosslike form, growing to about ¾ inch long and ⅓ inch broad (20 x 8 millimeters). They are yellow in color with slightly darker veins. The flowers are sweetly scented, with nectaries providing a food source for pollinators such as bees and flies. The nectaries are found at the base of the ½-inch (1-centimeter) long calyx tube.

The fruits are dry when ripe, narrow, and about 3 inches long (8 centimeters) with a distinct beak. The fruit splits lengthwise to release the seeds, although seeds may be retained for longer in the beak. The seeds are brownish black, roughly spherical and up to 1.9 millimeters in diameter.

The pollen beetles *Meligethes aeneus* and *M. viridescens* were thought by the discoverer of the plant to be the pollination agents, however, their effect may be more destructive than beneficial. Other beetles unique to the plant may be in part responsible for pollination.

High humidity

Out-breeding is promoted by the action of a self-incompatibility gene system which ensures that,

The sweetly scented flowers of *Coincya wrightii* (Lundy cabbage) bloom in their sole habitat in the world, the island of Lundy, in southwest Britain.

for good seed set, pollen must be transferred between plants. The species grows in exposed, open plant communities subject to high atmospheric humidity during the cooler months and great heat and high light intensity during the summer. Such conditions are not commonly encountered in the British Isles and this limits the species potential range.

Even on the tiny island of Lundy, this species is not widespread, only occurring patchily on the southeastern coast, where it extends over a distance of around 1½ miles (2.5 kilometers) and over an altitudinal range of around 66–394 feet (20–120 meters). Its chief habitat is on the steep sea cliffs of granite and slate where competition and grazing pressure are low. Where grazing animals are excluded, the plant can occur locally on flatter, more fertile ground, above and back from the cliff edges.

Population size fluctuates markedly, and in recent years numbers have ranged from a low point of about 320 in 1979 up to around 4,500 in 1994. A series of warm and dry summers and mild winters may have favored the plant and caused these recent increases.

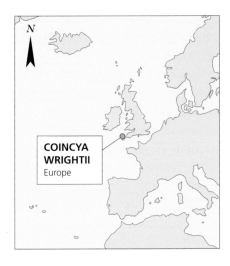

Introduced species

The chief threats to the species' survival are overgrazing and the spread of invasive shrubs. Young plants are eaten by domestic livestock as well as introduced rabbits, Sika deer, and Soay sheep. The spread of bracken (*Pteridium aquilinum*) and the alien, purple flowered *Rhododendron ponticum* locally threaten some colonies. Although there has been substantial control of the invasive shrubs under a Countryside Stewardship agreement, clearance has not so far been concentrated in areas where the Lundy cabbage occurs.

The species is in cultivation in one or two specialist collections and botanic gardens.

Fred Rumsey

COLOBUS MONKEYS

Class: Mammalia

Order: Primates

Family: Cercopithecidae

Colobus monkeys are found in various types of forest throughout central Africa. They are energetic primates, running and jumping through the trees and rarely venturing down to the forest floor. The name *colobus* is derived from a Greek word meaning "mutilated," referring to the formation of the colobus thumbs, which are either very small or absent. Without the thumb, the colobus has a more hooklike hand that aids in swinging on branches high in the treetops.

Both colobus monkeys and their close relatives, the langurs, are often called leaf-eating Old World monkeys by primate experts. Leaves require a great deal of digesting since they are mainly cellulose, a substance that is hard for the stomach to break down. To overcome this difficulty the colobus has developed a digestive system similar to that of the cow. A colobus monkey's stomach is pouched. Colobus monkeys do not, however, have cheek pouches for storing extra leaves, because leaves are always abundant where they live.

The nostrils of the colobus are close together, facing downward and outward. Its tail is not prehensile, unlike the tails of other monkey species. It does have hard pads on its bottom, which act as a cushion when the monkey is at rest.

The genus *Colobus* is divided into two groups, or subgenera: *Colobus*, made up of the various black-and-white species; and *Procolobus*, containing the red and olive species. The black colobus is a species of black-and-white colobus. There were originally thought to be many varieties of black colobus, but it is now accepted that there is just one species with many different coats. The olive colobus, once thought to be its own genus, is now generally grouped with the red colobus. Like the black-and-white colobus, the red colobus is divided into several subgroups.

The red colobus has a black body with chestnut head and arms, while the black-and-white colobus has short black hair with long white plumes that run down its sides. White fur accents the chin, cheeks, and forehead. The infants of some colobus species are born with white coats that gradually darken as they grow older.

Black-and-white colobus generally live in small groups of 8 to 15 individuals, usually one adult male, several females, and their offspring. These groups are sometimes called harems and tend to be territorial, with the males fiercely antagonistic toward one another. When males become sexually mature, they must leave their parental groups and live a solitary life until they can take over a group of their own.

Red colobus monkeys, however, have a very different social life. They tend to live in larger groups of 20 and sometimes as many as 80 animals, with many males and females. The red colobus appears to have one of the most complicated monkey societies. Red colobus are very unusual in that sexually mature females move to other groups while the males stay behind—the opposite of the black-and-white colobus.

Black-and-white colobus eat mainly leaves from a variety of trees. They don't require a large home range to get enough to eat. Red colobus prefer to eat only young leaves. This forces them to have a larger home range to obtain their food.

Black Colobus
(Colobus satanias)

ESA: Endangered

IUCN: Vulnerable

Length: 38–67 in. (97–170 cm), including tail
Weight: 12–32 lb. (5.4–14.5 kg)
Diet: Leaves
Gestation period: Unknown
Longevity: Unknown in the wild; up to 24 years in captivity
Habitat: Tropical rain forests and montane forests
Range: Congo, Gabon, Equatorial Guinea, southwest Cameroon

THERE ARE SEVERAL species of black-and-white colobus (with different colorations and markings), and all have suffered a lot of persecution from humans. They are hunted for meat, and their beautiful skins have long been used for adornment and for rugs. However, the black colobus is the rarest species of black-and-white colobus and is classified as endangered by the IUCN. Its habitat has been reduced by logging and agriculture. Logging places the black colobus in particular jeopardy. This monkey apparently does not do well in secondary forest, so transplanting it isn't possible.

The black colobus has a glossy black coat with hairs on the top of its head that are semi-erect and forward on the brow. Its facial skin is also black. It avoids eating large leaves and eats mainly young leaves and seeds.

While the black colobus may still be relatively abundant in

parts of western Gabon, all of its range is small and fragmented, and the destruction of its habitat is continuing. There are no accurate estimates of numbers for this species. However, a large population, estimated to number at least 50,000, survives in Gabon's Lope Reserve. More information on this monkey's distribution is urgently needed as is information on this monkey's status in the Congo in particular. The black colobus is banned from international commercial trade under CITES, but without preservation of its current range and protection against hunting, this species may face extinction in the early 2000s.

Red Colobus

(Procolobus badius)

The attractive coat coloration and distinctive face of this colobus monkey give it a particularly striking appearance.

IUCN: Lower risk

Weight: 11–24 lb. (5–11 kg)
Length: 34–55 in. (86–140 cm) including tail
Diet: Leaves
Gestation period: Estimated 120–150 days
Longevity: Unknown in the wild; possibly 30 years in captivity
Habitat: Rain forests, some savanna
Range: Portions of western and equatorial Africa

SOME EXPERTS DIVIDE the genus *Procolobus* into two species: the red colobus and the olive colobus. The olive colobus (*Procolobus verus*) is smaller than the black-and-white and red varieties and is characterized by its olive-gray fur. Well camouflaged in rain forests stretching from Sierra Leone to Nigeria, the olive colobus is listed as lower risk and its habitat is definitely vulnerable to deforestation.

The red colobus is listed by the World Conservation Union as lower risk, but many subspecies are also threatened. The following nine examples are all subspecies of the red colobus.

Miss Waldron's bay colobus (*Procolobus badius waldroni*)

Miss Waldron's bay colobus is listed by the World Conservation Union as critically endangered. It is found in western Africa, only in high forests in the southern Ivory Coast (east of the Bandama River) and in western Ghana. It is arboreal, found mostly in the high canopy of dense forest. It eats both mature and young leaves, but prefers a diet from the same trees favored by the local commercial timber industry. It is also hunted for its meat in Ivory Coast, and massive deforestation in Ghana between 1900 and 1950 reduced its habitat by 80 percent.

Because Miss Waldron's bay colobus has a very distinctive vocalization and travels in single file, it is an easy target for hunters. More education and study are needed if this endangered monkey is to continue to survive in the 21st century. Its population size is currently unknown, and no Miss Waldron's bay colobus exist in captivity.

Bay colobus
(*P. badius badius*)

The bay colobus lives in the high forests of Sierra Leone, Liberia, Guinea, and the Ivory Coast. In addition to leaves it also eats fruits and seeds. The major threats to its existence are hunting and loss of habitat. In Sierra Leone only four percent of its original range remains. Logging continues to decimate its home in the Gola Forest Reserve of southeastern Sierra Leone. The bay colobus represents an important source of protein for the local people, so its hunting is virtually uncontrolled there and in Liberia. Even so, it is a protected species. There are no bay colobus in captivity, and the monkey's current population is unknown.

Pennant's red colobus
(*P. badius pennanti*)

Pennant's red colobus is listed by IUCN as endangered and is found on the island of Bioko, which is part of Equatorial Guinea. In the middle of Bioko is an area known as Caldera de San Carlos, which seems to be the Pennant's main refuge. Due to a decline in the human population, there has been a slight, but promising, increase in this rare monkey's population. Hunting pressure has been reduced since firearms were outlawed in 1975.

There are no Pennant's red colobus in captivity, however, and this monkey's precise numbers are unknown. These factors, plus the fact that its range is limited by the ocean, make Pennant's endangered. If Caldera de San Carlos were established as a permanent reserve, this monkey could be better protected. Pennant's red colobus may also

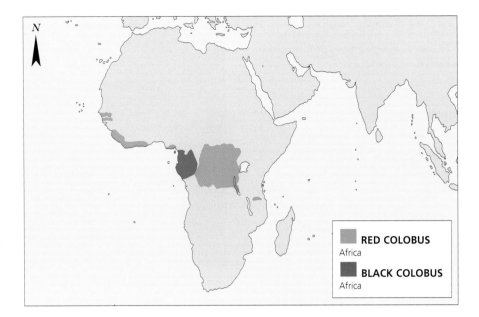

RED COLOBUS
Africa

BLACK COLOBUS
Africa

be found on the island of Pico Basile, but in total, probably fewer than 10,000 survive.

Bouvier's red colobus
(*P. badius bouvieri*)

Not found in any zoo, Bouvier's red colobus is listed by IUCN as endangered. It is found only in the Lefini Reserve in the Congo where it probably lives in the dense forests along the Lefini River and its tributaries. Bouvier's is heavily hunted for meat, and logging of its habitat is a major problem. The population of this colobus is unknown, but it is certain that very few animals remain. The Lefini Reserve is low on both funding and staff and cannot protect this monkey adequately. Without outside support, Bouvier's is probably doomed.

Preuss's red colobus
(*P. badius preussi*)

Preuss's red colobus is confined to northern Cameroon, along the Nigerian border in a forest just 37 miles (60 kilometers) wide and 75 miles (120 kilometers) long. Listed by both ESA and IUCN as endangered, the only

confirmed population of Preuss's red colobus is in the Korup National Park, where the total number of these monkeys is probably fewer than 8,000. Despite this park's protected status and the monkeys having been granted partial protection, the colobus here are still hunted at high levels. No Preuss's red colobus exist in captivity.

Uganda red colobus
(*P. badius tephrosceles*)

The Uganda red colobus is found in southwest Uganda, western Tanzania, and possibly Burundi and the eastern part of the Democratic Republic of Congo (formerly Zaire). The total population of this colobus is estimated to be in the low thousands. The monkey exists in relatively undisturbed rain forest and lives in groups of about 25 to 50 individuals. Its diet consists mainly of leaves from many different tree species, and feeding and foraging occupies about 45 percent of its daily routine. The major threats to the Uganda red are habitat destruction (often through cultivation), illegal production of

The black-and-white colobus is in more imminent danger of extinction than the red, but populations of both are severely depleted.

charcoal, and occasional forest fires. Hunting does not appear to be a problem. If the reserves and parks in its range continue to be adequately protected, the future of this monkey may be stable. The Uganda red is not known to have been bred in captivity. It is no longer listed by the World Conservation Union.

Tana River colobus
(*P. badius rufomitratus*)

The Tana River colobus is listed by both ESA and IUCN as an endangered species. This colobus is found around the Tana River in Kenya. In the late 1990s surveys indicated the total population as 1,100 to 1,300, down from an estimated 1,200 to 1,800 in 1975. More than 60 percent of these monkeys were found to occur outside the national reserve. However, overall protection measures have been improved, and related community activities have been initiated.

The Tana River colobus eats young leaves, fruit, and leaf buds and gathers in groups ranging in size from 12 to 20 individuals. Threats to its existence include forest clearance for agriculture and the widespread use of fires set to increase grass production. Another problem is the building of dams, which results in changes in the water table of the area. The effect of these changes is to increase the time it takes for the habitat to rejuvenate. The future for this colobus looks grave. Some steps have been taken to protect it, including a ban on international commercial trade

under CITES, but stringent habitat protection is also necessary if this species is to survive.

Uhehe red colobus
(*P. badius gordonorum*)

Also known as Gordon's red colobus, this monkey is endemic to Tanzania, being found only in the forest of the Udzungwa Mountains. The Uhehe red is listed as endangered by IUCN, with few animals remaining.

The Uhehe red colobus lives at high elevations and is usually found in groups of about 25 that include one or more adult males. Its diet is not very well known, but this monkey probably eats young leaves and some fruits, as do its red colobus relatives.

The Tanzania-Zambia Railway bisects the Selous Game Reserve, where the largest population of this colobus is found, dividing the monkey population in two. Agricultural encroachment, rubber plantations, fire, and hunting are all contributing factors in this monkey's decline. Uhehe reds are protected by law because they have Presidential Game status in Tanzania, but none exist in captivity and their future is in doubt. There are no

reliable estimates of numbers. However, a large population lives in the newly created Udzungwa National Park.

Zanzibar red colobus
(*P. badius kirkii*)

The Zanzibar red colobus is found only on the island of Zanzibar off the coast of Tanzania. The population is estimated at about 1,500, so this colobus is classified as endangered by both ESA and IUCN. It lives in areas of groundwater, swamp forest, and mangrove swamps. It prefers large groups of around 5 animals and is very tolerant of other neighboring groups.

The Zanzibar red colobus has unique white brows and an unpigmented nose. It is threatened by destruction of its habitat, and so far there has been no effective protection of its population. There are no Zanzibar reds in captivity, and if this monkey is to be saved, its range, including Jozani Forest Reserve, must be protected. This colobus is banned from international commercial trade under CITES. Plans are under way for an islandwide survey of this colobus.

Sarah Dart

California Condor

(Gymnogyps californianus)

ESA: Endangered

IUCN: Critically endangered

Class: Aves
Order: Falconiformes
Family: Cathartidae
Length: 45–55 in. (114–140 cm)
Weight: 20–23 lb. (9–10 kg)
Clutch size: 1 egg
Incubation: 42–50 days
Diet: Carrion
Habitat: Open brushy and semidesert country
Range: Arizona and southern California

THE HEAD AND NECK of the California condor are bare, with the skin being either pinkish or yellowish orange. The neck is ornamented with a ruff of fur-like feathers originating from the back and shoulder areas. The bird's plumage is entirely black except for white patches on the underwing linings and some white that shows above on the innermost flight feathers. In juveniles the head is either dusky or not colored.

No other bird so dramatically challenges a human being's notion of his own species' place in nature as does the California condor. This bird, better than any fossil, forces us to think about extinction as a natural process. Trilobites and dinosaurs represent extinctions that occurred without human causes or interference, for they disappeared long before the human species appeared. So if extinction is a natural process, what implications does this have for the future of the human race? Today, people tend to regard modern wildlife extinctions as a failing of humanity that spawns feelings of guilt and frustration. Since the 1970s humans have responded by attempting to prevent further extinctions. However, if extinction is a natural process, then interfering with or arresting that process may be just as unjustifiable as causing it prematurely. The future of the California condor may be the most celebrated example of how humans are dealing with the question of extinction. The California condor was already disappearing before modern civilization caught up with it two centuries ago.

The fossil record

Fossils show that since prehistoric times many condor or condorlike birds have lived and increased, then declined and disappeared. The closest relatives of the California condor were probably most prolific during the Pleistocene epoch, which began two million years ago and ended about 10,000 years ago. The California condor appears to be the last of its line. Its extinction would mean more than the end of a species—it would herald the end of a great lineage of birds.

The fossilized bones of California condors have been found in many states, including Florida and New York. This means that at one time the species occurred naturally over much of North America. By the time Europeans settled along the East Coast and began their move westward across the continent, the California condor was already in decline. The earliest settlers found the condor along the Pacific coast from southern British Columbia in Canada to the northern Baja Peninsula in Mexico. Apparently the species ranged farthest inland, and sustained its highest population, in southern California.

No one knows how many California condors were alive in the 1700s or the 1800s. Not until the 1940s were population estimates made, and by then fewer than 100 birds were believed to be alive. As the decades passed the population declined steadily enough that more precise counts were possible. By the mid-1980s only 27 wild condors survived.

Everything from the novelty of its size to its feeding and breeding habits makes the California condor particularly vulnerable to disturbance. The bird's breeding cycle is especially fragile. Only older adults breed; no immature birds have been known to do so. Condors take six years to reach maturity, but they may require more years than that to become successful breeders. Many larger bird species need several initial practice years before they acquire the parenting skills essential to raising chicks successfully. Females lay a single egg, which they may or may not replace if lost, probably depending on how late in the breeding season the egg is laid. After two months incubation, the chick remains in the nest for an additional five months, then depends on its parents for another six months after fledging. Raising a chick to this stage overlaps the following breeding season and usually keeps the same condors from

The California condor and similar birds have lived since prehistoric times. This condor was already disappearing before people began moving into California two centuries ago.

essentially eliminating whole condor generations. The population held steady until old condors began dying without young condors to replace them. Then the population fell rapidly.

First shot, then poisoned

Other factors exerted pressure on the California condors while the egg collectors were at work. Records show that 111 condors were taken between 1881 and 1910. No one can be certain how many condor killings went unrecorded. When a rancher saw a California condor feeding on a carcass, he could easily assume that the condor had killed his livestock and shoot the bird to prevent further losses. Other people shot condors for sport. Through the 1800s and into the early 1900s, killing birds of prey was considered good practice since it was commonly assumed that those birds took game that people could use for themselves.

Some ornithologists believe that the great birds also suffered indirectly from shooting, because the birds ingested lead bullet slugs or shotgun pellets when they ate carcasses that hunters had failed to recover. The ingested lead eventually caused poisoning and death. Other poisons in their habitat caused condors great harm as well, namely those used to kill livestock predators and insect pests.

The predator wars

Throughout the twentieth century, Americans made enormous efforts to tame the great wilderness of the West. Part of that challenge was to eliminate dangers, real or perceived, and to establish agriculture. Public

breeding in successive years. The usual productivity for a pair is one chick every other year.

Egg collecting, both for natural history investigations and for profit, flourished from the mid-1800s into the early 1900s. Bird species with high populations that lay several eggs per clutch—or even breed more than once per season—can sustain fairly high rates of egg collecting and suffer very little. However, laying a single egg every other year made the California condor extremely vulnerable to egg collectors. During the 30-year period from 1881 to 1910, collectors took at least 49 condor eggs, probably more.

Condors may live 40 to 45 years in captivity, probably somewhat less in the wild. This longevity may have camouflaged the effects of egg collecting for decades. The egg collectors were lands became valuable to private interests as a source of unlimited grazing for sheep and cattle, and governmental policies evolved that favored agricultural interests above other concerns. Eventually livestock producers convinced the federal government to declare war on wolves, lions, grizzly bears, eagles, and any other animal considered large enough to threaten livestock.

The federal government paid trappers for removing predators. Soon the government hired its own trappers to accomplish what private trappers could not. Predator control continued unabated as livestock producers received payment from the government for losses caused by predators. Eventually the goal became total eradication of offensive predators. Poisons such as strychnine, thallium, and sodium fluoroacetate (known as 1080) were preferred. One large carcass adequately laced with poison could kill carrion predators for weeks, even months, without requiring a trapper to visit and reset a trap.

Unfortunately large carcasses appeal to the California condor. The species evolved at a time when mammoths, bison, and camels were abundant. The California condor specialized in feeding on the rotting flesh of these great beasts. The birds could not distinguish between prey poisoned by bait and an animal that had died of natural causes. More regrettably poisons such as thallium and 1080 remain extremely potent in animals that die of it. Condors could die by eating an animal that had been killed from eating poisoned bait. No one can be certain how

many condors were unintentionally killed by poisons meant for other animals, but the extent and thoroughness of the predator control program leaves no doubt that many were lost.

Insecticides applied to food and fiber crops undoubtedly took their toll, too, although more indirectly. The pesticide known as DDT came into popular use after World War II. It worked especially well at controlling pests that damaged agricultural crops. However, DDT remains toxic for decades. When wildlife eat a little of it, the DDT is stored in their body fat and is then passed on to their predators. The DDT ingested by a predator begins to have a cumulative effect and can become lethal.

Adult birds can survive doses of DDT, but the DDT interferes with calcium use in the body. Females then lay eggs with too little calcium, and that means a thinner eggshell. Fragile eggs are easily broken and can fail to hatch. Eggs have tiny pores through which gases and water vapor are exchanged. A California condor egg may contain a normally developing embryo until water loss from the thin shell becomes too severe and the chick dies before it can hatch.

The California condor might have been able to withstand any one of these intrusions, but all of them pressuring the species at the same time was too much. Some naturalists and ornithologists recognized the condor's plight and fought on its behalf. A 1901 California law extended only modest protection by prohibiting the taking of nongame birds, their nests, or their eggs without a permit.

In 1937 the Forest Service set aside 1,200 acres (485 hectares) as the Sisquoc Condor Sanctuary in Santa Barbara County. Another 35,000 acres (14,165 hectares) were designated as the Sespe Condor Sanctuary in 1947, which was enlarged to 53,625 acres (21,700 hectares) in 1951. Some of this acreage prohibited public access. California legislation specifically protected the condor in 1954. Soon the bird was regularly monitored. The National Audubon Society hired a special condor biologist in 1965, and the U.S. Fish and Wildlife Service followed suit in 1966. Various technical committees and recovery teams operated from the 1950s into the 1970s. In 1967 the California condor was federally designated as endangered. A 1972 amendment to the Migratory Bird Treaty with Mexico extended protection to the condor. In 1973 the Endangered Species Act made it a federal offense to harm any species designated as endangered.

CALIFORNIA CONDOR
North America

▨ Historic range

The recovery efforts

A California Condor Recovery Plan was drafted, debated, and accepted as of January 1980. Since that time various measures have been taken to improve the quality of remaining condor habitat by closing roads, acquiring private lands within the habitat, providing supplemental feeding, and so on. Despite these efforts the species has continued to dwindle. To begin captive-breeding work, eight birds were captured in 1982 and six fledglings were taken in 1983. Then, in 1984 and 1985, four of the last five wild breeding pairs mysteriously disappeared. The Condor Recovery Team decided in 1986

The wingspan of the California condor is 8½ to 9 feet (2.6 to 2.75 meters). That of the larger Andean condor can be up to 10½ feet (3.2 meters).

to capture all the remaining California condors for an intensive captive-breeding program. The last wild condor was trapped in 1987. The birds have been housed at separate facilities in the San Diego Wild Animal Park and the Los Angeles Zoo to protect them from natural disaster and disease. Special handling techniques have been developed to make sure the condors remain "wild" and that they have the best possible chance to survive when released.

Bringing all the California condors into captivity was probably the most controversial wildlife management action ever taken in the United States. However, eggs have been produced, chicks have been raised, and the population has grown to 104 in captive-breeding facilities in

Escondido; Los Angeles; and Boise, Idaho. The captive-breeding colonies currently house 16 breeding pairs of condors, producing about 20 chicks each year. Reintroductions have also proved successful. Today there are 23 California condors in the wild—17 in the Los Padres National Forest in California and six in the Vermilion Cliff's region of Arizona's Coconino County.

This condor, however, remains critically endangered. It might have survived another 500 years or even longer if concern for preserving wildlife species a century ago had been as strong as it is today. Ornithologists might now be studying the natural decline of the California condor instead of battling to save it against all odds.

Kevin Cook

CONEFLOWERS

Order: Asterales

Family: Asteraceae (Compositae)

The name *coneflower* is used for several plant genera, but here we mean the genus *Echinacea*, which is nowadays well known as a popular herbal medicine used to stimulate the immune system. The genus contains nine species, all native to the eastern United States.

Long ago, Native Americans knew about coneflowers and used them medicinally. The active ingredients are known to have antiviral effects and also to stimulate white blood cell production. Coneflowers are widely cultivated for the herbal medicine industry, but wild plants are also poached by unscrupulous collectors. Collectors who dig up the plants pose a serious threat to wild populations of coneflowers, particularly the narrow-leaved purple coneflower, *E. angustifolia,* which is more potent medicinally than the more numerous and easily grown common purple coneflower, *E. purpurea.*

Coneflowers are also very popular garden plants valued for their purple, pink, white, or yellow flowers. Some of the species are very rare in the wild, with only a few, often small, populations known.

Neglected Coneflower

(Echinacea paradoxa var. *neglecta)*

IUCN: Endangered

Height: Up to 12–32 in. (30–80 cm) tall

Leaves: Basal clump and also some on the erect flowering stem, light green, strap shaped, hairy, the basal leaves up to 1 in. (2.5 cm) wide

Flowers: Solitary heads with light purple, pink, or white ray florets surrounding a central, conelike mass of disk florets

Fruit: Dry, nutlike, 1 seeded, each about 5 mm long

Habitat: Rocky prairies and open, wooded hillsides

Range: Arbuckle Mountain area of southern Oklahoma; possibly also in adjacent northern Texas

THE NEGLECTED coneflower is a showy and very rare plant closely related to the much better known yellow coneflower (*Echinacea paradoxa* var. *paradoxa,* the original variety of the species). The yellow in the English name is the paradox in the Latin name: the variety is unique in having bright yellow ray florets, whereas the usual color for coneflowers is a shade of pink, purple, or white. The yellow coneflower grows wild only in the Ozark hills of southwestern Missouri and adjacent northern Arkansas. The neglected coneflower is even rarer, known with certainty only from the Arbuckle Mountain area of southern Oklahoma.

Described for science

In September 1968, Ronald McGregor published a detailed and scholarly account of all the known species of coneflower. In January of the same year, he first described the neglected coneflower for science, in the journal *Transactions* of the Kansas Academy of Science. He mentioned several specimens of his new coneflower that had been collected in Oklahoma, but only one from Texas. The Texan plant was found in the 1840s, and no exact location was recorded at the time. Since then, nobody seems to have rediscovered the neglected coneflower in Texas.

The neglected coneflower is a perennial herb with unbranched, hairy stems. This species differs from the more common yellow coneflower not only in its flower color, but also in its natural distribution. Indeed, there is a large distance of about 200 miles (320 kilometers) between the neglected coneflower range in southern Oklahoma and the nearest populations of yellow coneflower in southwestern Missouri and northern Arkansas.

Harsh environment

The prairies and woodland glades (grassy openings in forests) where coneflowers grow can be extreme habitats: very cold in winter, with sub-zero temperatures, and very hot, often humid, in summer, with temperatures of 86 degrees Fahrenheit (30 degrees Centigrade) or more. They may also suffer long periods of drought. Plants have to be tough to survive here, and often have adaptations such as fleshy roots to store water and nutrients, or even leaves oriented in a north-south plane, so as to avoid the direct glare of the sun.

Threats to the neglected coneflower include changes in land use, such as converting prairies into cultivated fields, or "improv-

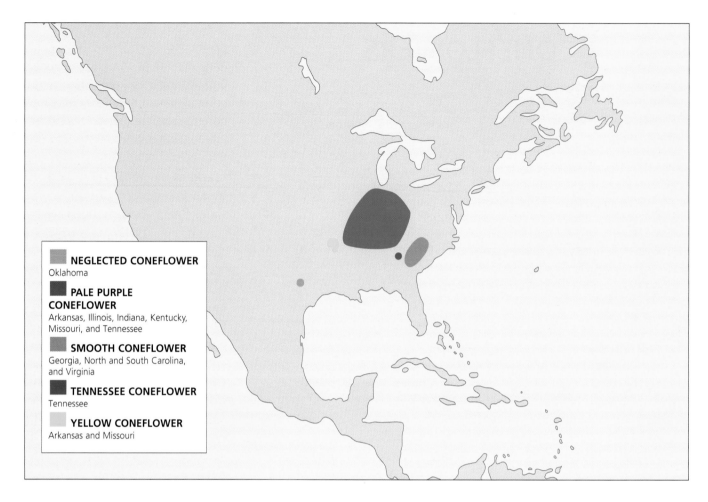

NEGLECTED CONEFLOWER
Oklahoma

PALE PURPLE CONEFLOWER
Arkansas, Illinois, Indiana, Kentucky, Missouri, and Tennessee

SMOOTH CONEFLOWER
Georgia, North and South Carolina, and Virginia

TENNESSEE CONEFLOWER
Tennessee

YELLOW CONEFLOWER
Arkansas and Missouri

ing" the grassland for grazing animals by fertilizing and introducing alien grasses. Those plants growing in woodland habitats are probably less at risk if the woodland is periodically cut for timber, because they depend on open sites within the woodland and do not survive well in heavy shade. However, clear-cutting of the neglected coneflowers' forest habitat, followed by conversion to cultivated fields or industrial or residential developments, would be disastrous for the coneflowers. Another threat could be the digging up of plants for their roots to be used in herbal medicine.

The neglected coneflower could be conserved by protecting its habitats from adverse change or destruction, ideally in official conservation areas.

Pale Purple Coneflower

(Echinacea simulata)

IUCN: Rare

Height: Stems 24–40 in. (60–100 cm) tall
Leaves: Spear or strap shaped, hairy, up to 1½ in. (4 cm) long
Flowers: Solitary heads, drooping, purplish pink, pink, or white florets
Fruit: Dry, nutlike, 4 mm long
Habitat: Limestone and dolomite glades, rocky open woods, prairies, and grassy hillsides
Range: Northern Arkansas, Illinois (rare), central Kentucky, and southeastern Missouri; also Indiana and Tennessee

IMAGINE FOLLOWING a narrow path through an Ozark forest in Missouri in early June. Everything around is green, with an abundance of lush foliage. Although the weather is hot and humid, the tree canopy overhead keeps the forest at a tolerable temperature. Suddenly the trees thin out in a small glade that is only a few feet across. The heat is like that of a furnace, where the sun beats down relentlessly. The ground is studded with rough rocks of dolomite, but in spite of these seemingly hostile conditions, the glade is full of grasses, sedges, herbs, and small shrubs.

Several blobs of purple suddenly appear above the grass: large, daisylike flower heads on top of erect, slender stems. This is the pale purple coneflower growing in its natural habitat.

Drooping purplish pink, pink, or white ray florets surround a cone of disk florets on the pale purple coneflower.

Glade dweller

The pale purple coneflower is a perennial herb with usually unbranched, hairy stems. Flowering occurs from the end of May to August. This species is most widespread in the state of Missouri where it grows in open limestone and dolomite glades.

There are actually two species known as pale purple coneflower: *Echinacea simulata* and *E. pallida.* The latter is much more common and widespread, and grows in most of the eastern United States, although it is most common west of the Mississippi River in Arkansas, Iowa, Illinois, Kansas, Missouri, and Oklahoma. The two species are very similar, but differ in the color and size of their pollen grains (yellow and small in *E. simulata,* white and large in *E. pallida)* and the

number of chromosomes in their cell nuclei. There is also a distinct geographical area occupied by *E. simulata* in which *E. pallida* is almost absent. In fact, the ranges of the two overlap by only 10 miles (16 kilometers). In the overlap zones, hybrids between the two species are common.

Name confusion

E. simulata was described for science by Ronald McGregor in 1968 as *E. speciosa.* However, the Latin name *E. speciosa* had already been used in 1849 for a different species (but which was no longer called that in 1968). The rules of scientific plant naming required that a different name be chosen for the more recent *E. speciosa.* Consequently Ronald McGregor renamed the pale purple coneflower *E. simulata* later in 1968.

Threats to the pale purple coneflower include radical

changes to its habitat, such as conversion to cultivated land or building. Plants growing in open prairies that were traditionally kept open by deliberate burning by Native American tribes are now in danger of being choked out by regenerating forest. For example, significant areas of southeastern Missouri that were known to be open grassland or savanna in the early 1800s are now dense forest. The removal of Native American people from this area put an end to the use of fire to keep the land open for wild grazing animals, and has allowed the natural climax vegetation (forest) to develop. Small, rocky woodland glades may provide a more stable habitat for the pale purple coneflower, since the soil in these glades is too thin for trees to grow well enough to form a proper forest.

Controlled fires

Conservation measures for the pale purple coneflower include securing the places where the species grows as nature reserves, protecting the habitat from destruction, and negotiating with landowners to be sympathetic toward the plant's habitat requirements when possible. Management of protected sites could include clearance of scrub and trees where necessary. Certainly the use of fire, where carefully controlled, is extremely effective at removing woody plants and thinning out coarse grasses so as to allow a rich growth of herbs, including the pale purple coneflower.

This species could also be cultivated to provide a backup in case wild populations are ever lost over a large area.

Smooth Coneflower

(Echinacea laevigata)

ESA: Endangered

IUCN: Vulnerable

Growth habit: Perennial herb with usually unbranched, hairless stems 20–60 in. (50–150 cm) tall
Leaves: Bluish green, hairless or slightly hairy, ¾–3 in. (2–7.5 cm) long
Flowers: Usually drooping, purplish to light pink ray florets surrounding a central, conelike mass of disk florets
Fruit: Dry, nutlike, 1-seeded fruits, each 4–5 mm long
Habitat: Open woods, glades, and limestone bluffs; also roadsides and cleared areas in woodland
Range: Northern Georgia, North and South Carolina, and Virginia

THE SMOOTH CONEFLOWER used to open its colorful purple flowers in six states of the United States. More than two-thirds of the historically known populations have now been destroyed, and the species is already presumed to be extinct in the states of Maryland and Pennsylvania.

Currently, three populations are known in Georgia, six in North Carolina, seven in South Carolina, and six in Virginia. Most of the smooth coneflower populations are very small, containing fewer than 100 plants; in fact four contain fewer than ten plants. The species was listed as endangered by the U. S. Fish and Wildlife Service in 1992, and there is now an officially approved recovery plan.

Smooth coneflowers are perennial herbs with usually unbranched hairless stems. Between 15 and 35 bluish green leaves occur in a basal clump. Some leaves are also found on the erect flowering stem. Flowering occurs from May to July.

Sunshine lover

Smooth coneflower usually grows on magnesium- and calcium-rich soils over bedrock such as diabase, gabbro, limestone, and marble. The best sites catch plenty of sunshine and have little competition from other plants, especially shrubs and trees. Coneflowers depend on periodic disturbances, such as grazing and fire to set back the gradual, natural buildup of shading and competing vegetation. The smooth coneflower, like most other coneflowers, cannot tolerate dense shade; also the species seems to need bare soil for its seeds to germinate successfully. Natural fires and large grazing and browsing mammals had a firm place in the historical ecology of the smooth coneflower's natural distribution. Now that those animals are gone or reduced in numbers, the open habitats loved by the coneflowers are reverting to shady forests.

Smooth coneflowers grow in open conditions and tend to receive more visits from pollinators, such as bees and butterflies, than plants growing in the shade.

The smooth coneflower has distinctive flowers in May to July, with drooping purple or pink ray florets.

Roadside populations

More cross-pollination means a greater seed production and also a greater flow of genetic information between plants, which helps to maintain diversity. The present distribution of smooth coneflower shows its dependence on periodic habitat disturbance. Of the 22 known populations, 16 are on roadsides, by trails, or on other rights-of-way.

This species is threatened by residential and industrial development; road construction, improvement, and maintenance; plant collecting; and the gradual buildup of woody vegetation in its natural habitat.

Controlled fires

The U. S. Forest Service has carried out controlled burning as a way of maintaining suitably open habitat for the species, and the results have so far been positive. Thinning of the forest canopy, followed by burning, has also been started at certain sites, and carefully timed mowing of vegetation may also prove beneficial. The collection and storage of seeds is planned in collaboration with the Center for Plant Conservation and its associated network of botanical gardens in the United States. Areas deliberately managed for the smooth coneflower's conservation will eventually become open, fire-maintained savannas.

One particular population of smooth coneflowers has been carefully monitored and the numbers of plants and seedlings have been counted every year. The numbers of plants have fluctuated, with 146 plants in 1995, 150 in 1996, 137 in 1997, and 156 in 1998.

These counts show that fewer plants now exist compared with the 250 individuals counted in the late 1980s. The population has declined because plants are dying, and also because few seedlings are successfully growing to maturity. In most years of the survey, no new plants became established, although four were established in 1989, one in 1991, five in 1992, and one in 1993. The death rate of mature plants varied between seven and 38 each year. Fortunately, seedlings and small plants were seen in the summer of 1998.

Tennessee Coneflower
(Echinacea tennesseensis)

ESA: Endangered

IUCN: Endangered

Growth habit: Perennial herb with unbranched or branched stems 4–16 in. (10–40 cm) tall
Leaves: In a basal clump and also some on the erect flowering stem, narrow, hairy, 2–6¾ in. (5–17 cm) long
Flowers: Mid-May to October, solitary heads with 12–17 spreading, pink or purplish pink ray florets ¾–1 in. (2–2.5 cm) long, surrounding a central, conelike mass of disk florets
Fruit: Dry, nutlike, 1-seeded fruits, each 4.5–5 mm long
Habitat: Dry, stony or gravelly hills and woodland glades
Range: Known only in three counties in central Tennessee

TENNESSEE CONEFLOWER is the rarest of all nine species of coneflower. It is known to grow wild in just five places in Wilson, Davidson, and Rutherford counties in central Tennessee.

The young flowering heads first appear as early as late April, and flowering takes place from the middle of May right up until October, reaching its peak during the months of June and July. The flowers of the Tennessee coneflower are often visited by butterflies and bees, and the seeds are eaten by birds such as cardinals and goldfinches.

Encroaching cedar

Tennessee coneflower grows in glades (natural or artificial clearings in woodland) where the bedrock is either exposed or covered by a very thin layer of soil. Such glades are often dominated by a conifer known as the eastern red cedar. This small tree species is actually a type of juniper *Juniperus virginiana*, rather than a true cedar. The eastern red cedar is an invasive tree of open areas, particularly in rocky glades and on cliffs, and left unchecked, it will eventually choke up a glade and shade out smaller plants. The Tennessee coneflower will not normally tolerate more than 50 percent shade.

The population of Tennessee coneflower in Rutherford County is found within a small area of about 15 feet (4.6 meters) in a parcel of land owned by a private corporation. One of the sites in Wilson County is also on private land, but there is another population inside the adjacent, publicly owned Cedars of Lebanon State Forest. All five populations are located within just 14 miles of

each other, and the greatest area occupied by any of them is no more than a few hectares. Population levels range from 3,700 plants to about 89,000 plants at each site. One of the two populations in Davidson County has now been reduced because of damage done during construction work. The coneflower's habitat falls within an area that is going through a phase of rapid development for housing, and this could pose a further threat to the survival of the species.

Not only is habitat destruction a threat but also the deliberate digging-up of plants for cultivation in gardens or for presumed medicinal properties.

The Tennessee coneflower apparently has rather ineffective methods of seed dispersal, which place a limit on the plant's ability to colonize new areas.

The main objectives in the Tennessee coneflower's recovery plan include improving the man-

The Tennessee coneflower has pink or purple flowers with distinctive, spreading ray florets.

agement and protection of the five existing populations, searching for new populations, maintaining populations in cultivation, and reintroducing the plant into the wild.

Cultivation

Maintaining a stock of pure bred Tennessee coneflower in cultivation would provide a back-up in case of extinction in the wild. It is actually illegal to sell the species across state lines, unless a permit is obtained from the U. S. Fish and Wildlife Service Office of Endangered Species. The coneflower is already in cultivation at the Missouri Botanical Garden in St. Louis, Missouri, as part of a network caring for populations of endangered plants in cultivation, known as the Center for Plant Conservation.

Yellow Coneflower

(Echinacea paradoxa var. *paradoxa)*

IUCN: Rare

Growth habit: Perennial herb with unbranched, hairy stems 14–33 in. (35–85 cm) tall
Leaves: In a basal clump, also some on the erect flowering stem, light green, strap shaped, hairy, up to 1⅗ in. (4 cm) wide
Flowers: Solitary heads, bright yellow ray florets surrounding central conelike mass of blackish disk florets
Fruit: Dry, nutlike, 1-seeded fruits, each 4.5–5.5 mm long
Habitat: Rocky prairies, open glades in woodland, treeless hill summits
Range: The Ozark hills of southwestern Missouri and northern Arkansas

THE YELLOW CONEFLOWER has become a popular ornamental garden plant in recent years because of its attractive flower heads. They are unique in having bright yellow ray florets, whereas the usual color for coneflowers is a shade of pink, purple, or white. Indeed, the yellow in this coneflower's English name is the paradox in the Latin name.

The yellow coneflower is well suited to the often difficult conditions of gardens in the American Midwest, characterized by the extremes of hot, often very humid summers and cold winters. This climate is typically found in the coneflower's only native habitat, the heavily wooded Ozark hills of southwestern Missouri and adjacent northern Arkansas.

The yellow coneflower blooms in June, its solitary heads displaying drooping yellow ray florets around a central conelike mass of blackish disk florets. Its leaves occur in a basal clump, with a few also on the flowering stem.

The yellow coneflower is threatened by land use changes, such as converting prairies into cultivated fields, or altering the grassland to make it more suitable for cattle by applying fertilizers and sowing vigorous, alien grass species. Another possible threat (as with all other coneflower species) could be the digging up of plants for their roots for use in herbal medicine.

The yellow coneflower's popularity in cultivation gives the species considerable protection against extinction should the wild populations ever decline to a

critically low level. Fortunately, the species is also being conserved in the wild by protecting some of its prairie habitats as nature reserves.

Prairie reserve

In Polk County in southwestern Missouri, La Petite Gemme Prairie was designated as an official Missouri Natural Area in 1977. The site covers 37 acres (15 hectares), ranging in altitude from 1,115 to 1,180 feet (340 to 360 meters). La Petite Gemme Prairie is owned by the Missouri Prairie Foundation, a private organization concerned with preserving native prairies in

Missouri. The prairie is currently managed by the Missouri Department of Conservation.

Natural and human-induced fires have for centuries played a vital role in the maintenance of prairie lands in America. The hot summer and autumn were probably the main season for such blazes, when there is plenty of dry grass and frequent thunderstorms. Today La Petite Gemme Prairie is managed with controlled burning, hay making, and resting on a rotation basis. Burning in the spring helps to control plants that are not native to this prairie habitat.

Nick Turland

The yellow coneflower prefers a rocky habitat with extreme seasonal temperature differences.

CONIFERS

Order: Pinopsida

Family: Pinaceae

Conifers are woody trees and shrubs that grow throughout the world, except in Antarctica. Most conifers are evergreen plants with needlelike or scalelike leaves. Seeds and pollen are born on separate male and female structures called cones.

Many species of conifer are listed by IUCN–The World Conservation Union. Several of these are Chinese species belonging to genera such as *Abies* (firs) and *Cathaya*.

China is a vast country with diverse geographical, climatological, and topographical features. These characteristics, as well as an unusual Pleistocene history, have contributed to the evolution of an extremely abundant and diverse gymnosperm flora.

Gymnosperms are woody plants, such as conifers, that produce naked seeds. China is the richest country in the world in gymnosperms. It is estimated that China has approximately 250 species representing 34 genera in 10 families. Many of these species are endemic to China.

Several new conifer species have been discovered in China only recently (*Cathaya argyrophylla*, 1958; *Abies beshanzuensis*, 1976; *A. yuanbaoshanensis*, 1980; *A. ziyuanensis*, 1980; *A. fanjingshanensis*, 1982; *Pinus squamata*, 1992).

Due to a drastic increase in China's human population and the resulting increase in human intervention in the natural world, many Chinese plant species have severely declined.

Cathaya is a monotypic genus of a single species. About 4,000 individuals of this species remain in five populations in central China. There is only one location for *A. fanjingshanensis* and only three individuals of *A. beshanzuensis* are known. Effective protection measures for these species are urgently needed.

Endangered conifers are not restricted to China, however. The Fraser fir of the United States is currently classified as vulnerable by IUCN–The World Conservation Union due to an introduced species of aphid (*Adelges piceae*).

Baishanzu Fir

Abies beshanzuensis

IUCN: Endangered

Growth habit: Evergreen tree, up to 56 ft. (17 m) in height and 30 in. (75 cm) in diameter

Leaf: ½–1½ in. (1–4 cm) long, 2.5–3.5 mm wide, bright green above, with two white bands beneath

Male cones: Solitary, pendent, spreading pollen by wind

Female cones: Solitary, erect, cylindrical, 3–5 in. (7.5–12.5 cm) long, 1⅓–1½ in. (3.5–4 cm) in diameter, pale brown or brownish yellow

Seed: About ½ in. (1 cm) long with 16–22-mm long wing, distributed by wind

Habitat: Deciduous broad-leaved forest on volcanic soil

Range: Mt. Baishanzu, Southeast China

WHEN THE BAISHANZU FIR was first discovered in 1976 by the Chinese botanist M. X. Wu, there were seven individuals at Mt. Baishanzu in Qingyuan county, Zhejiang province in southeast China. Now there are only three trees left. This species was recognized as one of the 12 rarest and endangered plants listed by the International Species Security Committee (ISSC) in 1987 and the Chinese Plant Red Data Book (1992). The habitat of this species is very fragile.

This rare and endemic species is a living fossil, a relic that existed when the region had a more oceanic climate in the Quaternary period. The main reason for the endangerment of this species is the glaciation that occured during this period. More recently expansive agriculture and fires, combined with poor regeneration, are thought to have been responsible for the decline of the species.

Exciting discovery

The discovery of the Baishanzu fir in southeast China was very exciting for paleoclimatic and paleogeographic researchers. Usually the modern distribution of firs (genus *Abies*) in China is limited to high altitudes of 9,850–13,000 feet (3,000–4,000 meters) or more northerly latitudes, where it is accompanied by spruces (*Picea*), larches

BAISHANZU FIR
China

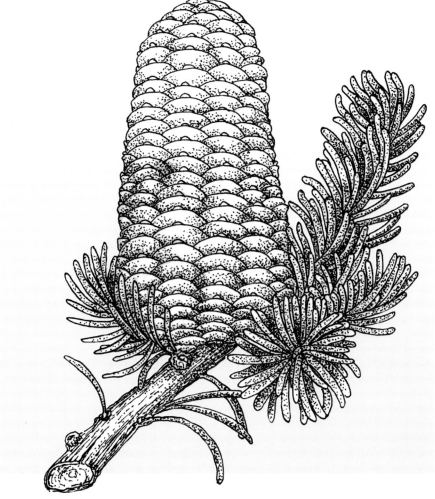

The winged seeds of the Baishanzu fir are held within the woody bracts of the female cone. The wings help the seeds to disperse in the wind.

(*Larix*) or hemlocks (*Tsuga*). The altitude of the trees on Mt. Baishanzu, however, is only 5,600 feet (1,700 meters), and this mountain has a relatively southerly latitude. No hemlock or spruce grow with this rare species. Instead, it grows among broad-leaf deciduous forest and its habitat is very different from that of firs found in southwest and northeast China. In late autumn and winter, when the leaves of other trees have fallen, the evergreen Baishanzu fir is readily distinguishable in the mountain valley.

Unfortunately, the remaining three individuals have only poor growth conditions.

Reproduction

The male cones release pollen in May. Female cones ripen in November of the same year. The winged seeds fall and are dispersed by the wind.

In order to protect this very endangered species, the Baishanzu Reserve was established by the local government in 1985. In 1992 it became Baishanzu National Reserve. The technicians in the reserve successfully grafted Baishanzu fir on to stock of the Japanese fir (*Abies firma*) in 1989. The grafted trees began to bear cones in 1997, but the main shoots are too limited to use for grafting. Some seedlings have been cultivated in the nursery recently but have not yet been transplanted to the original site.

Little biological knowledge about this species is available.

The biological background of Baishanzu fir needs to be studied in order to create effective measures for its protection.

Fanjingshan Fir
Abies fanjingshanensis

IUCN: Endangered

Growth habit: Evergreen tree, up to 72 ft. (22 m) in height and 25 in. (65 cm) in diameter, with resinous buds
Leaf: ½–1¾ in. (1–4.4 cm) long, 2–3 mm wide, bright green above, with two white stomatic bands beneath
Male cone: Less than ⅔ inch (1–1.5 cm) long, yellow with red spore scales, soon falling
Female bold: Solitary, barrel-shaped, with a flat tip, 2–2¼ in. (5–6 cm) long, 1¼–1½ in. (3.5–4 cm) wide, dark purplish-brown to dark brown.
Seed: Ovoid-conical, 6–8 mm
Habitat: Mixed coniferous-deciduous forest at 7,000–7,500 ft. (2,100–2,300 m)
Range: Mt. Fanjingshan, China

FANJINGSHAN MOUNTAIN, with its particular geographical position, ancient rock, indigenous forest vegetation, favorable ecological environment, and rich biological resources, is internationaly recognized as a UNESCO Biospher Reserve. Fanjingshan fir is a relict species, occurring only in inaccessible areas on Mt. Fanjingshan. It is distributed mostly on steep hills with gradients of 50–60 degrees, and it is restricted to slopes facing north, northwest, or

FANJINGSHAN FIR
China

northeast at an elevation of 7,000–7,500 feet (2,100–2,300 meters), forming coniferous-deciduous mixed forest with species such as *Tsuga chinensis* and *Acer flabellatum*. The Fanjingshan fir habitat is a route for cold air in winter. It is also rich in precipitation and fog. The cool and moist conditions are suitable for this species because its branches can withstand freezing and the weight of snow. The towering crowns of this species create a distinctive treeline on Mt. Fanjingshan.

Reproduction

The tree sprouts new growth rather late, usually in June. The male cones shed pollen in May and June; the female cones ripen in October and November.

In 1998, most of the mature trees died, beginning from the top of the tree. Abortive seeds were also observed. The reason for this is not known. There are a lot of mosses on the ground where Fanjingshan fir grows, especially bog mosses (*Sphagnum*), which hold water. This can

result in deep swamp conditions that affect the ability of tree roots to respire. Waterlogging might be a reason for the poor growth of Fanjingshan fir recently. Although this species is in a UNESCO Biosphere Reserve, no propagation experiments or conservation work have been carried out so far. Biological research must be carried out to find the reason for this species' decline.

Qiaoping Xiang

Fraser Fir

(Abies fraseri)

IUCN: Vulnerable

Subfamily: Abietoideae
Height: 30–40 ft. (9–12 m)
Width: 20–25 ft. (6–7.5 m)
Habitat: Temperate rain forest and mountain crests
Range: Lower Appalachian Mountains, United States

FRASER FIR IS an attactive, small- to medium-sized conifer that grows in the southeastern United States. It is named for the Scottish plant explorer John Fraser (1750-1811). The Fraser fir is also known as the she balsam, the southern balsam fir, and sometimes the southern balsam.

Notched needles

Fraser firs reach 30–40 feet (9–12 meters) in height and 20–25 feet (6–7.5 meters) across, forming a pyramidal shape with a stiff, horizontal, branching pattern. The shining, dark green needles (leaves) are ½–1 inch (1–2.5 centimeters) long and have a notch at the tip. When the

tree is young, the bark on the trunk is thin, smooth, and reddish, with numerous resin blisters that give off a characteristically pleasant scent. As the tree matures the bark turns gray brown and forms scaly plates.

Clouds of pollen

Fraser fir produces separate male and female flowers. The female flowers open in mid-May to early June and are found high in the uppermost canopy. The male flowers are arranged below the female flowers on the tree and yet are still located in the upper half of the tree. The male pollen is wind-dispersed and forms yellow clouds of pollen grains. The fruit is an erect, cylindrically shaped cone, 2–2½ inches (5–6 centimeters) in length. The seeds are held inside the woody bracts of the cone. The cones begin to open and shatter late in September through mid-October. The woody bracts, or scales, that make up the cone, form a sharp downward-curved point at the end. They are the only native fir to have this characteristic.

High flyer

The Fraser fir is restricted to heights of between 4,000–6,700 feet (1,200–2,040 meters) of the southern Appalachian Mountains from southwestern Virginia to western North Carolina and eastern Tennessee. This species prefers moisture-rich, cool to cold growing conditions that prevail in the temperate rain forest. The mountains that make up its range average 75 to 100 inches (1.9 to 2.5 meters) of rain a year, with a mean summer temperature of 60 degrees Fahrenheit (16 degrees Centigrade) or less. The winter

From above, the distinctive notched shape of the Fraser fir's needles can be clearly seen.

temperatures may average 30 degrees Fahrenheit (-1 degree Centigrade) and snow cover is usual. Fog helps to moderate temperatures and adds to the precipitation. At high elevations along the ridge tops and mountain crests this fir forms almost pure stands. Because it can hold the soil on the steep slopes and inhibit erosion, it plays a very important role in the creation of watersheds and the protection of the region's water quality.

In 1900 an aphid, the balsam woolly adelgid (*Adelges piceae*), was accidentally introduced from Europe to Maine on imported nursery material. In the eastern United States it attacks both the Fraser fir and the balsam fir (*Abies balsamea*). The balsam fir has proved to be the more resistant. The infestations spread from the lower to the higher elevations. A Fraser fir is killed 5 to 10 years after the initial infestation. On Mount Mitchell the mortality rate of the Fraser fir from 1955 to 1965 was estimated at over 1.5 million trees. Young and vigorous seedlings and saplings seem to live the longest.

Since *A. fraseri* and *A. balsamea* are closely related, it is hoped that they are similar enough genetically for the Fraser fir to develop similar resistance to the introduced adelgid.

Tom Ward

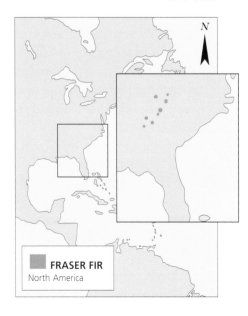

FRASER FIR
North America

Yinshan

Cathaya argyrophylla

IUCN: Rare

Growth habit: Evergreen tree, up to 79 in. (2 m) in height, to 130 in. (3 m) in diameter
Leaf: Dark green 1½–2½ in. (4–6 cm) long, up to 3 mm wide
Cone: Egg-shaped, 1¼–2 in. (3–5 cm) long, ½–1¼ in. (1.5–3 cm) in diameter, pale brown or chestnut at maturity
Seed: Egg shaped, 2–2½ in. (5–6 cm) long, dark olive green, irregularly spotted; wing ⅖–⅗ in. (10–15 mm) long
Habitat: Needle-leaved and broad-leaved mixed forests on limestone
Range: China (Guangxi, Hunan, and Sichuan provinces)

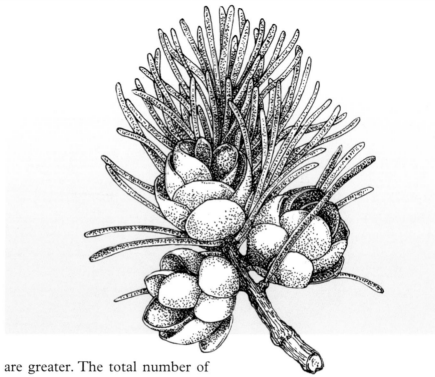

The seed producing cones of the yinshan appear pale brown or chestnut when mature. Low seed production is one of the factors contributing to this species' decline.

THE YINSHAN WAS discovered in 1958 at Huaping, Longsheng County, Guangxi Province, China, by botanists conducting fieldwork in the area. At first a seedling was found, and then specimens with cones were collected. The plants were immediately recognized as being unique, belonging to a single species genus *Cathaya*. Through extensive field investigations this species has now been found at more than 30 sites.

The yinshan is a rare, relict species endemic to southern China. It is found in the subtropical mountain areas, where its populations are very scattered. Colonies consist of from one to a few individuals, or at most several dozen, except at Laotizi, Jinfo Mountain, where numbers

are greater. The total number of individuals with a height greater than 3 feet (1 meter) is less than 4,000. The soils where this species can survive are made of limestone, shale, and sandstone, and are slightly acid. The leaf is recognizable by its impressed midrib and two conspicuous white bands on its lower surface.

The yinshan grows along the crests of isolated caplike rocky mountains and in crevices of sheer precipices and overhanging rocks with shallow soil. None of the existing colonies are easily accessible. The natural reproduction of the yinshan depends to a large extent on the density of the

forest. It regenerates well within thin stands, but its seedlings and saplings are rare in dense stands. Seedlings require some shade, but the older trees tend to create too much shade, and prevent the healthy growth of yinshan seedlings and saplings.

Low seed production

The yinshan is often found mixed with broad-leaved trees and is shaded by them. At pre-

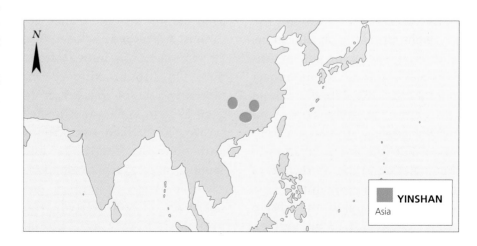

YINSHAN
Asia

sent, most of the yinshan communities are in the early or intermediate stages of community succession. In the later stages of succession, the yinshan might be replaced by some of the invading broad-leaved tree species that dominate this vegetation. This is currently an important factor limiting the enlargement of the populations of yinshan. Low seed production and low germination rate are other factors resulting in this species' rarity.

Reproduction

Flowering and pollination take place in May. The pollen is spread by the wind from male cones to female cones. Fertilization occurs in June of the following year. The female cones are pale brown, ripening in Octo-ber and becoming chestnut brown when mature. The seeds are dark olive-green and egg-shaped. They are between 2–2½ inches (5–6 centimeters) long and are irregularly spotted. The seeds also possess wings up to ⅝ inch (15 millimeters) in length.

Fragmented population

Large climatic changes during the Quaternary period have resulted in a decrease in the number of individuals and the discontinuous distribution of yinshan populations over a large area. Increasing human activity has caused the fragmented populations to decline further. The distances between these populations act as a barrier to reproduction. The trees in a given stand tend to only reproduce with one another. This has led to a loss of genetic diversity, resulting in the further decline of the yinshan and the shrinkage of its distribution range.

Protection

At present, every known population has been placed under protection by local governments and departments. Several nature reserves (Jinfo Mountain and Wunong in Sichuan, Huaping and Jinxiu in Guangxi, and Chengbu and Linxian in Hunan) have been established where the emphasis has been placed on the protection of the yinshan. This species is successfully grown in the arboretum in Xinning County, Hunan. Also, some Yinshan trees have been grafted on to *Pinus elliotii* and are being cultivated successfully there.

Qiaoping Xiang

Hawaiian Coot
(Fulica americana alai)

ESA: Endangered

IUCN: Vulnerable

Class: Aves
Order: Gruiformes
Family: Rallidae
Subfamily: Fulicinae
Length: 14–16 in. (36–41 cm)
Weight: Up to 25⅓ oz. (717 g)
Clutch size: 4–10 eggs; 6 average
Incubation: 23–27 days
Habitat: Ponds and marshes
Range: Hawaiian Islands

THE BODY OF THE Hawaiian coot is dark slate gray. The head is somewhat darker, even appearing black at a distance, but is actually a rather shiny green or blue at close range. The undertail is white. The bird's large, pointed, white beak forms a shield that extends between the eyes beyond the forehead onto the forecrown. The upper shield may be white, pale blue, or yellowish orange to bright red. These coots may have a pale black ring near the tip of the beak, particularly those birds with red shields.

When floating on water, coots resemble ducks in their size and general appearance. Coots, however, have pointed beaks that are flattened from side to side—unlike the duck's beak, which is flattened top to bottom. Also, coots' long toes are lobed rather than webbed. These large, peculiar toes are easily seen because coots frequently leave the water to rest and preen their feathers on dry land. They also go ashore to forage for seeds and shoots. Swimming coots pump their heads back and forth as if trying to boost their momentum, appearing as if strings were attached from their head to their feet, so one stroke pulls the head back and the next stroke pulls it forward again. To take flight, coots must run across the water a short distance. They feed on aquatic plants, seeds, vegetation, invertebrates, and fish.

How many coots?

Bird experts disagree on how many species there are in the coot genus *Fulica*, counting from eight to ten. According to some ornithologists the Hawaiian coot is a separate species (*Fulica alai*). Traditionally, however, the

Hawaiian coot is considered a subspecies of the American coot (*Fulica americana*), which has a smaller shield.

Unlike its counterparts in North America, the Hawaiian coot does not migrate. It remains in the same general vicinity year-round. At breeding time the Hawaiian coot builds a large, floating mound of vegetation which it usually anchors to rooted aquatic plants. The mound may be 2 feet (61 centimeters) or more in diameter. The nest cup is about 6 inches (15 centimeters) across and a couple of inches (five centimeters) deep. The mound's weight lets it ride low in the water, so the eggs may actually be right at or only slightly above the waterline.

The Hawaiian coot is threatened by a range of different factors. Freshwater marshes have been drained for agriculture and land development. Many estuaries have also been lost to development. As a species' habitat disappears, it usually follows that the species will decline. Other problems that have been cited as potential threats to the Hawaiian coot, include predation by exotic mammals such as rats, mongooses, dogs, and cats.

Chemical polution

Pesticides may also pose certain hazards. Hawaii's agriculture depends heavily on various chemicals that may adversely affect the coots. One possible danger could be herbicide runoff into marshes, where the poison may kill aquatic plants the coots need as food or cover. More specific studies are needed to determine the actual effect of such herbicides. While draining

marshes destroys coot habitat, exotic plant species such as water hyacinth (*Eichhornia crassipes*) also degrade habitat quality by choking waters with too much dense vegetation. Coots prefer open water with scattered patches of vegetation. Preserving this type of environment is an important consideration.

Coots are aggressively territorial. Intolerant of their own kind, they are quick to attack intruding coots, which may be the reason for describing an ill-tempered person as an "old coot." To avoid constant fighting, coots have several feather displays and postures that advise other coots to beware. Still, only so many coots will fit into a given body of water. If that

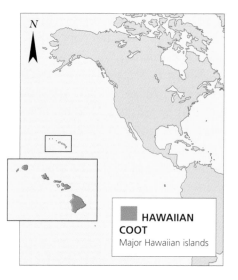

HAWAIIAN COOT
Major Hawaiian islands

The Hawaiian coot is traditionally considered a subspecies of the American coot (*Fulica americana*), shown here.

water area is made smaller by exotic plants or is degraded by pollution, fewer coots can breed on it. Also, Hawaiian coots use saltwater ponds and brackish estuaries mainly during non-breeding periods. They do not nest on salt water, thus not all available habitat is suitable for all aspects of the bird's life.

The Hawaiian coot was considered a game bird for many years. Never really prized as table fare, it was shot mostly for sport. It was finally protected from hunting in 1939. Now considered endangered, the Hawaiian coot is covered by the Endangered Species Act. Population counts and estimates through the 1970s usually tallied about 2,000 birds, with more found in some years, less in others. Census work conducted from 1980 to 1986 averaged about 1,800 birds. Hawaiian coots are found on all Hawaiian islands except Lanai. The various wildlife refuges on these islands are all managed to benefit the Hawaiian coot and other Hawaiian wildlife.

Kevin Cook

Coral Plant

(Berberidopsis corallina)

IUCN: Endangered

Class: Magnoliopsida
Order: Violales
Family: Flacourtiaceae
Life form: Evergreen
scrambling shrub or liana
Height: Climbing to 30 ft.
(10 m) or more
Leaves: Evergreen, oval with
spiny margins
Flowers: Coral red or scarlet
clusters, hanging down
Pollination: Possibly pollinated
by the green-backed firecrown
hummingbird (*Sephanoides
sephanoides*). Propagation in
the wild might be
predominantly by
suckering/layering of shoots.
Habitat: Streambanks in
densely shaded coastal
rain forest
Range: Southern Chile

The attractive red hanging flower clusters of the coral plant or coral vine (*Berberidopsis corallina*) can only be seen in a few locations in the coastal rain forests of southern Chile.

THE STRIKING SIGHT of this rambling vine, scrambling through trees and shrubs and cascading down to the ground, with its attractive scarlet hanging flowers, is now tragically almost a thing of the past. Always rather restricted in range and found only in the coastal mountains, or cordilleras, of the Concepción, Arauco, Cautón, Valdivia, and Osorno provinces of southern Chile, it is now perhaps known only in a few areas: Concepción, the Quebrado Honda, and Fundo Colcura forests.

The coral plant, also known as the coral vine, was originally described by the British botanist J.D. Hooker in 1862 from a collection made by Richard Pearce for a horticulturalist firm called Veitch's. The same firm established them in cultivation in the British Isles shortly afterward. For many years this cultivated plant was thought to be the only member of its genus. However, recent work has established the true affinities of a second species, *B. beckleri*, which grows in the montane rain forests of Queensland and New South Wales, Australia. With another Australian genus containing a single species, *Streptothamnus*, *Berberidopsis* forms an isolated tribe, Berberidopsideae, within the very large family of Flacourtiaceae. It is considered to be among the most primitive of the ten recognized tribes, and in its climbing habit, pollen shape, and anatomical characteristics it is unique. This has led some botanists to suggest that these three species deserve to be recognized in their own family, the Berberidopsidaceae.

The coral plant flowers from December to April and again in August, fruiting in December. In cultivation in the northern hemisphere flowering occurs in late summer. The fruit are berry like but without pulp and contain 12 to 24 shiny brown seeds.

Woven baskets

Not only is the coral plant of commercial interest for its horticultural merit, but in Chile it has been traditionally used by Native Americans of the Mapuche tribe for making baskets and other woven goods—one of their main sources of income. The removal of the plant for this trade is, however, less of a threat to the remaining populations than the habitat destruction that occurs through commercial forestry plantations and agriculture.

The species is in cultivation in some Chilean gardens but is perhaps more frequently cultivated in the British Isles, where it may be found for sale in some garden centers. It thrives only in cool, humid areas that recreate its South American home; some of the best examples can be seen in gardens on Atlantic coasts from Scotland to North Wales. A project based at the Royal Botanic Garden, Edinburgh, is distributing selected plants of known origin to safe sites throughout Britain and Ireland for conservation. Specimens in cultivation in the British Isles have not previously produced seed. Whether this is through lack of a pollinator, genetic self-incompatibility, or some other factor, may only be resolved by current research. It is possible that most cultivated coral plants may derive from a very limited number of introduced plants.

Fred Rumsey

CORAL PLANT
South America

COTINGAS

Class: Aves

Order: Passeriformes

Family: Cotingidae

Cotingas have long baffled those who study them. Although species are similar and obviously related to each other, they are also very different. In short they are as varied as the tropical landscape in which they evolved.

Ornithologists believe the cotingas developed from primitive songbirds after South America and Africa drifted apart 100 million years ago. There are several songbird families, such as manakins and tyrant flycatchers, that are sometimes grouped with cotingas. Some ornithologists consider the entire cotinga clan as a subfamily of the tyrant flycatchers. Attempting to classify birds correctly is an important

undertaking. The categories to which ornithologists assign birds represent relationships of behavior, anatomy, evolution, and more. As new information becomes available, such as the discovery of new fossils or new species, ornithologists reorganize the categories to show more accurately how various species are related. Understanding the relationships among bird groups influences our interpretations of natural phenomena, such as migration and the separation of continents. Understanding these factors helps measure what we know about our planet and how we can help endangered wildlife.

From the giant, crow-sized umbrella birds to the tiny calyptura, the cotingas show remarkable adaptations. Some sport wattles (fleshy growths that dangle from the face like on a turkey), and nearly all have

modified wing feathers. The cotingas' colors range from dazzling orange to brilliant blue and nearly every other hue—even black and snow white.

Birds of tropical forests, the cotingas mainly occupy the Amazon Basin of northern South America. However, a few species inhabit Yucatán in Mexico and a few others live as far south as São Paulo in Brazil.

If becards are included in the cotinga family, then the rose-throated becard (*Pachyramphus aglaiae*) extends the family as far north as southern Texas and southern Arizona.

Having evolved in tropical forests, cotingas are vulnerable to human activities that lead to the cutting or clearing of those forests. Several species are currently threatened, but more field research may eventually prove that additional species are in jeopardy.

Banded Cotinga

(Cotinga maculata)

ESA: Endangered

IUCN: Endangered

Length: 7½ in. (19 cm)
Weight: 2⅓ oz. (65 g)
Clutch size: Probably 1–2 eggs
Incubation: Unknown
Diet: Probably small fruits
Habitat: Humid forests
Range: Southeastern Brazil

THE BANDED COTINGA makes a stunning impression with its remarkable colors of blue and rose. It is just one of seven species known as "blue cotingas," all of which are in the genus *Cotinga*. The blue of these birds is especially rich and lustrous, but as is the case in all blue birds, it is a deceptive effect. Feathers contain no chemical pigment which is truly blue. Red, yellow, orange, brown, black, and some greens do occur in feathers, but the blue in the feathers is from scattered and reflected light, as is the blue color of the sky.

The male cotinga is uniformly bright blue above with darker, blue-black wings and tail. The chin, throat, and belly are a deep purplish rose, and a bright blue band runs across the breast. The undertail is also bright blue. The beak is dark gray to blackish and then becomes lighter at the base. The legs and feet of the bird are dark gray. The female banded cotinga is not blue but dark gray above and slightly paler below.

Unfortunately more is known about blue feathers and the relationships of cotingas than about the birds themselves. Just like its relatives, the banded cotinga spends its life high in the trees of thick forests, where people on the ground cannot follow and study them well. Specimens collected for museums allow ornithologists to study anatomy and relationships among species, genera, families, and so on, but specimens do not provide information on behavior. Such things as how long the birds take to build nests, how long they incubate their eggs, or how they call to each other or recognize their mates can only be studied by observing live birds.

What is known about banded cotingas is that their habitat is disappearing. They prefer primary forests, which are forests

Many members of the family Cotingidae are found in the tropical forests of the Amazon basin.

that have not been cut down or cleared. They apparently shun secondary forests—those forests that grow back after the original forests have been cut. Although specific research has not verified this view, it is reasonable to assume it is the case because the few banded cotinga populations that remain all inhabit small patches of primary forest. Banded cotingas do not occur in the available expanses of secondary forest which have grown up following timber cutting and agricultural clearing.

The banded cotinga is one of many species found in the coastal forests of eastern Brazil. The bird is one of many animal species that are threatened by the heavy cutting of these forests. If the remaining primary forests should be lost, the banded cotinga could also be lost.

White-winged Cotinga

(Xipholena atropurpurea)

ESA: Endangered

IUCN: Vulnerable

Length: 7½ in. (19 cm)
Weight: Unknown
Clutch size: Unknown
Incubation: Unknown
Diet: Small fruits
Habitat: Coastal forests
Range: Eastern and southeastern Brazil

■ WHITE-WINGED COTINGA
Brazil

■ BANDED COTINGA
Brazil

THE WHITE-WINGED COTINGA has two close relatives in the genus *Xipholena*. None of them have been studied well in the wild, so little is known of their natural history. However, more observations have been made of the white-tailed cotinga (*Xipholena lamellipennis*) and the pompadour cotinga (*Xipholena punicea*) than of the white-winged species.

Both of these other two cotingas have been seen to perform ritualized display flights in which the white wings common to all three species flash brightly against the dark forest. Male pompadour cotingas engage in a chase type of behavior, where the dominant male appears to fly at another male to drive him off. The second male may, likewise, displace a third male cotinga before the first male approaches to displace the second male yet again. It is possible white-winged cotingas do this too, but such behaviors have not been observed in them because no specific field studies have been done on this now rare species.

The male white-winged cotinga is a very dark purple with a short brownish purple tail. The wings are bright white, as are the eyes. Females are gray or brownish gray overall with some white in the wings. As a bird of Brazil's coastal forest, the white-winged cotinga has suffered from habitat destruction. The existence of fewer birds makes finding and studying the species more difficult, and the density of its forest habitat also makes the species harder to study.

Like the banded cotinga, the white-winged cotinga prefers primary forests. Its dwindling population has not adapted to forest regrowth.

Kevin Cook

COUCALS

Class: Aves

Order: Cuculiformes

Family: Cuculidae

Subfamily: Centropodinae

Coucals inhabit various habitats in Africa, Madagascar, southern Asia, and Australia. Ornithologists have traditionally regarded them as a subfamily of the cuckoo family, but some experts have recently proposed dividing the cuckoo family into five smaller families. The 27 to 30 species of coucals would represent one distinct family. This classification system has not been widely accepted yet, but ornithologists are studying it.

The coucals are mostly large terrestrial birds, somewhat pheasantlike. They are well adapted for life in forest undergrowth, shrub land, or even dense grasslands. Coucals have stout, slightly decurved beaks. Like cuckoos, they have long tails. Also like cuckoos they have two toes pointing forward and two toes pointing backward. Coucals build their own nests and raise their own young, rather than laying their eggs in other birds' nests as do Old World cuckoos. Coucals' nests are typically ball-shaped masses of leaves and grasses with an entrance on the side. A few species even build entrance chambers.

Coucals are especially known for their loud nonmusical calls, which they usually give while hidden among vegetation. They also hiss and screech.

Green-billed Coucal

(Centropus chlororhynchus)

IUCN: Endangered

Length: 17 in. (43 cm)

Weight: Unknown

Clutch size: 2–3 eggs

Incubation: Unknown

Diet: Unknown, but probably insects and some small vertebrates such as lizards

Habitat: Foothill forests with dense undergrowth, especially of dwarf bamboo

Range: Western and southern foothills of central mountain region of Sri Lanka

THE HEAD, LOWER back, rump, and tail of the green-billed coucal are black with a purple sheen. The neck, upper back, and breast are a shiny metallic brown, appearing either bronze or copper. Chestnut patches are visible on the wing and shoulder, and the wing feathers are dull colored at the tips. The leg, foot, and toe are black. The bird has an exceptionally large, slightly decurved beak and is ivory colored with a faint green hue.

The green-billed coucal has become Sri Lanka's rarest bird. Habitat loss is to blame for its plight. Sri Lanka has cut its native forests, not only to produce lumber products for the world market but also to create jobs for its citizens. Plantations of pine, teak, and eucalyptus have been established to sustain timber production. Rubber and tea are also important cultivated crops. Sadly, neat rows of cultivated trees (called stands) do not reproduce the traits of the original plant communities that form animal habitat. Although some animal species are adaptable and find tree plantations and other agricultural land satisfactory, most species do not. In 1988 a pair of green-billed coucals was found in an area where the vegetation was mostly disturbed by human activities. Dwarf bamboo, which the green-billed coucal is believed to prefer, was conspicuously absent. No green-billed coucals were seen in a nearby

Coucals are mainly large, somewhat pheasantlike birds that spend most of their time on the ground. They are known for their loud nonmusical calls and also hiss and screech.

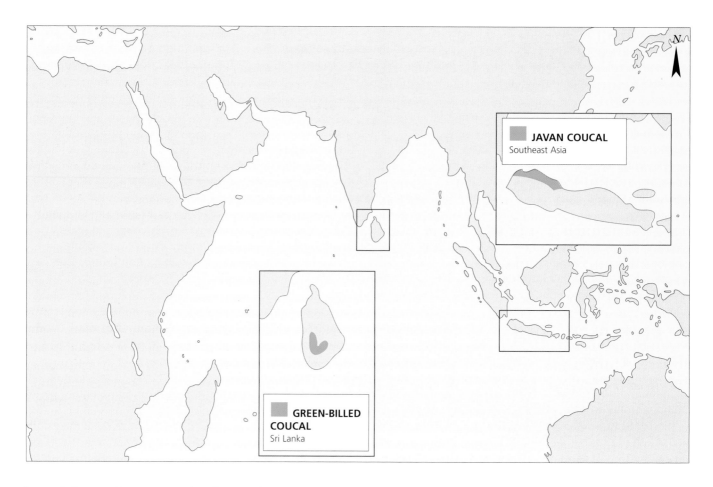

JAVAN COUCAL
Southeast Asia

GREEN-BILLED COUCAL
Sri Lanka

logged forest that was seeing its second growth. It seems that the green-billed coucal generally does not use second growth or other disturbed forest habitats. The bird's unwillingness to occupy artificial plant communities indicates that the habitat has lost something essential for its survival. What the missing ingredient or ingredients might be remains unknown.

How does it nest?

Specific needs of food or nesting cover can be lost when natural plant communities are destroyed. The green-billed coucal has not been studied, so its natural history is not well known. Its nest is reported to be a rounded mass of small sticks, roots, and grasses lined inside with green leaves. The nests are usually found 3 to 6½ feet (about 1 to 2 meters)

above ground in thorny shrubs. The green-billed coucal's peculiar beak might mean that it has a more specialized diet than its more common relative the greater coucal (*Centropus sinensis*). This possibility needs to be investigated carefully. If the bird does have a specialized diet, learning what it is could lead to the discovery of the missing ingredient in artificial habitats that prevents the green-billed coucal from adapting.

Rarely sighted

In the 1880s the green-billed coucal was described as common but almost impossible to view. Most people who encounter the green-billed coucal only hear it, and this makes historical estimates of its population and range suspect. The green-billed coucal sounds so much like the more

abundant greater coucal that birds which are heard but not seen could be misidentified. Still, the bird certainly must have been more abundant when its habitat was more extensive.

Dwindling habitat

By 1955 people knew the bird's habitat was dwindling, and the bird showed no signs of adapting to altered habitat. By 1989 one Sri Lankan authority on birds bemoaned that Sri Lanka had been "developed to an almost unimaginable extent."

The area that once supported green-billed coucals now supports the densest human population on the island. Protecting the green-billed coucal depends on preserving the last remnants of its native forests and on studying its natural history to learn what its special needs are.

Javan Coucal
(Centropus nigrorufus)

Length: 16 in. (41 cm)
Weight: Unknown
Clutch size: Unknown
Incubation: Unknown
Diet: Unknown
Habitat: Dense shrubberies, thickets, and lowlands
Range: Western Java and extreme southeastern Sumatra in Indonesia

THE JAVAN COUCAL is blackish brown with cinnamon coloring on the shoulder and on the outer flight feathers. The feet and toes are thick and strong. The tail is moderately long and the beak is slightly decurved. Since it is more adaptable to change than the green-billed coucal, the Javan coucal has adapted to some second-growth plant habitats. Very little is known of this bird's natural history. The Javan coucal inhabits lowland shrub communities of western Java and extreme southeastern Sumatra. The Sumatran population may already be extinct, and the Javan population is jeopardized by the conversion of lowland areas to agricultural uses.

The coastal lowlands of the island are cleared and developed for fish ponds and rice paddies. Many of the ponds are saltwater facilities used to raise shrimp. Harvesting 154,000 short tons (140,000 tonnes) of shrimp each year, Indonesia has become a major shrimp-producing country, second only to China in the eastern hemisphere. Indonesia also produces carp and other freshwater fish. Those areas unsuitable for shrimp or carp ponds are used for growing rice. This aggressive agricultural and aquacultural growth is important to the Indonesian economy because the shrimp and rice reach international markets. However, such large-scale production has destroyed most of the lowland habitat that once supported the Javan coucal.

Giving up already developed areas to recover the Javan coucal is an unrealistic expectation, but the remaining lowland shrub habitat must be preserved. In addition studies could reveal how managing second growth could benefit the bird.

Kevin Cook

COUGARS

Class: Mammalia
Order: Carnivora
Family: Felidae

Cougars (also known as pumas, panthers, or mountain lions) form a group of 30 subspecies of shy, solitary animals. They are the largest cats of the genus *Felis*, averaging about the same size as a leopard, and tend to be buff to brownish or grayish in color.

Cougars were once the most widespread mammals in the New World besides humans and were found in a wide range of habitats. They can thrive in forests, lowland tropical forests, swamps, grasslands, dry bush country, or any other area with adequate cover and prey. They wander in large ranges that extend up to 250 square miles (650 square kilometers) if the habitat permits it. The only time they have a fixed home is when the female is rearing her young. Otherwise, cougars will take temporary shelter in caves, rock crevices, or other areas where they can conceal themselves.

These large cats stalk their prey, killing it by leaping on the victim's back. Deer make up the cougar's most common food source, and an individual kills from one deer every 16 days to feed itself to one every three days when a female is feeding large cubs. The kill is dragged to a sheltered area, partly eaten, then covered with leaves or other items. The cougar will then return to consume more over the next several days.

The cougar does not have a specific breeding season, but most births in North America occur in late winter and early spring. Females usually give birth every other year, and the gestation period is between 90 and 96 days. The number of offspring can vary from one to six but is commonly three or four.

The cougar rarely attacks human beings, although seven people have been killed by these animals in Canada and the United States since 1900. Even so, people have long been afraid of this cat, considering it a threat to themselves and also to domestic animals. Therefore, the cougar has been intensively hunted since the arrival of European settlers.

By the early twentieth century the cougar population was severely depleted. Today there may be 16,000 individuals left. California provides the cougar complete protection, but Texas still allows it to be killed at any time. Other western states and Canadian provinces permit regulated hunting. Continued hunting and loss of habitat threaten the cougar's survival.

Eastern Cougar
(Puma concolor cougar)

Florida Panther
(Puma concolor coryi)

ESA: Endangered

IUCN: Critically endangered

Body length: Male 50–77 in. (125–195 cm); female 28–60 in. (70–150 cm)
Tail length: Male 28–31 in. (65–80 cm); female 21–32 in. (55–80 cm)
Shoulder height: 23–27 in. (60–70 cm)
Weight: Male 145–225 lb. (65–100 kg); female 80–130 lb. (35–60 kg)
Diet: Mammals of various sizes
Gestation period: 90–96 days
Habitat: Forested areas
Range: Eastern United States and formerly Canada

THE EASTERN COUGAR was said to be extinct as long ago as 1946, but since then there have been repeated sightings of the animal throughout its range. Unfortunately it is difficult to know for sure if the reported animal is the eastern cougar or another subspecies. While there is no conclusive evidence that the cats observed were the eastern cougar, the sightings have encouraged ongoing speculation about the rumored extinction of the animal. Today the eastern cougar has been virtually eliminated from eastern North America. In Canada the main population is found in southwestern British Columbia.

Like other cougar subspecies, the eastern cougar lives in forested areas where game is abundant. Deer is its primary source of food. Together with loss of habitat, the decline in prey has posed a major threat to the eastern cougar. Unfortunately it is still considered a threat to people and livestock and is in constant danger of being persecuted by humans. In the past "ring hunts" were popular, in which a group of hunters would surround an area and have free rein to kill all wildlife encountered. The largest of these hunts took place in

The Florida panther is one of the most critically endangered mammals in the world. Efforts to help it recover are in full force but may not be adequate to save this animal.

Pennsylvania in 1760, when 200 hunters formed a circle 30 miles (48 kilometers) in diameter and closed in on the animals in the area. The spoils of the hunt were 114 "mountain cats," 112 foxes, 11 buffaloes, 109 wolves, 198 deer, 18 bears, 41 pumas, and about 500 smaller animals.

Another subspecies, the Florida panther (*Puma concolor*

coryi), is a medium-sized animal with a broad, high skull. The favorite prey of this cat is also deer, which it kills by stalking, then springing and biting at the neck in much the same way as other felids. Food is needed about every seven days, or more frequently by nursing mothers. Wild hogs are another major food source for this cat, and many believe that this additional prey may have helped the Florida panther survive when its other eastern relatives could not. The cat also will eat various other mammals as well as reptiles and occasionally insects. There has never been a documented attack on a human by a Florida panther.

The male Florida panther wanders a range of up to 250 square miles (648 square kilometers) in search of prey, substantially further than do western mountain lions, which have a greater density of prey to hunt. The female travels less, from 70 to 90 square miles (180 to 230 square kilometers). Both roam continuously, though slightly less after feeding, and usually travel alone except when breeding or rearing offspring.

Former range

The Florida panther is one of the nation's most critically endangered animals. Listed as endangered since 1967, it formerly ranged from eastern Texas and western Louisiana and the Lower Mississippi River Valley to the southeastern states, including Arkansas, Mississippi, Alabama, Georgia, Florida, and parts of Tennessee and South Carolina. Today the cat's distribution is uncertain, but the only confirmed populations are in south

Florida in the Big Cypress and Everglades regions. The estimated total population in the wild is between 30 and 50 animals. Statistics suggest that under current conditions, the Florida panther will be extinct within 25 to 40 years.

Increased sightings

As in the case of the eastern cougar, there have been numerous reports of sightings of the Florida panther across its former range, but none have been proved conclusively to be members of this subspecies. Many of these sightings are questionable, but the reports have increased steadily from the 1960s onward. It is believed that the subspecies was still relatively abundant, with a population of about 500 animals around 1900. Excessive hunting has been the primary cause of the cougar's decline, along with illegal killing and highway mortality. Habitat loss and the decline of prey populations have also played a part.

Many believe that today the continued increase of human activity within the animal's former range presents the greatest threat to the cougar's survival. Twice as many people live in Florida now as than in 1960. There simply is not enough public land in which the Florida panther may roam freely.

Other problems are challenging the critically small Florida panther population. Because so few of the cats remain, they have a significantly reduced gene pool. This has led to an increase in disease, genetic defects linked to inbreeding, and a high rate of abnormal sperm. Most conservationists believe there must be a group of at least several hundred animals to achieve a healthy, self-sustaining population. Recently another problem was discovered. A Florida panther was found dead of mercury poisoning in 1989. Extremely high levels of

While some cougars are endangered, others, like this California cougar, are not.

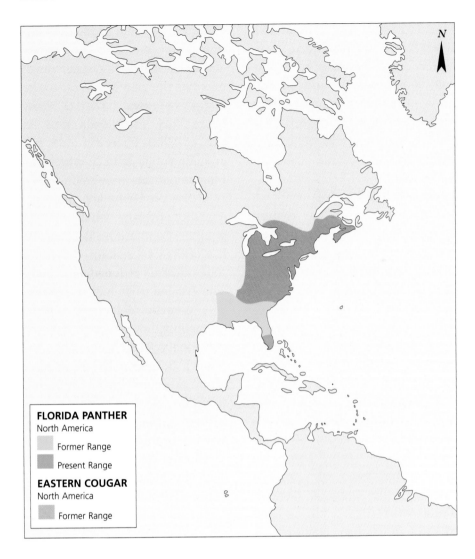

FLORIDA PANTHER
North America

Former Range

Present Range

EASTERN COUGAR
North America

Former Range

N

the two subspecies. Interbreeding would have occured naturally, helping the Florida panther remain genetically healthy. It is hoped that the introduced females will interbreed with the Florida panther and help to reduce the genetic problems caused by inbreeding without swamping the Florida panther gene pool.

Radio tracking

Scientists have been carrying out capture-and-tracking programs with the Florida panther for some time. Of the 30 to 50 animals in existence, 24 are fitted with radio collars that allow scientists to monitor the animals. Cougars are trapped in trees by hound dogs, then darted with tranquilizers. The cats are then given medical and genetic tests and various vaccinations.

Although the Florida panther's situation is bleak, the dedication of the state, together with a strong group of professionals, may help the subspecies survive. The acquisition and protection of this cougar's habitat is perhaps one of the most critical parts of the state's survival plan. State and federal governments have tried to accommodate this need by expanding national parklands in southern Florida and establishing the new Florida Panther National Wildlife Refuge.

Habitat acquired

About 300,000 acres (134,040 hectares) of habitat have been acquired in recent years, and more is expected to be obtained in the future. However, even these tactics may not be enough to save the cougar from extinction.

Elizabeth Sirimarco

the toxic element were found in its liver. Tests were run on other individuals, and although none had nearly as high a level of mercury in their systems, some had levels high enough to raise concern. The presumed source of the element was prey animals, which accumulate the mercury through eating aquatic food.

Recovery plans

The Florida panther has one of the strongest recovery plans of any endangered species. Since 1950 Florida has extended cougar protection while other states still viewed the animal as a pest. In 1973 the Florida panther gained federal protection under the Endangered Species Act.

Cooperative state and federal programs began in the 1980s.

During 1991 and 1992 a total of ten kittens were removed from the wild for a captive breeding program. However, in 1992 new data showed that the health of the wild population was continuing to deteriorate. The breeding program was reevaluated and a decision was made to stop captive breeding and try to restore the genetic viability of the remaining panthers in the wild. Several females of the Texas subspecies *Puma concolor stanleyana* were introduced into the Florida panthers range. The Texas subspecies' range used to overlap the Florida panther's range before human encroachment isolated

CRANES

Class: Aves

Order: Gruiformes

Family: Gruidae

Subfamily: Gruinae

Cranes have stimulated the human imagination in art and literature for thousands of years. These elegant birds have even shown their influence in some religions and folklore. Fossils indicate that cranes have been around far longer than have humans—extinct forms date back 40 million years. Some extant species, such as the sandhill crane, may have survived at least four million years.

Cranes occupy every continent except Antarctica and South America. Their long necks, legs, and feet make them well suited for the open country they inhabit. Their height allows them to see over vegetation to watch for predators. Most cranes inhabit marshes or grasslands associated with marshes and feed on large insects such as grasshoppers. They also feed on crustaceans such as crayfish and crabs. However, these same types of habitat have become very important to humans. All over the world people have drained marshes and converted them for agricultural use.

Sandhill cranes have adapted to drier croplands. During their autumn migrations they feed heavily on waste grain in wheat, barley, and corn fields. Unfortunately other species cannot adapt to changes in their environment so easily.

Many crane species have reacted to lost habitat by shifting territories. Some cranes no longer occupy traditional winter habitat but are establishing new wintering grounds elsewhere. Because cranes can live more than 20 years and because they have such low reproductive rates, their populations often decline very slowly. Alterations in their range plus their long life cycle and low rate of reproduction make it difficult for ornithologists to determine the status of some crane species. However, three kinds of cranes are definitely known to be having survival problems. These are the Japanese crane, the Mississippi sandhill crane, and the whooping crane.

Beautiful plumage patterns and stately behavior make cranes favorites among birders and nonbirders alike. Cranes' large size makes them easy to see and watch. Through the 1980s people showed a willingness to pay for seeing the spectacle of migrating cranes. Revenues generated by wildlife tourism could help pay the costs of preservation.

Japanese Crane

(Grus japonensis)

ESA: Endangered

IUCN: Vulnerable

Length: 40–48 in. (100–120 cm); stands 5–5½ ft. (1.5–1.7 m) tall

Weight: 13–15 lb. (6–7 kg)

Clutch size: 1–2 eggs

Incubation: 30–35 days

Diet: Insects, fish, frogs, salamanders, and grains

Habitat: Marshes in summer, fields and rivers in winter

Range: Eastern Hokkaido Island of Japan near Kushiro; Lake Khanka in Russia north of Vladivostok, extending west into Manchuria (China); the mainland birds winter on the Korean peninsula

THE UPPER AND LOWER body of the Japanese crane are entirely white. The wing is mostly white, but the middle and inner flight feathers are black. The forehead and forecrown are mostly bare and bright red; a white patch extends from eye to eye around the back of the head, tapering to a sharp point midway down the back of the crane's neck. The beak is greenish or horn colored.

The Japanese crane once symbolized long life and marital stability to the Japanese people. The honored bird inhabited the four large Japanese islands and ranged as far south as Taiwan and a portion of the Asian mainland across the Sea of Japan. For centuries the region's growing human population has applied steady pressure for more farmland and places for people to live. The demand for human space has grown particularly intense during this century. The crane has responded by slowly declining over the years.

At one time the Japanese crane was thought to have been lost in Japan altogether, but in 1924 about 20 birds were found on the island of Hokkaido. Political conditions in China and the former U.S.S.R. prevented outside investigations of Japanese crane populations in those countries. Russian ornithologists, however, reported some surviving birds in the 1950s, living at Lake Khanka north of Vladivostock. Although the mainland birds migrate to spend winters on the Korean peninsula, they do not cross the sea to mingle with the Japanese population. Nor do the Japanese birds leave their island. The two populations are isolated from each other.

The Hokkaido birds were discovered in a large marsh north of Kushiro. Known as the Kushiro Shitsugen, the marsh sprawls across 50,000 acres (20,235 hectares), or about 78 square miles (202 square kilometers). Because the site is so far north and in a cold climate, dead marsh plants do not decompose as they would in warmer parts. This dead but undecayed vegetation (mostly the reed *Phragmites communis*) forms extensive mats surrounded by living plants, interrupted by small pools and meandering streams. This marsh complex has proved of no value to human interests but is extremely valuable for the survival of the cranes.

Join the club

During the 1950s Japanese schoolchildren formed crane clubs after a unique winter visit by the cranes. The winter of 1952 was unusually cold, and the hungry cranes approached human settlements, where they pecked for waste grain. Schoolchildren bought corn and buckwheat to feed the cranes, and the birds returned the following year.

Winter feeding and counting the birds became primary activities of the crane clubs. The first count in 1952 yielded 33 Japanese cranes. As programs to feed the cranes in winter and protect their habitat progressed, the crane population recovered. The crane club count in 1962 was 184, and 222 by 1972. The Hokkaido Japanese crane population reached about 450 birds in 1991. In recent years the population has been estimated at 594 and increasing.

Virtually all the Hokkaido cranes are found within 35 miles (56 kilometers) of Kushiro. They do not migrate but they do move from the marshlands of the Kushiro Shitsugen in winter. Special feeding stations have been established for them in fields. Farmers and members of the crane clubs put out grain, such as buckwheat and corn, which the cranes readily accept. The cranes congregate at the feeding stations by day and roost in unfrozen rivers by night.

In addition to grain, cranes eat insects and fish, particularly the mudfish (*Misgurunus anguillicaudatus*), which is known locally and in the aquarium trade as dojo but named oriental weatherfish by the American Fisheries Society. Cranes will also eat amphibians, such as the common frog (*Rana temporaria*) and salamanders (*Salamandrella keyserlingii* and *Hynobius retardatus*).

While the Japanese population has grown, the mainland Asia population has declined for the same reason: habitat loss. The International Union for the Conservation of Nature (IUCN) estimates that as few as 600 to 800 birds survive in China, 300 to 350 in North Korea, and 200 to 300 in South Korea. The total population in the wild is estimated at 1,700 to 2,000 birds. The Japanese crane is banned from international commercial trade under CITES, the Convention on International Trade in Endangered Species of Wild Fauna and Flora.

Japanese culture has benefited from the recovery of the Japanese crane. Beginning with a national effort to raise money to feed the cranes in 1952, the Japanese people have regained their reverence for this ancient bird.

A black area encircles the long neck of the Japanese crane like a sleeve, extending farther down in back than in front. The neck of the female is lighter, or grayer, than the male's.

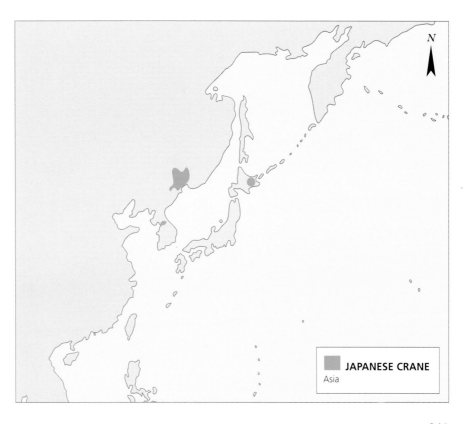

JAPANESE CRANE
Asia

Mississippi Sandhill Crane

(Grus canadensis pulla)

ESA: Endangered

Length: 34–40 in. (86–102 cm); stands about 4 ft. (1.2 m) tall
Weight: 10–14 lb. (4.5–6.4 kg)
Clutch size: 1–2 eggs
Incubation: 28–31 days
Habitat: Wetlands
Range: Jackson County, Mississippi

LONG BEFORE HUMANS appeared on earth, sandhill cranes filled the sky over North America. Their noisy, uneven trumpeting is still heard, as they bugle, rolling their Rs again and again in a call that sounds like, "KARRR-rrruh!" Over and over again they call. Their undisciplined chorus raises a clamor that can be heard from a great distance. For thousands of years sandhill cranes have gathered each autumn by the Platte River in central Nebraska. In recent years this spectacle has become an American national treasure.

Thousands of people visit the area's rural towns, filling the motels and campgrounds. They gather at the Platte River to thrill in witnessing a spectacular bird that has survived perhaps nine million years.

When the human species first explored the North American continent, sandhill cranes occurred coast to coast, north and south, east and west, inhabiting nearly every present-day state and province. As modern settlement took hold in the 1700s and began expanding rapidly in the 1800s, sandhill cranes disappeared from portions of their range. They withdrew from the Atlantic seaboard, the Midwest, and parts of the South.

Ornithologists now recognize six subspecies of sandhill cranes. The three most northerly subspecies migrate yearly between summer nesting habitat and wintering habitat. The three most

There are six recognized subspecies of sandhill cranes. They were once abundant and occurred from coast to coast in the United States. Unfortunately this is no longer the case. Sandhill cranes even need help to hatch their eggs.

southerly subspecies do not migrate but remain in the same habitat year-round. For many years nonmigratory sandhill cranes lived on the coastal plain of the Gulf states from Louisiana to Florida. Most of these birds slowly dwindled away as people converted marshes and prairies into cropland and tree plantations. One small population survived in extreme southeastern Mississippi, and in 1972 it was described as the sixth subspecies.

This subspecies is generally darker than other sandhill crane subspecies. Overall it is a neutral dark gray with some orange brown splotches scattered about the wing, neck, breast, and side. The lore, forehead, and forecrown are unfeathered and bright red; the cheek and chin are often pale. The bird's beak is long, straight, and pointed, usually dark gray or nearly black, and paler at the base. The innermost wing feathers (known as tertials) are long, almost plumelike, and extend out over the tail when the wings are folded. The Mississippi sandhill crane feeds on plant material, insects, crayfish, amphibians, and reptiles. This subspecies numbered perhaps 100 birds in 1920. By 1983 it had declined to just 40 wild birds.

Habitat loss

This coastal crane inhabits shallow marshes and dry savannas (grassy expanses with scattered trees and few woody shrubs). In the past natural fires set by lightning probably burned the savannas periodically. These fires would kill the woody plants and keep the land open for the grass communities known as prairies. During the late 1800s and the

opening decades of the 1900s, people cut the natural stands of loblolly pine (*Pinus taeda*), grazed cattle on the savannas, drained marshes, and planted crops where possible. By the 1950s pine plantations had become well established in the southern states. Growing trees efficiently on plantations meant suppressing fire, building roads, digging drainage ditches, and developing towns for workers.

Conservation efforts

The cranes retreated to isolated patches of habitat along forest edges where runoff formed marshes, to the edges of swamps and surviving savanna, and to young pine plantations where grassy openings existed between rows of trees. Complicating the birds' isolation are three main highways that have been built through their last stronghold. These highways opened land for development. Fortunately the Nature Conservancy purchased 1,709 acres (692 hectares) of vital habitat for the beleaguered cranes. Additional land has been purchased, with 18,000 acres (7,285 hectares) now protected in the Mississippi Sandhill Crane National Wildlife Refuge. Despite these efforts, the cranes have consistently failed to raise their young successfully in recent years. Either their eggs fail to hatch or the chicks die. No one has been able to explain this complete reproductive failure.

To compensate for this problem, specialists working to help the cranes recover have been taking one egg from each crane's nests. Because the cranes usually lay two eggs, that leaves one egg for the parent birds to tend. The

other egg is carefully hatched and the chick reared in captivity. Each December the captive chicks are released back into the wild flock. This technique has increased the wild Mississippi sandhill crane population to nearly 100 birds. Until researchers can find the cause of the subspecies' reproduction problems, the captive rearing-and-release technique will probably have to continue.

Whooping Crane
(Grus americana)

ESA: Endangered	
IUCN: Endangered	

Weight: 9–17 lb. (4–7.7 kg)
Length: 50–52 in. (127–132 cm); stands up to 5 ft. (1.5 m) tall
Clutch size: 1–3 eggs; usually 2
Incubation: 29–31 days
Diet: Primarily insects, clams, and crustaceans; some small vertebrates such as amphibians, rodents, and fish; occasional fruits and grains
Habitat: Shallow wetlands, wet grasslands, and coastal estuaries
Range: North America from extreme south-central Northwest Territories in Canada to the coastal plain of the Gulf of Mexico in Texas; cross-fostered birds migrate between Idaho and New Mexico but have wandered into Mexico

THE PLUMAGE OF the whooping crane is all white except for the black outer flight feathers. The crown, forehead, and jawline are bare and bright red. The beak is dark to straw colored. The legs and feet are black, and the toes are a pale flesh or a dull golden color. Young whoopers have rust-colored heads and necks.

The whooping crane once ranged over much of the North American continent. Fossil discoveries show that the species occurred coast to coast. Quite probably the whooping crane's preferred habitat declined as the last glaciers retreated, and the bird's continental distribution dwindled as well.

In historical times migratory birds moved as far north as the subarctic to breed, then traveled to the coastal plains of the Atlantic Ocean and the Gulf of Mexico to spend the winter. Small flocks of resident whoopers occupied the southern states from eastern Texas through Louisiana to Florida year-round.

Between these extremes the whooping crane inhabited the western and upper Midwest, particularly Iowa, Wisconsin, and Minnesota, plus much of south-central Canada. This area was once richly endowed with shallow marshes left behind by glaciers that disappeared thousands of years ago.

Experts agree that whooping cranes were never abundant, but they disagree on how many whooping cranes existed before modern human settlement began in the 1800s. Estimates range from as few as 1,300 to perhaps two or three times that number. By 1941 only 21 wild whooping cranes survived. They were split between a flock of 15 birds that moved between Canada and Texas, and six birds that remained in Louisiana. By 1948 the Louisiana birds had disappeared, and few people believed the species could survive. The

The attractive whooping crane is North America's tallest bird. Its size and its bright white plumage made it a conspicuous target for hunters, as well as for egg collectors and naturalists seeking specimens for museums.

drastic decline stemmed from three main causes: conversion of marshland to farmland, zealous egg collecting, and shooting.

Easy target

The whooping crane is North America's tallest bird. At up to 17 pounds (7.7 kilograms), with a wingspread of almost eight feet (2.4 meters), the whooper ranks among the continent's largest birds, too. Its size and bright white plumage made it a conspicuous target for hungry settlers and curious naturalists seeking specimens for museums in the United States and Europe.

Despite the low population reached in the 1940s, whooping cranes continued to migrate to Aransas National Wildlife Refuge in Texas each winter. No one knew for sure where they spent their summer, although immatures appeared with adults each autumn at Aransas.

Breeding grounds

The breeding grounds of the last wild whoopers were discovered accidentally. A pilot flying over Great Slave Lake in Canada spotted two adults in 1952. A single bird was found in the general vicinity the following year.

In 1954 a fire started in a remote section of Wood Buffalo Park, which lies just south of Great Slave Lake between Alberta and the Northwest Territories. Two men were dispatched in a helicopter to appraise the fire. On their return flight they spotted two adult whooping cranes and a chick inside the park. Later fieldwork proved Wood Buffalo Park to be the last breeding stronghold of the whooping crane. Those last few

nests became crucial to a daring experiment.

The U.S. Fish and Wildlife Service began recovery efforts in 1967, relying on an extensive breeding effort. As part of this endeavor, American and Canadian biologists began removing one egg from whooping crane nests. These eggs were put in sandhill crane nests in Idaho.

Cross-fostering

Additional eggs were taken from captive whoopers and also placed in the sandhill nests. When the eggs hatched, the sandhills raised the whooper chicks as their own. This breeding technique is called cross-fostering.

The eggs survived the move and hatched well. The young whoopers migrated with the sandhills from Idaho through Wyoming and Colorado into New Mexico. Success ultimately depended upon whether the cross-fostered whooping cranes would recognize each other when they reached breeding age at about four years of age.

The cross-fostered whooping crane flock grew to more than three dozen birds by the 1980s. Unfortunately several birds died when they flew into power lines and fences, and at least one was killed by a golden eagle. On top of this a lopsided ratio of males to females developed. Not a single pair has formed in that flock, so no mating has occurred. Now only eight whooping cranes remain in the flock.

In 1989 a second captive flock was established at the International Crane Foundation in Baraboo, Wisconsin, a conservation organization dedicated to the preservation of cranes world-

wide. In addition to birds from the Patuxent center, some of the Baraboo cranes have been used for reintroduction efforts.

Captive success

In 1991 captive whooping cranes bred successfully on their own. This has encouraged ornithologists to believe that captive-bred birds, which have better chances for survival and breeding, might be available to release into the wild. Until this event occurred, captive females were artificially fertilized. With natural mating now occurring among captive birds, young whoopers can learn the courtship rituals before they are released into the wild.

In February 1993 a nonmigratory flock of 14 captive-reared whooping cranes was reintroduced on the Kissimmee Prairie in Florida. Since then more than 45 further birds have been released at this site, and annual releases of about 20 birds each are scheduled for years to come. In addition at least 18 whooping cranes have been transferred to a facility in Calgary, Canada, to establish a third captive flock.

Atificial insemination

Biologists are evaluating sites in Canada for a later reintroduction of a migratory flock of whooping cranes. Artificial insemination has also proved successful in increasing the number of eggs laid by captive cranes.

The gains whooping cranes have made can be deceptive. Captive flocks and artificial insemination are no way for a species to survive. They are only intermediate steps to recovery. Many of the same problems that originally endangered the whooping crane still exist. The cross-fostering program did produce some benefits. Whooping cranes almost always lay two eggs. Biologists discovered that those birds left with only one egg better tended their single chick and had more chicks survive to migrate than did those birds caring for two chicks.

The wild flock has consequently grown dramatically, and today the total population of whooping cranes consists of 300 known birds, with about 180 of these living in the wild.

The whooping crane is banned from international commercial trade under CITES, the Convention on International Trade in Endangered Species of Wild Fauna and Flora.

More wildlife management

Although the whooping crane remains a highly endangered species, its margin of survival has expanded. Perhaps more surprising than the bird's partial recovery is that it managed to survive in the social, political, and academic climates obtaining at the time. In the 1940s wildlife management was just emerging as an academic program in universities and was in its infancy as a profession. Early wildlife management meant preserving recreational hunting by preserving the prey of hunters.

No one ever pretended the whooping crane was a game bird that could be recovered for hunting purposes. Society had yet to recognize any responsibility for the recent extinction of passenger pigeons, heath hens, and Carolina parakeets, and no state or federal laws existed to empower an agency to protect endangered species. The whooping crane struggled through three decades of human misjudgment.

Finally the Endangered Species Act of 1973 mandated that the federal government be responsible for endangered species. Wildlife management matured beyond protecting animals for hunting and Americans began to form a conscience about preserving other life-forms. The law became a tool for protecting a species' right to exist. No other species, except for the bald eagle, contributed as much to the passage of this landmark legislation as did the whooping crane.

Kevin Cook

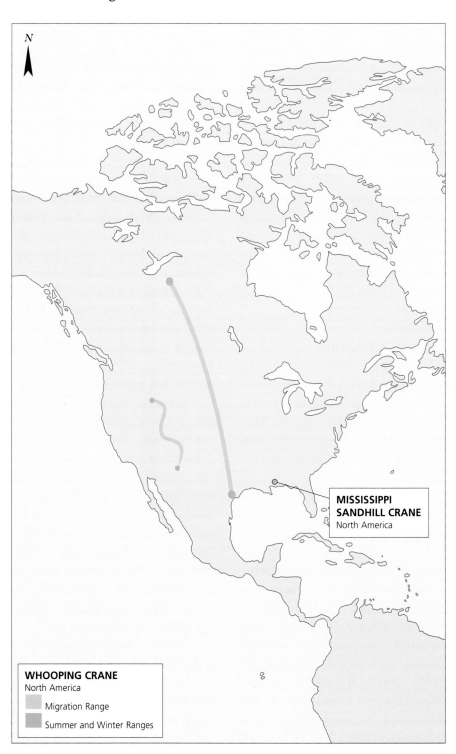

MISSISSIPPI
SANDHILL CRANE
North America

WHOOPING CRANE
North America
Migration Range
Summer and Winter Ranges

CRAYFISH

Phylum: Arthropoda

Class: Crustacea

Order: Decapoda

Crayfish are part of the order that includes shrimps, lobsters, and crabs. *Decapoda* means "ten feet," which is what crayfish have, counting their two large pinching claws. This order alone contains about 10,000 species. Although primarily a marine group, the Decapoda occur in fresh waters and have invaded terrestrial environments. All members of this order also have antennae or feelers and generally a hard shell and claws.

Certain species of crabs, lobsters, and shrimps make this group of great importance as a food resource to people. The Decapoda also play a valuable role in aquatic ecosystems as predators, herbivores, omnivores, and scavengers, and they are important in the diet of many predatory organisms, especially fish.

Giant Freshwater Crayfish

(Astacopsis gouldi)

IUCN: Endangered

Length: Up to 30 in. (76 cm)

Diet: Omnivorous

Habitat: Freshwater lakes, rivers, and streams

Range: Tasmania, Australia

ALTHOUGH INFORMATION on the distribution and habits of Tasmania's giant freshwater crayfish was reported as early as 1870, it was not until 1936 that the animal received a formal description and species name. It is classified in the family Parastacidae, or the Gondwana crayfish.

The giant freshwater crayfish is not only the largest of the crayfish, but it is also considered to be the largest freshwater invertebrate in the world. It has been recorded at lengths in excess of 30 inches (76 centimeters) and at a weight of almost 10 pounds (4.5 kilograms), with unofficial weights given of over 13 pounds (5.9 kilograms). Today individuals of up to 16 inches (41 centimeters) and 4.4 pounds (2 kilograms) are considered large. Because of its impressive size, the giant freshwater crayfish has been sought as food by native Tasmanian fishers and by generations of Australian settlers.

The giant freshwater crayfish is found only in the northern portion of the island of Tasmania, where it occurs in lakes, rivers, and streams that drain north into the Bass Strait, as well as in the Arthur River system in the northwest. The Bass Strait separates Tasmania from the Australian mainland. The giant freshwater crayfish is known to range downstream into brackish waters with the tides.

This crayfish inhabits cool, shaded waters with temperatures up to 70 degrees Fahrenheit (21 degrees Celsius). It ranges from deep areas to more shallow, rapidly flowing sections. This crayfish prefers deep, log-filled pools. A critical habitat requirement is the presence of rocky or woody cover that offers protection against predators. The giant freshwater crayfish is omnivo-rous, eating both plants and aquatic insects. The major element in its diet is probably bacteria, protozoa, and fungi found on aging plant material.

Mating takes place in the autumn, with eggs being carried by the female during winter and hatching in the spring. Young remain with the mother in late spring and summer. Females reproduce only every second year. The offspring are slow growing and reach maturity late, with some individuals living to as many as 30 years.

Fishing regulations

The population size varies from site to site, depending upon fishing pressure. The fishing season extends from early August through late April. A fisherman is permitted to catch a maximum of 12 animals in excess of five inches (13 centimeters) long (measured by the length of the hard-shelled body). Retaining females with eggs or young is not permitted. In areas with higher fishing pressure, as little as five percent of the population may be mature animals; in more inaccessible regions the percentage of mature individuals may reach 50 percent. However, these crayfish are so rare that even in the areas in which mature populations are highest it is difficult to catch as many as 12 legal-sized animals.

Habitat modification, especially from land clearance and overfishing, has contributed to the rarity of this species. Of additional concern is the introduction of aphanomycosis, or crayfish plague, to Australia. The plague is caused by a fungus that occurs on North American crayfish without serious consequences.

N

GIANT
FRESHWATER
CRAYFISH
Tasmania, Australia

However, the fungus was introduced into Europe and has had devastating effects on the native fauna there. Since studies of this fungus on certain Asian and Australian species have shown it to be equally devastating to these animals, it would be expected to threaten the survival of Australian crayfish species.

In 1969 a reserve was established at Caroline Creek, Mersey River drainage, in northwest Tasmania. The reserve encompasses an area that includes less than two miles (3.2 kilometers) of stream in which no fishing is permitted. A recent survey has found few giant freshwater crayfish within this protected zone, and none of legal size. Fishing regulations still do not provide sufficient protection for breeding populations. The reserve has been overfished and the landscape modified, including the addition of a plantation that grows an exotic pine species.

Additional protected areas where the giant freshwater crayfish can thrive need to be established, and the modification of fishing regulations is essential to secure larger reproducing populations in the wild.

Hell Creek Cave Crayfish

(Cambarus zophonastes)

ESA: Endangered

IUCN: Critically endangered

Length: Unknown
Diet: Detritus
Habitat: Subterranean cave waters
Range: Stone County, Arkansas

FIVE SPECIMENS OF this Arkansas cave crayfish were first collected in 1961 but were not formally described for another three years. It belongs to the family Cambaridae, or cyclic crayfish. Only eight specimens are known to exist in zoological collections. As is typical for cave species, this crayfish is albino (unpigmented) and has reduced eyes.

The Hell Creek Cave crayfish is known only from Hell Creek Cave in Stone County, Arkansas. An examination of over 170 caves in north-central Arkansas has not revealed any more populations of this rare species, which occurs only in waters of subterranean limestone channels.

Hell Creek is a typical wet cave—muddy and subject to flooding during significant storms or lengthy wet seasons. Approximately 150 feet (45.7 meters) inside the cave entrance lies a pool that ranges from one foot to at least 20 feet (30 centimeters to 6.1 meters) deep. This pool is fed by a narrow, shallow stream located in a passageway extending 1,400 feet (427 meters) farther into the interior of the cave. Water from the cave pool eventually emerges through three springs that lie about 150 feet (46 meters) from the cave entrance. The Hell Creek Cave crayfish has not been found outside the deep pool. Nothing is known of the feeding or reproductive habits of this species. Only one female carrying eggs has been observed, and this occurred in the month of May.

Cave environments lack the presence of light. Since green plants cannot grow without light, animals are dependent upon material brought into the cave system by creatures that move between the surface and the cave or by the replenishment of the cave's aquatic system by surface waters. The materials that are imported into the habitat may be a food source or may provide the necessary nutrients to support bacteria, protozoa, and fungi that, in turn, are consumed by the crayfish.

Bat droppings

Hell Creek Cave was at one time a summer roost for the endangered gray bat (*Myotis grisescens*). Evidence suggests that a colony of approximately 16,000 gray bats used the cave, but there have not been large numbers of bats in the cave for several years. This demonstrates the impact that disturbing one endangered species can have on another. With the growing absence of gray bats from the cave, the nutrients from their droppings were lost. Now the crayfish must rely upon nutrients from surface waters. The crayfish's egg production and population size are extremely limited and are directly affected by nutrient levels.

The population size of the Hell Creek Cave species is unknown. Channels that can be penetrated by people represent only a fraction of the subterranean system, so measuring the population is difficult. The largest number of crayfish sighted by scientists in a single trip was 15 individuals in 1983. The total population is estimated at fewer than 50 individuals.

Vulnerable to change

There are no known predators for this species. Because the crayfish are limited to a stable environment, they display a low productivity level, late sexual maturity, and a population that is consistent with the low levels of nutrients available in the cave environment. Therefore, they are especially sensitive and vulnerable to changes in their habitat. In addition, groundwater pollution increases this species' vulnerability to extinction.

The Arkansas Natural Heritage Commission now owns a 160-acre (65-hectare) tract that includes the entrance to Hell Creek Cave. Gating the entrance of the cave system could provide protection from cave use and potential collectors of the crayfish while still permitting the entry of bats. It is also important to carefully monitor the crayfish population. However, of equal importance is protecting the source of the cave's replenishment, known as a recharge area, which is largely on private property. Potential threats within this recharge zone include the growth of a nearby city, groundwater pollution and altered drainage patterns, three industrial opera-

tions, lowered groundwater levels from human water use, and a nearby state highway that in the past has had a 4,000-gallon (15,140-liter) gasoline spill. The crayfish is also at risk from collection. Taking away an adult could have a dramatic effect on the population.

Conservation

To guard against deteriorating water quality, conservation and management agreements should be undertaken with local industry. Additional lands should also be acquired in the recharge zone. The continued search for cave systems in the area that might harbor the Hell Creek Cave crayfish is also worth considering.

Nashville Crayfish

(Orconectes shoupi)

ESA: Endangered

IUCN: Critically endangered

Length: Unknown
Diet: Probably omnivorous
Habitat: Freshwater streams
Range: Mill Creek, Tennessee

THE NASHVILLE CRAYFISH is known to exist only in a small stream system called Mill Creek, located in Davidson County and a small portion of Williamson County, Tennessee. Davidson County is dominated by the city of Nashville and its suburbs.

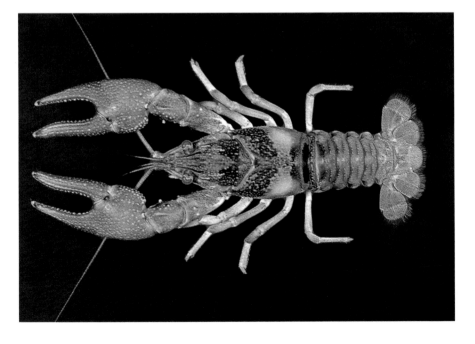

The Nashville crayfish apparently exists in only a single small stream system in Tennessee.

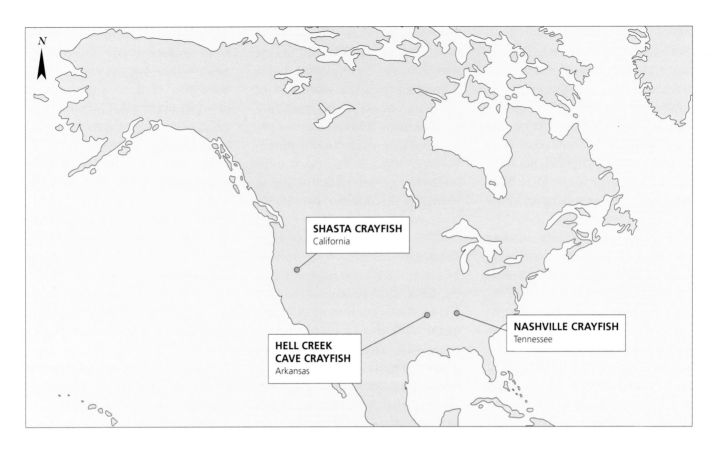

The first thorough survey of the crayfish in the Nashville, Tennessee, area was conducted by Robert Fleming in the late 1930s. Fleming surveyed a wide range of habitats and collected all but one of the crayfish species now known from this region. One crayfish, which he identified as the subspecies *Cambarus propinquus sanborni* (no common name), was later determined to be a new species and described in 1948 as *Orconectes shoupi*. It has since acquired the common name Nashville crayfish. It is part of the family Cambaridae, or cyclic crayfish.

Habitat

Within the Mill Creek system are other species of stream-dwelling crayfish and two burrowing species. The most common stream crayfish in the area is *O. placidus* (no common name), which does not occur in the Mill Creek system but dominates rocky areas in the surrounding streams. The Mill Creek system is typical of streams that drain into the Inner Nashville Basin, flowing over bedrock with gravel runs, scattered limestone slabs, and smaller rocks. Sandy and silty areas occur in pools, backwaters, and along stream margins. Downstream portions of the system are generally more turbid and silty, reflecting greater human activity in the area. In the Inner Nashville Basin limestone forms conspicuous rock slabs. Their fragments, weathered and broken from the flat-lying deposits, form the critical habitat of the Nashville crayfish, ranging from areas of riffles to pools.

Females carrying eggs during the spring seek isolated areas along shore. Other crayfish also inhabit the system, being found in pool areas and along stream margins. In Sevenmile Creek, the largest tributary in the system, and in smaller tributary streams, members of an unnamed species are more common.

Although many specimens of the Nashville crayfish have been collected during the last 15 years, biological information from these collections has not been compiled. From a few available collections it seems that males molt into reproductive form in late summer and fall, while the females lay eggs in late winter and early spring. Nothing is known of the growth, aging, and diet of this species. Crayfish generally are omnivorous and opportunistic feeders, and this may also apply to the Nashville crayfish.

During July 1985 the Nashville crayfish was found to comprise 90 percent of the crayfish fauna at eight sampling sites in Mill Creek and 40 percent of the species at four locations on Sevenmile Creek. At two additional sites on Mill Creek the Nashville crayfish was approximately equal in number to another as yet unnamed species from the same genus.

A target for predators

As is typical for crayfish, an array of predators, especially vertebrates, hunt this species for food. Among the potential predators would almost certainly be the raccoon (*Procyon lotor*).

A comparison of three sites surveyed between 1969 and 1976, with a follow-up study done in 1984, showed the Nashville crayfish to be still common at one, still uncommon at another, and reduced at the third. The last site had been drastically altered by the removal of streamside woodlands and the recontouring of the streambanks. Streamside trees and vegetation are important to the crayfish, since they provide shade and filter out some of the silt and pollutants in runoff. The replacement of trees by grasses also tends to alter the depth, bottom type, and bank cover of the stream.

The Nashville crayfish dominates the Mill Creek system, while *O. placidus* is the predominant crayfish in surrounding streams. The natural process that excludes the more successful *O. placidus* from the Mill Creek system is unknown. The alterations to the system by human growth have not upset this process, but the consequences of future changes are unknown.

The Nashville crayfish is certainly affected by stream modifications and degradation of water quality. One of the greatest threats is the continued development of the basin, especially construction in the floodplain.

Soils in the area are thin, and flat bedrock areas are common. This gives rise to rapid runoff and flooding of low-lying areas. Regions that are easily flooded create a demand for environmental changes to protect property that include paving, which contributes to runoff, degradation of water quality, and siltation. Spills and occasional discharges have occurred and have contributed to the degradation of water quality.

No recovery plan

At the moment no specific action has been undertaken to preserve the Nashville crayfish. The species needs to be monitored, biological information needs to be gathered, streamside buffer areas need to be preserved, and continued building in the floodplain needs to be curtailed. The preservation of farmlands upstream will help to maintain water quality in the basin. Potential threats to the Nashville crayfish from the more successful and widespread *O. placidus* also need to be researched.

Noble Crayfish

(Astacus astacus)

IUCN: Vulnerable

Length: Unknown
Diet: Omnivorous
Habitat: Freshwater streams, rivers, and lakes
Range: Europe; transplanted to portions of Asia and Africa

ALTHOUGH THE NOBLE crayfish has been known for many centuries, its presently accepted

species name dates back only to Carolus Linnaeus, the Swedish naturalist who established the modern scientific method of naming plants and animals. In 1758 the noble crayfish was the first species of crayfish to be named, and it has been an important fisheries species in Europe for centuries. It is a member of the Astacidae family, or river lobsters.

This species is typically colored in browns and greens on the back, with the underside of the first pair of claws turning to a dark red or reddish brown. Because the noble crayfish was raised in fisheries, its original range has been somewhat obscured. The noble crayfish is believed to be primarily a species of northern and eastern Europe, including portions of France eastward to the western republics of the Russian Commonwealth, and from the southern portions of the Scandinavian countries southward. It is absent from the Italian and Balkan peninsulas. This species has been introduced into various parts of Europe, western Asia, and North Africa.

The noble crayfish occurs in a wide variety of habitats ranging from streams and rivers to lakes. These habitats are typified by cool, well-oxygenated waters with sufficient foliage cover. In areas of its range that overlap with members of the genus *Austropotamobius*, the noble crayfish is more common in the larger streams and rivers, while the smaller *Austropotamobius* prefers smaller streams. Cover providing a daytime retreat ranges from rocky and woody debris to dense stands of submerged aquatic vegetation. The noble crayfish also burrows into stream banks.

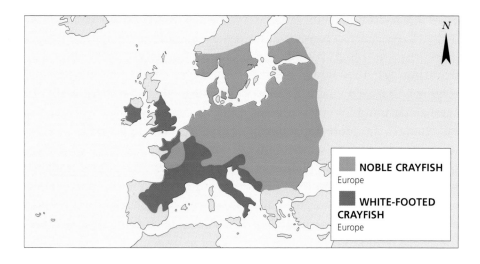

NOBLE CRAYFISH
Europe

WHITE-FOOTED CRAYFISH
Europe

Opportunistic feeder

The noble crayfish feeds on both living and dead plant and animal matter. Diet can vary according to region and the age of the animal. Living animal matter is preferred over dead matter and usually includes aquatic insects, crustaceans, worms, sponges, bryozoans, and mollusks. Crayfish crush the thin mollusk shells with their lower jaws (mandibles). In turn birds, mammals, and fish all like to prey on the noble crayfish.

As is common for such a wide-ranging species, this crayfish's reproductive cycle varies with latitude. Mating typically takes place during the autumn, with subsequent egg laying. The eggs are carried over winter, and hatching occurs during the spring and summer.

Juveniles leave the mother in summer. The males mature in three to four years, while maturity in the females requires four to six years or more, depending on climate.

Ravaged by plague

Population sizes of this species vary due to outbreaks of aphanomycosis (crayfish plague) and competition from introduced species. The crayfish plague was first noted in northern Italy in the 1860s. It spread throughout Europe, decimating or eliminating populations of native crayfish.

The crayfish plague is caused by a fungus (*Aphanomyces astaci*) known to occur naturally only in North American crayfish. There appears to be a relationship between the plague fungus and its North American host crayfish that does not exist in European or Australian crayfish species.

Although the crayfish plague in Italy was not detected until the 1860s, the first recorded introduction of a North American crayfish did not occur until 1890. This species, the spinycheek crayfish (*Orconectes limosus*), was transplanted into the Oder River in Germany to replace stocks of the noble crayfish that had been decimated by the crayfish plague in the late 1870s.

The plague source

Even though the crayfish plague in Europe predates the introduction of the spinycheek crayfish, the North American crayfish are still assumed to be the source of the disease, since the fungus occurs naturally in the spinycheek crayfish. Further introductions of North American crayfish and the use of infected fishing gear (traps and nets) helped spread the crayfish plague across Europe and affected populations to varying degrees.

The noble crayfish is vulnerable not only to the crayfish plague but also to competition from newly introduced species from North America and from a Eurasian species. The spinycheek crayfish has displaced some noble crayfish, as has the Eurasian long-clawed crayfish (*Astacus leptodactylus*). The red swamp crayfish (*Procambarus clarkii*), a native of North America, has not at this time come into contact with the noble crayfish, but there is reason for concern.

Devastating acid rain

Additionally, habitat alteration, water use, and overfishing have contributed to the declining numbers of the noble crayfish. Acid rain is especially devastating because it decreases the number of young and prolongs the hardening of a crayfish's new shell after molting.

In Europe many approaches have been tried to preserve the native crayfish, including regulations to control pollution, reintroductions of the noble crayfish to its habitat, and fishing rules governing size, catch limits, seasonality, numbers and types of traps, and areas open to fishing.

Action required

Continued pollution abatement and preservation of the noble crayfish habitat is important. Regulations need to be more widespread concerning the introduction of exotic species and the use of exotic crayfish for bait. With research it would be possible to breed a strain of noble crayfish that is resistant to the plague, helping return this species to many parts of its former range.

Shasta Crayfish

(Pacifastacus fortis)

ESA: Endangered

IUCN: Critically endangered

Length: Unknown
Diet: Unknown
Habitat: Freshwater springs
Range: Shasta County, northern California

THE SHASTA CRAYFISH is a member of the Astacidae, or river lobster, family. It was first described in 1914 by Walter Faxon from specimens collected by the U.S. Fisheries Commission in 1898. These animals were obtained from Hat Creek near Cassel and from Fall River near Fall River Mills in Shasta County, California. Both streams are part of the Pit River system, which drains the northeast corner of California before becoming part of the Sacramento River system.

From the Shasta crayfish's discovery in 1898 through a 1975 study done for the U.S. Fish and Wildlife Service, a survey of the California crayfish in the late 1950s was the only other time this little-known species was reported. The researcher at that time was unable to collect any specimens of the Shasta crayfish, although he received reports from residents that they had recently caught crayfish or had

found young ones in the stomachs of trout. It was assumed that these reports referred to the Shasta crayfish, since it was the only known crayfish species that had ever been reported from the area. It is probably on the basis of these reports that Riegel added a new locality to the crayfish's range, one-half mile (800 meters) northwest of Cassel. This new site in the Hat Creek drainage between Rising River Lake and Baum Lake lies near one of the original Shasta crayfish localities.

The range of this species in the Fall River and Hat Creek systems is below 3,400 feet (1,035 meters) in the former and 3,200 feet (975 meters) in the latter system, with only one additional site outside these two. This site, Sucker Spring, is a small spring that runs to the Pit River, which lies between the mouths of the two known drainage systems.

The Shasta is unique among North American crayfish for its typical dark greenish to dark brown to blackish color pattern on the back and generally dark orange color underneath the large claws. The crayfish's dorsal

color allows it to blend in with the rock or gravel lava common in the area. Blue individuals of the Shasta crayfish with a lighter orange to yellow belly are also known, especially from the Sucker Spring site.

The Shasta crayfish's closest relative, the sooty crayfish (*P. nigrescens*), was at one time common in the vicinity of San Francisco and was described as blackish. The first specimens of the sooty crayfish ever reported were purchased in the markets of San Francisco. Crayfish from certain sites may appear to be generally black, but this is from dirt deposits that are shed with the exoskeleton of the animal when it molts.

The Shasta crayfish prefers clear, cool waters, typically near spring sources of streams and lakes. Springs are noteworthy for their low variation in annual temperatures. A significant limiting factor for the Shasta crayfish is the availability of shelter in the

The pattern on the back of the Shasta crayfish makes it a unique species. The color of its back permits it to blend in with its surroundings.

form of rocks. Most crayfish have been collected under rocks on a clean, firm gravel bed. This species, as is typical for surface-dwelling crayfish, is nocturnal and uses rocks for shelter during the day. Its diet is unknown, although in the laboratory it has fed on worms and limpets.

Mating appears to take place in late September and October, and eggs are laid in late October and November. The female carries the large eggs under her abdomen through the winter. The numbers of eggs are estimated to be between 14 and 66, depending upon the size of the female. This is a low number of eggs for a surface-dwelling crayfish. Hatching begins in late May, with the young remaining with the mother until mid-July. Most individuals live about four years.

Only one predator

All crayfish are important in the food chain, and the Shasta crayfish could be expected to be a food source for an array of predators, especially vertebrates, but trout are the only probable predators reported to date. However, the Sucker Spring site was converted to a raceway for raising trout (by stabilizing the banks with lava rocks), and although trout were present, the Shasta crayfish maintained a reproducing population by using the lava rock walls as shelter.

The existence of exotic species of crayfish within the Shasta crayfish's range threatens this animal's survival. Reduction and modification of the Shasta crayfish's habitat through increased land use and water demands are threatening its survival as well. Agricultural development, power plants and

human population growth have all affected surface and subsurface waters in the crayfish's range. In addition, the introduced virile crayfish (*O. virialis*) and signal crayfish (*P. Lenisculus*) in the Fall River-Hat Creek area are competitive threats to the survival of the Shasta crayfish.

A tough competitor

The virile crayfish, a native of the Midwest and nearby Canada, has been shown to supplant native species in other parts of the country where it has been introduced. Virile crayfish were introduced into California ponds in Butte County for use in laboratories. This introduction probably occurred between 1939 and 1941, and a study of California crayfish in the 1950s found the species spreading through Butte and into Colusa, San Joaquin, and Yolo Counties.

The presence of the virile crayfish in and around recreational waters is probably the result of fishermen releasing unused bait. By the late 1970s the range of the virile crayfish had expanded upriver to the mouth of Sucker Spring, and by the early 1980s the crayfish had migrated farther upriver to Pit River Falls. As of 1990 the range of the virile crayfish included lower portions of Lake Britton, including lower Burney Creek, and the downriver portion of Fall River. Although this species is not living in Shasta crayfish areas, its inevitable encounters with that species will almost certainly result in more Shasta crayfish decline.

The signal crayfish, a native of the northwest (including Canada), has been introduced into other

parts of the west and Europe. Its closest relative, the sooty crayfish, vanished from the San Francisco Bay area after the introduction of the signal crayfish.

In 1975 the signal crayfish was found in a nearby isolated locality (Crater Lake, Lassen County, California) where it was actively fished. Since the isolated site also contained a new population of trout, the crayfish may have been accidentally introduced with the trout or added to the lake as a food source for the fish. By 1978 the signal crayfish was found with the Shasta crayfish at Baum and Crystal Lakes. By the early 1980s the signal crayfish was also found in lower Hat Creek and lower Fall River, and by the mid-1980s it occupied Sucker Spring. As of 1990 it was found in the upper portion of the Fall River system, where the Shasta crayfish is primarily concentrated.

Since 1975 the populations of Shasta crayfish at Crystal Lake and Sucker Spring have been seriously reduced as a result of the introduction of the signal crayfish. Similar consequences are expected from contact with the virile crayfish. The total Shasta population was estimated at 3,000 in 1998—a 50 percent decline from the 1988 estimate.

Ongoing studies

The three species of crayfish in Shasta County are still being studied, and regulations prohibiting the use of crayfish as bait have been enacted. Judging from the trends since 1975, there is a definite need for finding an isolated area that can support populations of the Shasta crayfish. The species must be introduced to new regions where it does not now occur, and portions of its range must be restocked following the elimination of newly introduced species.

White-footed Crayfish

(Austropotamobius pallipes)

IUCN: Vulnerable

Length: 3–5 in. (7.5–13 cm)
Diet: Omnivorous
Habitat: Freshwater streams, rivers, and lakes
Range: Europe

THE WHITE-FOOTED CRAYFISH is one of two small European crayfish that display green-to-brown hues along the back. The animal's common name is derived from the white color usually found on the underside of the major claws. Occasionally two rows of darker brown, broken stripes are evident on the top of the abdomen. Larger individuals up to 4¾ inches (12 centimeters) are more often found in lake habitats, with the largest individual reported to have been a little less than 5½ inches (14 centimeters). The white-footed crayfish is a member of the Astacidae family, or river lobsters.

The white-footed crayfish is native to western Europe (including the British Isles), ranging from Spain and France eastward to the former Yugoslavia. Unlike the noble and long-clawed crayfish, the white-footed species is less desirable as a commercial food item, so it has not been transplanted as frequently.

The white-footed crayfish's preferred habitat ranges from the clean, unpolluted waters of rivers to small streams and lakes, from the mountains to the lowlands. This species is generally found under rocks or in burrows along stream bottoms or banks. In areas where it occurs with the noble crayfish, the white-footed crayfish dominates the smaller streams, while the noble crayfish is found in larger bodies of water. The white-footed crayfish tolerates higher temperatures and lower oxygen levels than the noble crayfish.

The white-footed crayfish is omnivorous and is itself preyed upon by fish. The reproductive cycle of the white-footed crayfish varies with latitude and elevation. Mating takes place in the autumn, and the female carries the eggs over winter. Hatching occurs in the spring and summer, depending upon water temperatures. Females smaller than 2 inches (5 centimeters) have been observed carrying eggs, although most females with eggs are larger. The numbers of eggs carried by each female is related to the size of the individual and varies from region to region.

Maturation takes about three years but may occur in two. The time taken also varies among geographic regions, with some individuals maturing as late as five or six years of age in areas with colder climates.

Crayfish plague

One of the most serious obstacles to the survival of the white-footed crayfish is the crayfish plague. Besides this, actual or potential problems exist because of the introductions of three species of North American cray-

fish: the signal (*Pacifastacus leniusculus*), spinycheek (*Orconectes limosus*), and red swamp (*Procambarus clarkii*) crayfish. The Eurasian long-clawed crayfish also competes with the white-footed species. The white-footed crayfish has disappeared from parts of its range where the spinycheek crayfish has spread or been introduced.

Other exotic species are now found within the range of the white-footed crayfish as well. Interbreeding between the populations could cause further decline in the white-footed crayfish. Other threats to this species are pollution, habitat alteration, and overuse of its waters.

Fishing regulations

The white-footed crayfish has been eaten for centuries in Europe and continues to be harvested today. To insure that overfishing does not speed up the demise of this species, fishing regulations have been established limiting catches. In addition, scientists are monitoring the effects of pollution on this crayfish as well as undertaking more transplantation of crayfish.

Continued pollution control and wise use of water resources will improve aquatic habitats in Europe. In addition, breeding plague-resistant strains of white-footed crayfish would permit restocking the species within its range. In areas now containing introduced species, eradicating the exotic crayfish may be necessary, and sites containing the white-footed crayfish should be isolated and quarantined while other suitable sites are reclaimed and restocked.

Raymond W. Bouchard

CREEPERS

Class: Aves

Order: Passeriformes

Family: Drepanididae

Subfamily: Psittirostrinae

Creepers belong to the unique family known as the Hawaiian honeycreepers. These songbirds form a diverse group, with each species having adapted to particular aspects of native Hawaiian forests.

Understanding the relationships among the honeycreepers has proved difficult. Some are specialized for feeding on nectar, while others feed primarily on insects. Some nest in cavities, others in the open. Some are colored bright red, yet others are dull green or even black. Some have very peculiar beaks, some have very plain beaks.

Similar birds inhabit different islands, which has further confused their status as species or subspecies. To add to our confusion, beyond physical or behavioral traits or island distribution, some honeycreepers retain native Hawaiian names while others bear English names.

The creepers were for many years considered part of the *akepa* species in the genus *Loxops*. This opinion was revised in the 1980s. The creepers are now classified into five species in two genera.

Hawaii Creeper

(Oreomystis mana)

ESA: Endangered

IUCN: Endangered

Length: 4½–5 in. (11–13 cm)

Weight: ½ oz. (14 g)

Clutch size: Probably 2 eggs

Incubation: Unknown

Diet: Insects

Habitat: Forests with both ohia (*Metrosideros collina*) and koa (*Acacia koa*)

Range: Hawaii, Hawaiian Islands

VERY FEW VISITORS to Hawaii ever see the little green and yellow birds that cling to bark and creep up and down trees. The Hawaii creeper moves by releasing its grip, then hopping just a bit before gripping again. Its progress is a hesitant, jerky movement which totally lacks the fluid motion of walking. This behavior suits the Hawaii creeper well because it finds food hidden in the crevices and fissures of tree bark. It will eat a variety of bark-dwelling insects, but grubs (beetle larvae) seem to be the Hawaii creeper's favored prey.

The upperparts of the male Hawaii creeper are olive green, but the underparts are paler, or more yellow and less green. The chin and throat are white. The lore is black, as is the area around the eye, giving a masked look. The beak is light and less decurved than the beaks of some creepers. The female looks essentially the same as the male of the species but lacks the mask.

These thoroughly arboreal birds build their nests behind loose bark and in well-protected forks on horizontal tree limbs. Only three Hawaii creeper nests have ever been found, and only two have been described in writing. The first, located in 1903, was never described. Accounts of the second, which was found in 1976, were never published. The third nest was discovered in January 1978, 75 years after the discovery of the first nest.

Observers of the most recently discovered nest noticed that the birds used small twigs, lots of lichen, and much spider webbing. The finished nest was well camouflaged. However, the birds abandoned the nest, so additional information is still lacking.

Once abundant, the Hawaii creeper has declined as the forests on Hawaii have dwindled. Largest of the Hawaiian Islands, Hawaii historically supported forests that were diverse in character because of its varied elevation and the effect of prevailing winds. The forests were both wet and dry and extended from nearly sea level to a very high timberline on the island's volcanoes. Some trees grew 12,000 feet (3,660 meters) above sea level. The timberline is an irregular feature partly because of lava fields formed by still-active volcanoes and partly because of heavy grazing.

The Hawaii creeper occupied all the forests around the island, although some observers in the early 1900s wrote that the bird usually lived above 3,600 feet (1,100 meters). Whether this elevation limit was the result of some natural habitat barrier or of early human disturbance of lower forests is uncertain. In the 1980s the Hawaii creeper inhabited forests between 3,000 and 7,000 feet (915 and 2,135 meters).

A fragmented range

The species' population was estimated at 24,780 birds in 1986. Such a large figure seems accept-

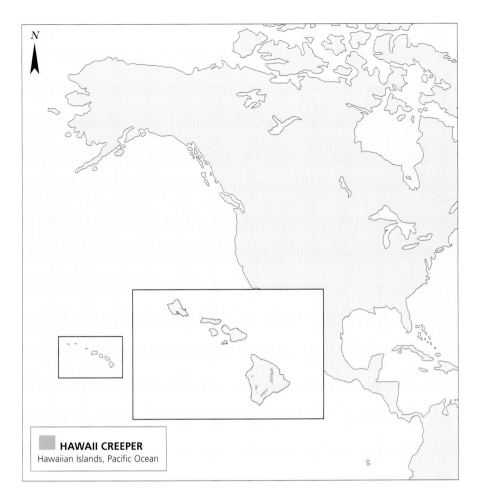

HAWAII CREEPER
Hawaiian Islands, Pacific Ocean

The plan to preserve the Hawaii creeper includes public education and habitat protection as the key elements. Education means focusing on instilling respect for these unique birds. Habitat protection includes not only stopping the cutting and clearing of the forests but managing the forests to maintain the quality essential to the birds. Steps should be taken to eradicate many exotic plants such as banana poka (*Passiflora mollissima*) and strawberry guava (*Psidium cattleianum*), as well as exotic animals such as pigs (*Sus scrofa*), mongooses (*Herpestes auropunctatus*), and black rats (*Rattus rattus*).

Molokai Creeper
(Oreomystis flammea)

ESA: Endangered

IUCN: Extinct

Length: 5 in. (13 cm)
Weight: ½ oz. (14 g)
Clutch size: Unknown
Incubation: Unknown
Diet: Probably insects
Habitat: Wet forests of ohia (*Metrosideros collina*)
Range: Molokai, Hawaiian Islands

OBSERVERS REPORTED the Molokai creeper as abundant in the 1890s, but since then it has declined rapidly and thoroughly. The last verified sighting of a live Molokai creeper occurred in 1963. Many hours of searching by ornithologists, amateur bird enthusiasts, and bird survey

able when compared to other endangered Hawaiian birds with populations numbering only in the dozens. However, despite the large population estimate, the Hawaii creeper remains endangered because its habitat is fragmented. The bird no longer occurs widely across the island but is confined to two large and three small forest parcels.

The largest forest tract containing the Hawaii creeper lies east of Mauna Kea and stretches about 33 miles (53 kilometers) southward along the 5,000-foot (1,525-meter) elevation contour to just northeast of Mauna Loa. The second largest tract lies southeast of Mauna Loa. Two smaller Hawaii creeper populations are known in forested areas southwest and west of Mauna Loa. The fifth population is west

and north of Hualalai on the central west side of the island.

More important, those factors that have endangered or destroyed other species continue to operate on Hawaii. Since the early Polynesians arrived around C.E. 700, humans have steadily invaded the islands, bringing with them exotic plants and animals that have changed the landscape significantly.

Human presence on the islands has also caused enormous destruction to the forests. The forests are cut for raising crops, grazing, logging, and urban expansion. Now visitors to Hawaii seldom see the Hawaii creeper and its honeycreeper relatives because these birds survive only in forests that are far removed from the usual features that attract tourist attention.

The last verified siting of a Molokai creeper was in 1963. Despite the efforts of ornithologists and amateur bird enthusiasts, this bird remains an elusive species.

teams have failed to discover any surviving populations.

The male Molokai creeper is bright red overall with reddish brown wings and tail; the feet and toes are light. The bird has a light beak that is thin and straight. The female has orange-brown upperparts. Her chin, throat, and upper breast are orange and the belly is buff. The sides are a light yellow brown.

Virtually nothing is known about the Molokai creeper's natural history. Its nests and eggs were known to early ornithologists, but the essential details were not recorded. The bird is known to have behaved like other creepers in moving over tree trunks and large branches. Apparently it often hung upside down in its quest for food, but its specific diet was never discovered. With so little known about a species, explaining its disappearance is largely speculation.

Dramatic wilderness

The fifth largest of the Hawaiian Islands, Molokai extends 38 miles (61 kilometers) east to west and about 10 miles (16 kilometers) north to south, covering approximately 261 square miles (676 square kilometers). It lies between Maui and Oahu. Molokai rises to an elevation of 4,970 feet (1,515 meters) toward its east end. There dramatic sea cliffs and deep valleys render the landscape less useful to humans.

The Olokui Plateau is surrounded by cliffs nearly one-half

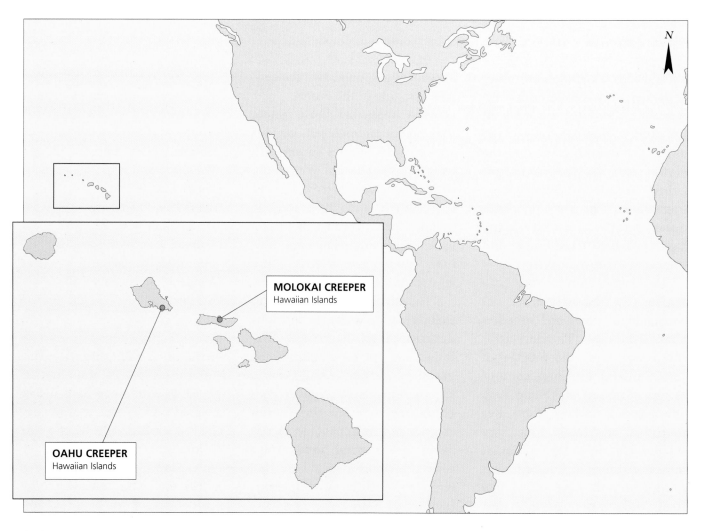

MOLOKAI CREEPER
Hawaiian Islands

OAHU CREEPER
Hawaiian Islands

mile (800 meters) high and remains probably the most pristine of the state's wild lands. Whereas the flatter landscape of the island's western end has been almost entirely developed for agriculture and settlement, the east end remains forested. Although the U.S. Fish and Wildlife Service list this animal as being endangered, IUCN believes it to be extinct. Perhaps somewhere in the forests of this rugged area there may still be small numbers of the elusive Molokai creeper.

Oahu Creeper
(Paroreomyza maculata)

ESA: Endangered

IUCN: Critically endangered

Length: 4½ in. (11 cm)
Weight: ½ oz. (14 g)
Clutch size: 2 eggs (known from a single nest found in 1901)
Incubation: Unknown
Diet: Insects
Habitat: Forests, probably of ohia (*Metrosideros collina*)
Range: Oahu, Hawaiian Islands; last seen in the Koolau Mountains, north of Honolulu

OF ALL THE MAJOR Hawaiian Islands none has been more drastically altered by people than Oahu. Third largest of the islands, it also supports the largest and densest human population in the state. Very little primary forest remains. That which survives is badly degraded by exotic plant and animal species. Despite these conditions the Oahu creeper survives. Occasional sightings provide hope that enough habitat remains for this species to continue to sustain a small population.

The male Oahu creeper is olive green on the upperparts, which contrasts with golden yellow underparts. The forehead and cheek are also golden yellow, but the lore is blackish with a dark green line extending behind the eye. The tail of this species is short, and the beak is thin and mostly straight, with the upper half darker than the lower. The female has a gray-green crown, nape, and upper back, fading to a more olive green on the rump. She has a pale whitish-yellow green lore and line over the eye, with the same color smudged on her cheek and extending onto a clear chin and throat, washing to a brighter whitish yellow on the side and belly. The wing features two white bars.

The bird's natural history was not well recorded when the species was still abundant in the late 1800s and early 1900s. Consequently very little detail is known about this creeper. For many years it was considered just one of six subspecies of the Hawaii creeper (*Oreomystis maculata*), each of which inhabited a different island.

This lumped classification led early ornithologists working in the Hawaiian Islands to write about the Hawaii creeper in general terms and to combine observations of birds seen on different islands. It was supposed that a subspecies would show similar behaviors from island to island. As each of the subspecies was reconsidered and eventually distinguished with full species status in the 1980s, the information that was once generally applied to all the birds no longer adequately described the individual species. Slight differences in nesting habits and feeding behaviors indicate that it is risky to apply general information to each island's creepers when there is little direct evidence to go on.

Beetle eater
For example, one observer noted in 1903 that the Oahu creeper fed heavily on a certain beetle (family Carabidae) that insect experts found difficult to collect. The bird was probably able to find the beetle in parts of trees that human insect collectors could not safely reach. However, this particular beetle was not specifically noticed as a food source for creepers on any of the other islands. Therefore, it would be incorrect to say that all Hawaii creepers eat that beetle.

Follow-up studies to verify these early observations are not always possible in the case of extremely rare species. The fact that the birds survive only in low numbers in remote habitats make field studies too expensive in terms of time and other resources.

Unfortunately the details of a species' natural history are necessary for developing specific recovery plans based on that species' life needs. Until populations of rare species such as the Oahu creeper can recover enough to justify natural history studies, the best strategy for conservation is habitat preservation.

Kevin Cook

CROCODILES

Class: Reptilia

Order: Crocodylia

Family: Crocodylidae

The crocodile family consists of 15 species of large armored reptiles that exist in tropical regions around the globe. They share the order Crocodylia with alligators, caimans, and gharials. Most crocodiles live near freshwater shores in the warmer regions of the earth. The species of this family all share an unmistakable, lizardlike appearance.

A crocodile can move on land, sliding on its belly or galloping short distances by moving its forelegs and hindlegs. These reptiles, however, move most efficiently in the water, using back-and-forth movements of the body or stroking with their tail. They can also float, leaving only the nostrils, eyes, and ears above the surface.

Crocodiles are generally large in size, with some species reaching up to 23 feet (7 meters) or more. They have large jaws and long teeth of variable form and size. As in the case of all members of this order, the teeth are not used for chewing but for seizing and holding prey.

Crocodiles tear pieces of flesh from their prey by planting their teeth firmly and then quickly rolling over in the water on the long axis of their body. The roll is repeated, and once a mouthful has been torn off, the crocodile raises the top half of its head above water, forcing the piece deeper and deeper down its throat with jerking movements.

Crocodiles are voracious eaters, including all types of animals in their diet, from insects to vertebrates. Most will eat anything they can overpower and consume. If a crocodile attacks something too large for it to swallow, it will bite into the prey and twist rapidly, tearing chunks from the prey's body. Young crocodiles feed primarily on insects, worms, and small fish. As they grow older they prefer turtles and larger fish. Older crocodiles add birds and small mammals to their diet. A few large crocodiles occasionally will attack people.

Crocodiles and other Crocodylia lay eggs. These are white and hard-shelled. Crocodile eggs are about the same size as the eggs of chickens or geese. The females construct nests, where the eggs remain until the young are born. The offspring are ready to feed themselves soon after hatching and grow rapidly until they reach sexual maturity. Captive crocodiles live to a greater age than any other animal except turtles.

There is a low survival rate for crocodile offspring. In each generation a small number may die from disease but many more are lost to predators, which include lizards, various mammals, crabs, and mature crocodiles. From these causes, an estimated 50 to 90 percent of young crocodilians are lost in the first two to three years of their lives.

As they mature, young crocodiles are often killed by large male crocodiles attempting to drive them from their territories. Under normal circumstances one or two percent of wild hatchlings will survive to sexual maturity. When the numbers of a species are already low, years pass before the few young that do survive are able to breed and contribute to their population.

People have always hunted crocodiles because of the danger they pose to domestic animals and occasionally to humans, but this did not affect the populations for many years. The use of firearms seems to have coincided with the increased value of crocodile hides, and the animals were suddenly in danger.

Because crocodiles are prized for their hides, species all over the world were depleted by indiscriminate hunting during the 1950s and 1960s. In addition, the crocodiles' natural habitat is being lost to environmental development around the globe. For these reasons, more than half the species of crocodiles are classified as threatened or endangered.

In the 1950s and 1960s hundreds of thousands of crocodiles were killed, primarily for their hides. At the height of the trade, up to eight million skins were traded each year. One New York company alone was tanning 1.5 million hides annually. By 1969 all 23 species of crocodilians were endangered or decreasing in number. However, with the creation of the Convention on International Trade in Endangered Species of Wild Fauna and Flora (CITES) in 1973, international trade controls came into effect. Sustainable management also became a priority, and ranching became more common. Most species of crocodilians have since begun recovering from decline.

Unfortunately prohibiting slaughter has not always been enough to help these reptiles replenish their numbers. Legislative attempts often are not enforced. However, new ways of helping endangered animals are seeing increased success. For example, in the late 1960s programs were launched to save shrinking crocodile species, and organizations recently have released captive-reared individuals into the wild.

Captive rearing is accomplished by capturing eggs from the wild, or taking those laid by captive adults, and incubating them in captivity. These captive-bred animals are later released into the wild once they are capable of protecting themselves against predators.

American Crocodile

(Crocodylus acutus)

ESA: Endangered

IUCN: Vulnerable

Length: Average 12 ft. (3.7 m); maximum 15 ft. (4.6 m)
Clutch size: Approximately 40 eggs
Diet: Fish
Habitat: Coastal areas, mangrove swamps, brackish bays; also in lakes and lower reaches of large rivers
Range: Central Mexico to northern South America, Cuba, Dominican Republic, Jamaica, Haiti, and southern Florida

THE AMERICAN CROCODILE has the widest range of any crocodile in the New World. It is also the only one found in the United States. This reptile was once widespread and often abundant but is now severely depleted throughout its range, primarily because of overexploitation for hides from the 1930s to the 1960s. Today the principal threat is habitat destruction, although continued hunting is problematic in some countries. A majority of countries where this crocodile is found have mangement programs in place that call for complete protection, but only a very few countries actually enforce these provisions. This means that remaining populations of the American crocodile are still subject to persecution. The primary threat of overexploitation of hides is now accompanied by habitat loss and other effects of human activity. Most of what we know about the species comes from observation of the Florida population.

The American crocodile is the only species of crocodile found in the United States. Today its numbers are severely depleted—primarily because of commercial exploitation of its hide.

The American crocodile is a large, slender-snouted species that prefers quiet waters, although larger individuals may enter deep bays at night. This species is primarily found in Central America, its range extending from central Mexico through Central America on both the Pacific and Caribbean coasts. The only populations that persist are found in areas that tend to be inaccessible to people, but even these remnants are subject to exploitation and ever-increasing damage to the environment. The densest group discovered in recent years was found at Lago Enriquillo, a salt lake in the southwest Dominican Republic, where some 200 remain. This

Cuban Crocodile
(Crocodylus rhombifer)

ESA: Endangered
IUCN: Endangered

Length: Up to 12 ft. (3.7 m)
Clutch size: Unknown
Diet: Fish, turtles, and small mammals
Habitat: Freshwater swamps to brackish water in places
Range: Zapata Swamp in Matanzas Province of Cuba

population has been the subject of intensive conservation action in recent years, and a program of protection has led to the population now being considered stable. However, a program to establish a genetic reserve of 130 individuals transferred to the Dominican National Zoo was unsuccessful.

The island of Jamaica once boasted an abundant population of American crocodiles, perhaps comprising some 2,000 adults as recently as 1969. A survey in 1975 revealed only 41 crocodiles, the decline being due to hide hunting and wetland drainage. Today, however, the American crocodile is relatively plentiful in areas along Jamaica's southern coast and farming of the species is being discussed.

In the United States, the American crocodile has never been found anywhere but on the southernmost tip of the Florida peninsula. Populations were once found as far north as Palm Beach County and Biscayne Bay, but today nesting areas are restricted to the Florida Bay area. While breeding numbers are low, they have remained steady in recent years in the central Florida Bay-Key Largo region. Today the

The Cuban crocodile is endemic to Cuba. It was once widespread across the island, but it is now found in a single swamp in the Matanzas province.

estimated population is between 200 and 400 individuals, with 25 to 30 known breeding females. In recent years there has also been a slight increase in the number of nests created. Most nest sites are within the Everglades National Park, and the U.S. population of the crocodile will be considered endangered until all nest sites are adequately protected.

The American crocodile has enjoyed only nominal protection from governments in Central America, and these measures are usually not adequately enforced. Meanwhile, in Venezuela a small number of captive-reared American crocodiles have been released into the Jatira reservoir. Plans are also underway to release the species into the country's Cuare National Wildlife refuge. In Colombia the government agency responsible for wildlife conservation requires that the farms licensed to breed American crocodiles return five percent of their hatchlings to the government to restock habitats.

AS IS THE CASE WITH most crocodiles, the Cuban was once severely threatened by hide hunting. In recent years a more important concern has been to protect pure-blooded specimens of the species. About 30 years ago, when the Cuban crocodile was threatened by agricultural development, most individuals were relocated to enclosed areas in Cuba's Zapata Swamp. Unfortunately American crocodile populations were also moved into this environment, and as the two species began to breed, hybridization occurred. In the 1980s there was another relatively large population living in Lanier Swamp on Isla de Piños, but following the introduction of the common caiman (*Caiman crocodilus*), the pure-bred Cuban crocodile disappeared. By the 1980s pure-bred Cuban crocodiles were greatly outnumbered by the hybrids. Most of the remaining pure Cubans have been transferred to a separate enclosure where management has been greatly improved.

Today the species is protected by law in Cuba. Two government-operated farms specialize in breeding Cuban crocodiles to preserve the species. These farms also serve as a tourist attraction and provide hides for commercial use. The total population in the wild is believed to number 3,000 to 6,000. Efforts are under way to ensure that this population remains protected, but it remains extremely vulnerable because of its restricted distribution. A captive-breeding program is also under way in the United States, coordinated by the American Zoo and Aquarium Association.

Estuarine Crocodile

(Crocodylus porosus)

ESA: Endangered

Length: Up to 23 ft. (7 m)
Clutch size: 25–90 eggs
Diet: Young eat primarily shellfish, insects, and small fish; adults also consume vertebrates
Habitat: Typically brackish waters, but also rivers and freshwater swamps
Range: Sri Lanka, eastern India, and Bangladesh, through coastal Southeast Asia, to the Philippines and western Carolines; south through Indonesia to Papua New Guinea and northern Australia; and east to the Solomon Islands and Vanuatu

THE ESTUARINE, OR saltwater, crocodile is the largest crocodile species in existence, making it perhaps the most greatly feared of the Crocodylidae family. It is also considered the largest of existing reptiles. One individual was reported to have reached 30 feet (9.1 meters) in length, but this figure was probably determined from the length of a preserved skull and cannot be considered certain. The largest estuarine in recent years was a male found drowned in New Guinea—it measured 20 feet 4 inches (6.2 meters).

This species is the only true saltwater crocodile. While estuarine crocodiles exist primarily in brackish waters, large river estuaries, deltas, and coastal swamps, some are found in deep rivers and freshwater swamps far from tidal influences. Sometimes individuals have been spotted far from their breeding ranges. One male was found at sea hundreds of miles north of New Zealand.

The estuarine feeds during both day and night if food is available. When they are young, the animals feed mainly along the water's edge on small fish, crabs, and insects. As they mature, estuarine crocodiles will eat virtually any mammal they can catch at the shore. When this crocodile sees its prey, it briefly moves toward it on the surface of the water, then aligns its head with the object. Next it swims underwater until it is just in front of the prey. With its jaws open, it lunges forward and captures its meal. The larger the crocodile, the larger the prey it can consume.

The male estuarine reaches sexual maturity at approximately 16 years of age, while the female reaches maturity at ten years old. The animals become territorial at about two and one-half years, long before breeding starts. They tend to nest in the wet season, and the nesting lasts for a three- to five-month period.

The estuarine crocodile is especially prized for its hide because of the relatively small size of the belly scales and the larger area without bone. Because its commercial value is so high, the species is now severely depleted and declining through most of its range. The largest populations are found only in northern Australia and in parts of New Guinea.

In 1975 India launched programs to conserve two species of

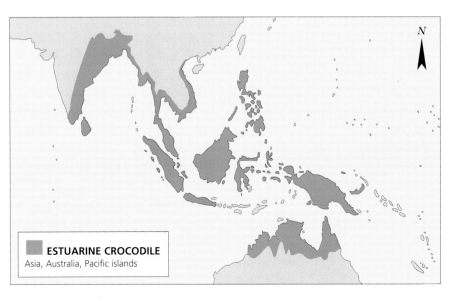

ESTUARINE CROCODILE
Asia, Australia, Pacific islands

crocodiles that exist in that country: the estuarine and the mugger. Both programs have had positive results. At nine rearing stations more than 1,200 estuarine crocodiles were produced and then released into the Bhitarkanika Sanctuary, where the species now breeds. In other parts of the country, another 24 individuals have been released. Relatively few saltwater crocodiles were found at Bhitarkanika when the sanctuary was created, but a census taken in 1988 counted 433 individuals, suggesting a 40 percent survival rate of the captive-bred specimens.

Morelet's Crocodile
(Crocodylus moreletii)

ESA: Endangered

IUCN: Data deficient

Length: 8 ft. (2.4 m)
Clutch size: 20–45 eggs
Diet: Fish
Habitat: Quiet, shallow freshwater swamps, backwaters, streams, ponds, and lagoons
Range: Central and Atlantic states of Mexico to the Yucatán Peninsula, southward through Belize and northern Guatemala; may occur in Honduras

MORELET'S CROCODILE was not considered a separate species until 1924, having been confused with both the Cuban and the American crocodiles. It shares with these a rounded protruber-

AMERICAN CROCODILE
Southern North America to northern South America, and Caribbean

AMERICAN CROCODILE, CUBAN CROCODILE
Caribbean

MORELET'S CROCODILE
North America, Central America

ORINOCO CROCODILE
South America

ance in front of the eyes and is relatively small, although animals of 9 feet (2.7 meters) are known to exist.

This freshwater reptile is able to reproduce earlier than other species, at about five years of age. This could be a major factor in the Morelet's survival because it has more years in which reproduction is possible. Morelet's crocodile is a mound-nesting animal. The female will tear up plants and gather leaves and twigs in a central heap.

Nesting usually occurs from April to June before annual floods, and incubation takes about 80 days. The hatchlings are about 6 or 7 inches (15 to 18 centimeters) in length. Because the mother remains near the shoreline nest so that she can protect her offspring, she is an easy target of human predation.

Morelet's crocodile is especially prized for its hide. Like the estuarine, or saltwater, crocodile, it has especially beautiful belly skin that produces a smooth, flexible leather. Only 50 years ago, 1,000 hides might be sold at market in a single day. Exporting of hides has been outlawed in Belize, and all crocodiles are protected by legislation in Mexico and Guatemala. However, the legislation is not enforced consistently and poaching still occurs.

It is becoming more and more difficult to sell and export the hides, however, which makes hunting Morelet's crocodile less attractive. Many of the remaining hunters are not professionals and therefore have little interest in the survival of the resource they are exploiting. Professional hunters usually leave a certain number of adults in an area and will avoid killing juveniles, while the amateur hunter will not. The ever-changing habitat in Mexico and Central America has added to the scarcity of this species.

Captive breeding

Morelet's crocodile can breed quite readily in captivity if conditions are right. For more than 15 years Zoo Atlanta in Georgia has been breeding this crocodile. Some captive-bred offspring have been released into the wild in Mexico and Belize. Since 1972 the Tuxtla Gutierrez Zoo in Chiapas, Mexico, has bred 60 offspring a year using six adult pairs. The hatchlings are raised in captivity for one year, then released in parts of Chiapas.

Mugger Crocodile
(Crocodylus palustris)

ESA: Endangered

IUCN: Vulnerable

Length: 13 ft. (4 m)
Clutch size: 10–46 eggs
Diet: Adults eat frogs, small mammals, and birds
Habitat: Any freshwater habitat, occasionally in brackish waters
Range: Centered on the Indian subcontinent, including parts of India, Nepal, Pakistan, Bangladesh, Sri Lanka; also Iran

THE MUGGER, OR marsh, crocodile is a large, fairly broad-snouted species that inhabits still or slow-flowing freshwater habitats, including rivers and man-made ponds or reservoirs. Numbers of this crocodile are depleted throughout its range, although certain areas possess greater populations than others. Today most individuals do not exceed 13 feet (4 meters), but in the past many reached a length of 16 feet (4.9 meters).

The fact that the mugger can adapt to human-made environments such as reservoirs and

Morelet's crocodile is especially prized for its hide. Only 50 years ago as many as 1,000 hides might have been sold in just a single day.

ponds is thought to be a positive factor in its survival. What may be the single largest population occurs in Hiran Lake, an Indian reservoir formed by a dam. Another major group of muggers occupies tanks in Sri Lanka that were constructed between 500 B.C.E. and C.E. 1300

The mugger basks on rocks in mid-river or on muddy banks where individuals can be inconspicuous when motionless. In drier months muggers occupy the deepest waters in their habitat but are known to wander several miles from dry rivers in search of water or food. Muggers tend to surround themselves with other mugger crocodiles of similar size, except during the breeding season, when males become territorial.

Grunting hatchlings

Females begin to lay eggs at the age of six, but the males tend to reach maturity later, usually at about ten years of age. Mating takes place in the open water. The female lays eggs in a nest chamber 14 to 20 inches (36 to 51 centimeters) in depth, dug at a distance from the water's edge and with a temperature of about 90 degrees Fahrenheit (32 degrees Celsius). The eggs are laid between late February and the first week of April, and incubation takes from 50 to 65 days. When the hatchlings are ready to emerge, they make grunting noises from within the nest. When the female hears them, she pulls the nest apart and releases the hatchlings into the water. Hatchlings are about 10 inches (25 centimeters) in length.

The mugger's populations were initially depleted by hide

hunting. Since hunting for the skin trade is now limited by protective legislation, the greatest threat today is set-net fishing, in which nylon gill nets are set across rivers or standing bodies of water. Any crocodiles found in the nets are clubbed to death. Another cause of depletion is egg predation by humans, as various tribes use crocodile eggs for food and medicinal purposes. Traditional Indian medicine men still believe in the curative powers of crocodile meat, fat, and various body parts. Such medicines are still available and demand a high price. Because the mugger tends to wander away from its nest, it is easy prey for hunters.

Habitat destruction is also a problem for the mugger crocodile as forests are cleared to the water's edge. The use of reservoir water for crop irrigation during the dry season also disturbs the climate of the mugger nests, resulting in a lower percentage of eggs hatching. The lower water levels also increase the chances that offspring will be caught by predators. The clearing of vegetation at the water's edge has taken with it the insects on which the juvenile crocodiles feed.

Protected by law

The mugger crocodile has legislative protection in Bangladesh, India, Iran, Nepal, and Pakistan. The animal is protected in Sri Lanka but can be hunted under a special license. India launched programs to conserve the mugger and the estuarine crocodile in 1975. Since that time the country has had success with captive-breeding programs. In 1990 a total of more than 2,000 young muggers from 31 rearing stations

were released in dozens of sites. Juveniles from these programs have been used to restock wild populations in at least 28 national parks, reserves, and crocodile sanctuaries in India. However, there is little additional mugger habitat available for further restocking, and the breeding centers have ceased producing offspring on the orders of the Indian government.

Scientists believe the future of the mugger crocodile in India is therefore uncertain. Pakistan has expressed interest in establishing a restocking program as well, but an important first step would need to be a survey of the status of populations in the wild.

Nile Crocodile

(Crocodylus niloticus)

ESA: Threatened

Length: Up to 16 ft. (4.9 m); typically 11 ft. (3.4 m)
Clutch size: 16–80 eggs
Diet: Young consume invertebrates, including insects, spiders, and crustaceans; adults consume fish and various mammals
Habitat: A variety of mainly freshwater habitats, notably larger rivers, lakes, and swamps
Range: Africa and Madagascar

THIS LARGE SPECIES is found in a variety of habitats throughout a wide area of Africa. It was once found throughout Africa and, because it can go out to sea like the estuarine crocodile, it was also found on various islands off the coast, including Madagascar.

In the early part of the 20th century the Nile crocodile was so prolific in what is now Tanzania that the government paid a bounty of up to three rupees to any hunter who killed one. In 1910 one cattle dealer earned approximately 5,000 rupees in two months. As late as 1950, 12,509 crocodile skins were obtained in Tanzania.

Nile crocodiles spend a large part of the daylight hours basking in the sun. When it becomes too hot, the animals may leave the sun in search of shade from nearby vegetation or they may partially submerge themselves at the water's edge. As the crocodiles cool down, they return to their basking until dusk, when they make their way back to the water. In this way these cold-blooded animals maintain their optimum body temperature. Only the dominant males of a group forego the sunshine. They spend their time swimming up and down their shoreline territory to discourage interlopers.

While young individuals mostly eat invertebrates, by the time they reach a length of 3 feet (about 1 meter) Nile crocodiles eat primarily fish. As these reptiles approach maturity, they are able to capture increasingly larger prey, including antelopes, zebra, warthogs, domestic goats, and cattle, and even animals as large as a Cape buffalo. Prey caught on land is often pulled into the water and killed by drowning. When the prey is large enough, a group of crocodiles may share the carcass.

Reproduction

Sexual maturity is reached at around 12 to 15 years of age, when the Nile crocodile is between 6 and 9 feet (1.8 and 2.7 meters) in length. The dominant male is established among mature males at the beginning of the mating season, and subdominant males are excluded from his

Certain groups of native people still hunt the Nile crocodile for food and medicinal purposes, and the animals are still frequently killed for the threat they pose to domestic animals and to humans.

territory. Some studies suggest that the Nile crocodile takes only one partner, at least during the sexually active portion of the reproductive cycle.

Protective mothers

The female deposits eggs into a hole on shore and buries them under 11 to 20 inches (21 to 51 centimeters) of soil. Females return to their first nest site each year and remain there after mating, defending it against other females until the eggs are laid. Both parents remain close to the nest throughout the incubation period, and the female does not feed during this time. When they are about to hatch, the offspring make a low noise and the female pushes the earth away so the young can make their way out of the nest. She then carries the hatchlings in her mouth to the water. The mother is extremely protective as the offspring hatch, even going so far as to attack humans on land should they come too close.

The hatchlings stay together for six to eight weeks, and the parents stay nearby to protect them from predators. When the offspring set out on their own they tend to dig burrows, often communally, which will offer them shelter for up to five years. The high degree of parental protection, together with the cooperation among young Nile crocodiles, seems to protect the hatchlings from predation.

Protection

As in the cases of most other crocodiles, hide hunting led to dramatic declines in Nile crocodile numbers from the 1940s to the 1960s. In western Africa

NILE CROCODILE
Africa and Madagascar

heavy hunting continued into the 1970s. However, this species now has legislative protection throughout much of its range and is also protected through export restrictions. Illegal trade is thought to be insignificant. Nonetheless in western Africa this species is believed to remain severely depleted, although little survey data exists. In eastern and southern Africa the Nile crocodile is now relatively secure and abundant. As a result, ranching programs with CITES-approved exports of skins are under way in Botswana, Ethiopia, Kenya, Malawi, Mozambique, South Africa, Tanzania, Zambia, and Zimbabwe. Madagascar and Uganda also export skins under approved quota systems.

Habitat destruction

Destruction of the Nile crocodile's habitat remains a problem, however, as more and more pressure is put on the African environment by humans: forests are cleared, swamplands are drained, waters are used for irrigation, and nest sites are trampled by domestic cattle. Increased use of water for recreation plays a role in the destruction of habitat, too, and fisher's gill nets often trap and drown crocodiles.

Orinoco Crocodile
(Crocodylus intermedius)

ESA: Endangered

IUCN: Critically endangered

Length: 10–16.5 ft. (3–5 m)
Clutch size: 15–70 eggs
Diet: Fish, small mammals, and birds
Habitat: Lakes and deep, slow stretches of large rivers
Range: The Orinoco drainage of Venezuela and eastern Colombia

THE ORINOCO CROCODILE population is extremely depleted and the animal is almost extinct throughout its small range. The animal was common in the 1930s, but today it is possible that only about 1,500 nonhatchlings survive in the wild. The Orinoco is a particularly shy and elusive species and is therefore difficult to count.

A survey carried out in the 1970s in the Colombian Orinoco plains revealed only 280 adult individuals within more than 155,000 square miles (400,000 square kilometers)—an area that included most of the crocodile's range in Colombia. While juveniles and a certain number of adults can be assumed to have gone uncounted, the numbers are still disturbingly low.

The total estimate of the Orinoco crocodile population in Colombia is a mere 500 individuals, compared with presumed primordial numbers in the hundreds of thousands. The situation in Venezuela is similar. A recent survey found 273 individuals and the estimate for the total wild population is just 1,000.

Dry season wanderers

This slender-snouted, freshwater species prefers wide and deep waters in large rivers during the dry season but wanders over great distances during the wet season. Individuals may occupy lakes and pools to avoid strong river currents. The species builds nests in holes dug in sandbanks high above the river. Nesting occurs in January or February, and hatchlings emerge between late February and late March. The female protects the hatchlings for a variable period of time.

The Orinoco is one of the most severely depleted of all the crocodile species. The Orinoco's hide was in great demand due to the crocodile's relatively large size and fine belly skin. Hide hunting began in the 1920s but had declined considerably by 1948 simply because there were so few crocodiles left that they were no longer exploitable. A minimum of 250,000 hides were taken from the Colombian range in the 1930s and 1940s.

The Orinoco crocodile is protected in both Colombia and Venezuela, but legislation is difficult to enforce. Virtually nothing is known of the status of this crocodile in Colombia today and surveys are urgently needed. The Colombian government is developing an experimental breeding program, and captive breeding of crocodiles for release into the wild is being undertaken at the Estacion de Biologia Tropical Roberta Franco in Villacencio. A trial release program is being considered for the El Tuparro National Park. In Venezuela remnant populations can be found but are under threat from a variety of factors, including habitat destruction, egg collecting, and the capture of animals for sale.

Four centers in Venezuela are breeding and rearing this critically endangered species for release into protected habitats. In April 1990 the first group of 31 captive-reared young Orinoco crocodiles were released into a Venezuelan wildlife refuge. Since then more than 1,020 others have been released into three protected areas and several private ranches. Periodic surveys and monitoring have been undertaken but need to be better developed. The Metro Zoo in Miami, Florida, has had success breeding the Orinoco crocodile and has established a long-range breeding program.

Philippines Crocodile
(Crocodylus mindorensis)

ESA: Endangered

IUCN: Critically endangered

Length: 9–10 ft. (2.7–3 m)
Clutch size: 10–30 eggs
Diet: Unknown
Habitat: Freshwater marshes, small lakes, ponds, and tributaries of large rivers
Range: Philippine Islands

THIS SPECIES OF relatively small crocodiles is severely depleted, with an estimated 500 to 1,000 animals remaining in the world. There are no longer any large populations of the Philippines crocodile left.

Although little is known about the natural habitat and history of the Philippines crocodile, it appears that the nest is constructed during the dry season. One captive female constructed a nest mound and produced three clutches of 13, 7, and 14 eggs. She defended the nest actively, lunging with her mouth open when disturbed. The incubation period was 85 days, but most of the eggs were infertile.

Farms, fish, and mines

The initial threat to the Philippines crocodile was hide hunting, but today the destruction of its habitat for agriculture and aquaculture projects poses an ever-increasing hazard. As the Philippines government endorses the construction of ponds, rice paddies, and plantations, the populations of the crocodile have become more and more imperiled. Pollution of waters has also caused depletion of the species.

In 1980 the Smithsonian Institute/World Wildlife Federation began the Philippines Crocodile Conservation Project. Under this plan Silliman University on the Philippine island of Negros set up a captive-breeding station. To date, Silliman University has a single breeding pair and 23 Philippines crocodiles. With stock from the Silliman University project, breeding programs are under way at the Gladys Porter Zoo in Brownsville, Texas, and at Melbourne Zoo in Australia. The Gladys Porter Zoo has repatriated some of its hatchlings to the Philippines.

Siamese Crocodile

(Crocodylus siamensis)

ESA: Endangered

IUCN: Critically endangered

Length: 10–13 ft. (3–4 m)
Clutch size: 20–48 eggs
Diet: Primarily fish
Habitat: Lowland freshwater lakes and swamps
Range: Thailand, Cambodia, Vietnam, Indonesia, Laos and Malaysia

LITTLE IS KNOWN about the natural history of the Siamese crocodile. It is a moderate-sized species said to feed mainly on fish. Nonaggressive, it is thought to pose no threat to humans when plenty of fish is available.

A captive population of Siamese crocodiles in Samut Prakan mates during December through March; most females lay eggs in April and May. The females build mound nests of vegetation, and the clutch hatches in 67 or 68 days at about 90 degrees Fahrenheit (32 degrees Celsius). At lower temperatures incubation may take 80 to 90 days. The female guards her nest during incubation, and when the young make a low noise from within the eggs prior to hatching, she helps them emerge by uncovering the nest.

The Siamese crocodile is extinct throughout almost all its range. In Thailand, for example, it is almost extinct in the wild. Surveys have confirmed the presence of only two wild adults, one in Pang Sida National Park and another in Ang Lue Nai Wildlife Sanctuary. The Mekong River basin and associated wetlands in Cambodia and Laos appear to have the only remaining large populations, but these are also fragmented and depleted.

Fortunately there are extensive captive-breeding programs in Thailand and Cambodia and smaller programs in Vietnam, Laos, and Indonesia. Zoos in North America also hold more than 130 Siamese crocodiles, and there are seven in Europe. Captive breeding has also been undertaken in Russia and Japan, while in Thailand the government is implementing a variety of recommendations from crocodile specialists and a national crocodile mangagement plan has now been drafted. Reestablishment of viable populations in the wild in protected areas is considered to be a feasible proposition, but there is extensive interbreeding with the estuarine species and maintenance of the purity of the Siamese crocodile stock needs to be encouraged.

Elizabeth Sirimarco

See also Alligators, Caimans, and Gharials

The Siamese crocodile is extinct throughout most of its range. In Thailand, where the species was once the most common, there are reportedly only 200 individuals remaining.

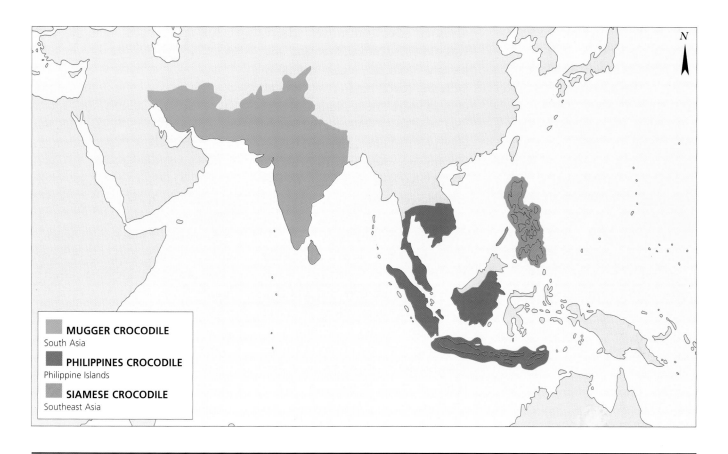

MUGGER CROCODILE
South Asia

PHILIPPINES CROCODILE
Philippine Islands

SIAMESE CROCODILE
Southeast Asia

CROWS

Class: Aves

Order: Passeriformes

Family: Corvidae

About 38 species make up the genus *Corvus*, which includes the common raven (*Corvus corax*), largest of all the songbirds, as well as magpies, jays, and nutcrackers.

One crow species or another occupies all the continents of the world except South America and Antarctica, and all the major islands except New Zealand.

Of all the birds, crows are generally regarded as being the most intelligent and most capable of learning.

Many species have complex social behaviors, but not all crows form large flocks. Crows lack any musical songs but utter various harsh croaks, caws, and other noisy chatter.

Hawaiian Crow
(Corvus hawaiiensis)

ESA: Endangered

IUCN: Critically endangered

Length: 19 in. (48 cm)
Clutch size: 5 eggs known, but recently only 1–2 eggs in captivity
Incubation: Unknown
Diet: Fruits, insects, birds, mice
Habitat: Open forests of ohia (*Metrosideros collina*) or mixed ohia and koa (*Acacia koa*) forests
Range: Hawaii, Hawaiian Islands

TWO MYSTERIES SURROUND the Hawaiian crow. First, it only inhabits the island of Hawaii, despite available habitat on the other large islands. Most crows are strong fliers and the Hawaiian crow is no exception. It should have been able to fly easily to the other islands. Second, its population collapsed in the 1980s for no apparent reason.

Described as abundant in 1900, the Hawaiian crow (or *alala* in the native Hawaiian language) declined slowly through the middle decades of the 1900s. Special surveys to monitor its population were begun and have been conducted annually for many years. The crow's population fell from 200 to less than 150 through the 1970s.

By 1986 only 12 birds could be found on the crow survey. Two birds were heard in 1987, but none were sighted on the crow survey. The bird was probably irretrievably doomed before the U.S. Fish and Wildlife Service

371

(U.S.F.W.S.) approved a recovery plan in 1982.

Eight birds were held at the Olinda Endangered Species Breeding Facility on Maui in 1987. One pair nested and laid a single egg, but the egg failed to hatch and the female died. By 1992 only 11 Hawaiian crows remained in the wild and ten more were in captivity.

Ornithologists suspect that land development destroyed much of the crow's habitat. It prefers tall ohia trees (*Metrosideros collina*) but is also found in forests mixed with ohia and koa (*Acacia koa*). The crow favors various fruits and insects, which it finds by rummaging through leaf debris on the ground. It has even been seen taking nectar, as well as mice and other small animals. Through the 1800s and into the 1900s the Hawaiian crow occupied all the habitat between 1,000 and 8,000 feet (305 and 2,440 meters) above sea level, noticeably on the slopes of the Hualalai and Mauna Loa volcanoes. It was abundant enough that people hunted it until that activity was outlawed in 1931. However, the crow was already declining by then. Besides losses from shooting and habitat loss, the crow probably suffered from having its habitat degraded by exotic plant and animal species. Exotic plants vastly changed the character of Hawaiian forests, outcompeting native plants that are necessary to the crow's existence.

Genetic problems

A final problem probably resulted from the Hawaiian crow's low numbers. Inbreeding, a situation caused by a breeding population with too few individuals and genes that are too similar, may account for the reduced fertility of eggs in recent years. During the 1980s the Hawaiian crow suffered an almost complete failure to produce offspring. Inbreeding has not been proven as the cause, but it is likely.

Conceivably a few birds could survive in the wild, escaping detection. The Hawaiian crow is, however, a big, dark bird of open forests, where it can be easily seen when it flies. If this bird is to survive, its future will depend on whether a very few captive individuals can produce young.

Mariana Crow

(Corvus kubaryi)

ESA: Endangered

IUCN: Critically endangered

Length: 15 in. (38 cm)
Weight: Unknown
Clutch size: 1 egg known; more likely
Incubation: Calculated at 18–21 days
Diet: Plants, including flowers, fruits, seeds, leaves, and bark; animals, including insects, lizards, small snakes, and young birds
Habitat: Both primary and secondary forests
Range: Guam and Rota, Mariana Islands

A PERSON WHO hears a bird pounding on a forest tree usually suspects it to be a woodpecker, but on Guam it could be a crow. The Mariana crow uses its beak to hit trees so it can remove the bark, behind which it finds insects and possibly small lizards. This behavior may have led to the bird's bark-eating habit, which is unique among crows.

The Mariana crow is also unique for being the only crow in the part of the Pacific Ocean known as Micronesia. Micronesia is made up of the Northern Mariana Islands, the Caroline Islands, and the Marshall Islands, located about 3,200 miles (5,150 kilometers) southwest of Hawaii. The Mariana crow lives on only two islands, Rota and nearby Guam (a territory of the United States). The

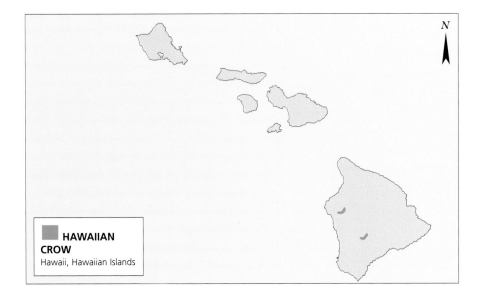

HAWAIIAN CROW
Hawaii, Hawaiian Islands

N

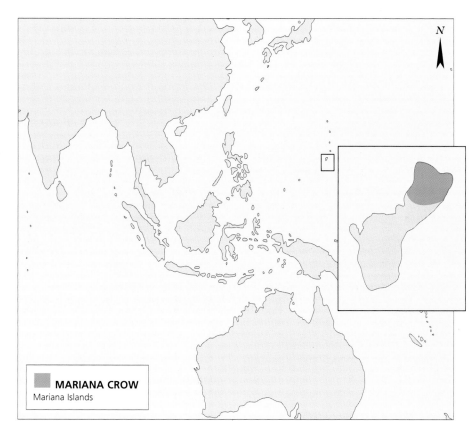

MARIANA CROW
Mariana Islands

forest destruction must also be considered in deadly combination with the snake.

As a forest species, the Mariana crow has adapted well to an arboreal lifestyle. It nests as high as 40 feet (12 meters) above ground in elaeocarpus (*Elaeocarpus sphaericus*) and constructs its nest from tree materials such as twigs and fibers of coco palm (*Cocos nucifera*) leaves. The Mariana crow often drinks the rainwater that collects in the bases of pandanus (*Pandanus* sp.) leaves and feeds in the canopy and on the forest floor.

After the breeding season, the Mariana crow may travel in flocks of three to 13 birds, but pairs defend breeding territories as large as 1 square mile (2.6 square kilometers). Obviously the smaller a forest is, the fewer breeding pairs it can accommodate. Removing the forest, then, severely impairs the crow's ability to sustain its population. Unfortunately, protecting the forests is not enough to save birds such as the Mariana crow. When exotic species such as the brown tree snake become established in an area, the quality of the habitat substantially decreases, reducing the habitat's ability to support native wildlife.

The U.S. Fish and Wildlife Service has a research program aimed at finding a way to control the brown tree snake because it is a problem on many other islands besides Guam. Additionally, several zoos have cooperated with the American Association of Zoological Parks and Aquariums to protect and recover Guam's forest birds through captive-breeding programs.

Kevin Cook

Rota population has remained fairly steady, but the Guam crows have seriously declined. Only 50 crows survived on Guam when the U.S. Fish and Wildlife Service listed it as an endangered species in 1984. Two factors probably explain this decline.

First, the Mariana crow is a forest species that once inhabited most of Guam's 209 square miles (541 square kilometers). Most of Guam's forests have been cut, so the bird now occupies only the northern third of the island. It does use secondary forests but prefers primary forests. Guam's best remaining primary forest is on the grounds of Anderson Air Force Base. The United States Air Force protects the forest as a wildlife sanctuary.

Second, the Mariana crow has become vulnerable to an exotic predator—the brown tree snake (*Boiga irregularis*). This snake became established on Guam in

the 1940s. No one knows exactly how the brown tree snake got to Guam, whether it was intentionally or accidentally, but its presence has become a critical problem for native birds. The snake originally occurred in Southeast Asia and feeds particularly on birds and birds' eggs, although it eats other vertebrates, too. Both nocturnal and a good climber, the brown tree snake has the ability to reach birds that nest either on the ground or in the trees. Even though the Mariana crow has been seen eating small brown tree snakes, the exotic serpent has no significant predators on Guam, so its population has grown rapidly. Its only constraints are food and cover, both of which have been abundant.

A deadly combination

The brown tree snake has been suspected as the primary cause of forest bird losses on Guam, but

CUCKOO-SHRIKES

Class: Aves

Order: Passeriformes

Family: Campephagidae

Cuckoo-shrikes are neither cuckoos nor shrikes. They are true songbirds in their own family of about 70 species. Some species inhabit portions of Africa, while others occur in India, Nepal, and southern China. Most species live in the island-rich area between Australia and Asia.

Individual birds do not wander much, and none are migratory. This means the cuckoo-shrikes are separated on islands, so they do not breed with each other. The result is that a few species have specialized into as many as 33 subspecies. Many cuckoo-shrikes are quite colorful, but some are patterned in grays, black, and white, much as are the true shrikes (family Laniidae). Almost all the cuckoo-shrikes grow peculiar feathers on their lower backs. These feathers have stout shafts but little or no vane, which makes them almost spine-like. The birds can erect these sharply pointed feathers during courtship and possibly use them as a defense against predators.

Ghana Cuckoo-shrike

(Campephaga lobata)

IUCN: Vulnerable

Length: 7½ in. (19 cm)

Weight: 1–1¼ oz. (28–34 g)

Clutch size: Unknown, but related species lay 2–3 eggs

Incubation: Unknown

Diet: Insects and small seeds

Habitat: Lowland rain forests

Range: Western Africa

FOR YEARS THE Ghana cuckoo-shrike was known from only five specimens. This situation is not surprising considering where the bird lives. Its preferred tropical forest habitat receives up to 20 feet (6.1 meters) of rain a year. Warm weather and ample rain provide good growing conditions for plants, so the region's forests can be very dense. Even if the area could be reached without trouble, vegetation makes many forest animals, particularly small birds, hard to find. The Ghana cuckoo-shrike was undoubtedly overlooked for years.

An alarming rate of forest cutting and other habitat-destroying activities prompted several studies of west African birds in the 1960s and 1970s. When looked for, the Ghana cuckoo-shrike was found. For example, the species was not known to occur in Liberia until the late 1960s. Iron mining on Mount Nimba in central Liberia (near the borders with Guinea and Ivory Coast) destroyed much of the mountain and its forests in the 1960s. Studies were begun to determine whether the last forested areas of Mount Nimba should become a national park. Between 1967 and 1971 ornithologists in the study groups collected 18 specimens of the Ghana cuckoo-shrike, all from a place where it had never been detected before.

Males of the species are mostly dark, and the head and throat are a shiny blackish green. The back is green, and the rump and underparts are rufous to chestnut. The wings are black and green and the tail is black with yellow tips on the outer feathers. The eyes are dark red with bright orange wattles beneath. Female cuckoo-shrikes are lighter than males. The head and throat are not so deeply colored as in males', nor are they shiny. The feathers on the fore-head and crown show yellow green. The rump and lower back are yellow green and the underparts are yellow.

Forest destruction

Some ornithologists suspect that forest cutting has made the bird more detectable. Quite possibly more birds are trying to live in smaller patches of habitat. However, any habitat, whether forest or prairie, can only provide food and cover for a finite number of individual animals. Once a certain bird species uses all the available food and cover, that habitat area cannot support any more individuals of that species. Forest destruction has been so extensive in western Africa that not enough woodland remains to support all the animals in the numbers that it once did. The Ghana cuckoo-shrike has never been found in Guinea. Forest habitat appropriate for the species once existed in that country, but it has all been cut.

Ornithologists disagree about the relationship of the Ghana cuckoo-shrike to the eastern wattled cuckoo-shrike (*Campephaga oriolinus*). Some believe the two birds are the same species; others believe they are distinct. They differ in color and range. The eastern wattled cuckoo-shrike inhabits forests from Cameroon south into the Democratic Republic of Congo (formerly Zaire). It is not as rare.

No direct action had been taken to preserve the Ghana cuckoo-shrike as of the late 1990s. The species would benefit indirectly from international programs to protect rain forests.

Mauritius Cuckoo-shrike

(Coracina typica)

ESA: Endangered

IUCN: Vulnerable

Length: Unknown
Weight: Unknown
Clutch size: 2 eggs
Incubation: Unknown
Diet: Mostly insects, but also small fruits
Habitat: Mostly primary forests; some secondary forests
Range: Mauritius in the Indian Ocean

WHEN PORTUGUESE sailors landed on Mauritius in 1507, birds such as the Mauritius cuckoo-shrike thrived in the island's forests. The parade of human activities over the next three centuries left 27 bird species extinct—some on Mauritius and some on the neighboring islands of Réunion and Rodrigues. Together, these islands make up a group known as the Mascarenes. Volcanic in origin, they have never been attached to a continent by land

bridges. The islands' isolation in the Indian Ocean allowed their flora and fauna to develop one-of-a-kind characteristics.

Best known as the home of the now extinct dodo bird (*Raphus cucullatus*), Mauritius sheltered many unique forms of life. Lying 600 miles (965 kilometers) east of Madagascar, the island had never been inhabited by humans. Its 720 square miles (1,865 square kilometers) were almost entirely covered in forests. Besides the Mauritius cuckoo-shrike, these forests sheltered the Mauritius kestrel (*Falco punctatus*), the pink pigeon (*Nesoenas mayeri*), the Mauritius olive white-eye (*Zosterops chloronothus*), the Mauritius parakeet (*Psittacula eques*), the Mauritius black bulbul (*Hypsipetes olivaceus*), and

the Mauritius fody (*Foudia rubra*). All of these bird species are now considered threatened or endangered.

Mauritius became a Dutch territory in 1598. For the following half-century the Dutch used Mauritius as a sailing landfall for food, water, and fuel. In 1644 they established a penal colony there, and people have permanently inhabited the island ever since. Human habitation required cutting forests for lumber, to make room for food crops, firewood, and other necessities. As the forests were cleared, forest-dwelling birds declined.

People also brought animals to the island. Some were livestock deliberately established for human use. Others, such as the crab-eating macaque (*Macaca*

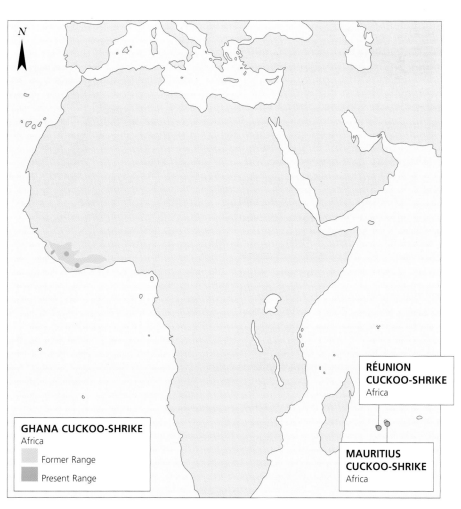

N

GHANA CUCKOO-SHRIKE
Africa

Former Range

Present Range

RÉUNION CUCKOO-SHRIKE
Africa

MAURITIUS CUCKOO-SHRIKE
Africa

fascicularis), were intentionally released as novelty species. A few species, such as the black rat (*Rattus rattus*), became unintentionally established. Animals in all these categories have proved almost as lethal to Mauritius' bird population as the cutting of the forests. Exotic animals prey on native species and compete for nesting space and food. A native bird forced into habitat of marginal quality due to the presence of exotic species can find it extremely difficult to survive.

Adaptable bird

The Mauritius cuckoo-shrike originally inhabited nearly all of Mauritius. Significant expanses of the forest had been cut by the 1860s, but the cuckoo-shrike was still found in all remaining forests. People continued shooting the bird for food even as its habitat dwindled. By the early 1900s the species survived only in small forests of southwestern Mauritius. More than some endangered birds on Mauritius, the cuckoo-shrike has shown a willingness to accept second-growth habitat, although the greatest numbers of them still occur in primary forest. It even inhabits some shrub land.

When feeding, the Mauritius cuckoo-shrike picks insects from leaves and twigs in the forest canopy. It also takes a few small seeds and fruits, possibly adding small lizards on occasion. Where thicketlike second growth replaces cut forest, the cuckoo-shrike does look for food in the lower vegeta-

tion. This adaptability to habitat conditions helps the species survive only for a short time.

Habitat loss results in surviving populations of a species being located in small areas. Already small populations of birds such as the Mauritius cuckoo-shrike then become more vulnerable to predation and competition. Black rats and crab-eating macaques both take eggs and nestlings. Additional nest losses may be caused by the red-whiskered bulbul (*Pycnonotus jocosus*) and Indian myna (*Acridotheres tristis*). These exotic birds may also compete with the cuckoo-shrike for food and nesting sites. The Mauritius cuckoo-shrike suffered total failure of all known nests well into the 1970s. How much of this loss was caused by the presence of exotic predators is not known.

Secretive bird

In the late 1980s ornithologists estimated that about 450 Mauritius cuckoo-shrikes survived in the Macabee/Bel Ombre Nature Reserve. Figures in the 1970s included a low of 100 pairs to a high of 190 pairs. However, the cuckoo-shrike is secretive and easily overlooked. A higher figure was also reported that included juveniles and unpaired adults.

Several protective measures should help the Mauritius cuckoo-shrike. Hunting the bird has been illegal for decades, but it is unclear how strictly shooting laws are enforced. Some primary forest has been protected.

Attention has also been given to agricultural plantings that might benefit the species. Finally, a scheme for predator control, especially of the macaques, has been proposed.

The Réunion cuckoo-shrike is found on the island of Réunion east of Madagascar in the Indian Ocean. This illustration is of a related member of the *Coracina* genus.

Réunion Cuckoo-shrike

(Coracina newtoni)

ESA: Endangered

IUCN: Endangered

Length: 7 in. (18 cm)
Weight: Unknown
Clutch size: 2 eggs
Incubation: Unknown
Diet: Mostly insects
Habitat: Dense forests and thick scrub, particularly of tamarind (*Acacia heterophylla*) and heath (*Philippia abietina*)
Range: Réunion, east of Madagascar in the Indian Ocean

SINCE PERMANENT settlement of the island by people began in 1691, Réunion has suffered many of the same environmental problems as Mauritius. Several unique birds have either become extinct or are now perilously endangered, including the Réunion cuckoo-shrike.

At 970 square miles (2,510 square kilometers), Réunion ranks as the largest of the Mascarene Islands. It lies 475 miles (765 kilometers) east of Madagascar and about 125 miles (200 kilometers) southwest of Mauritius. The flightless dodo could not reach Réunion, but a flightless relative, the Réunion solitaire, already lived there.

No specimens of the solitaire were preserved and no remains have been found to verify its existence. However, enough material was written and drawn about the bird by early visitors to Réunion that most ornithologists accept its existence as fact. Like the dodo, the Réunion solitaire became extinct, but not until the early 1700s.

Small birds such as the Réunion cuckoo-shrike survived early settlement on the island. Their small size allowed more of them to inhabit a parcel of habitat. They could also fly to escape danger and they were naturally secretive. However, these traits could protect the cuckoo-shrike for only so long.

Introduced animals

Human presence on Réunion has meant drastic changes. Native forests have been cut to make room for agriculture. Livestock and exotic animals, such as the black rat (*Rattus rattus*), were introduced, either accidentally or intentionally. The deer *Cervus timorensis* was introduced as a game animal because the islands lacked large mammals suitable for recreational hunting. The deer browse the forest undergrowth, thereby damaging habitat quality for native wildlife.

People also brought birdlime with them to Réunion. Birdlime is a sticky material obtained from mistletoe, holly, and other plants. When smeared on twigs or other likely perches, it catches small birds that can then be collected for eating. Laws enacted to protect Réunion's birds have not succeeded in ending the use of birdlime, and poaching remains a serious problem.

The population of the Réunion cuckoo-shrike steadily declined as the human population grew and exerted more demands on the land. The bird probably suffered further losses as a result of three severe cyclones in the 1940s. Some ornithologists thought the Réunion cuckoo-shrike had become extinct by the 1950s, but it survived and by the 1970s its population had grown enough to be encouraging. Despite the bird's slight recovery, however, a problem has remained.

Avian malaria

The Réunion cuckoo-shrike has failed to occupy all the available habitat that still remains. There are two possible explanations. First, the bird was known to feed on certain beetles (*Oryctes* sp.) that lived on native palms. The palms were removed to make space for the cultivation of more commercially valuable trees and crops. The beetles disappeared and the palms now survive only at higher altitudes, so loss of food is one possibility. Second, mosquitoes that carry and transmit avian malaria were accidentally introduced to Réunion. The mosquitoes do not survive higher in the mountains where the cuckoo-shrikes now live.

Programs to continue clearing Réunion's forests have been reevaluated. Some tourism development has been stopped. Proposals to introduce the wild boar (*Sus scrofa*) have been defeated and recommendations for reducing the deer population have been made. The status of the Réunion cuckoo-shrike cannot be accurately determined until potential habitat on the island is surveyed and questions about food supply and disease are answered.

Kevin Cook

See also Bulbuls, Fodies, Mauritius Kestrel, Parakeets, Pigeons, and White-eyes.

Cui-ui

(Chasmistes cujus)

ESA: Endangered

IUCN: Critically endangered

Class: Actinopterygi
Order: Cypriniformes
Family: Catostomidae
Length: 26 in. (66 cm)
Reproduction: Egg layer
Habitat: Water column and rocks
Range: Pyramid Lake, Nevada

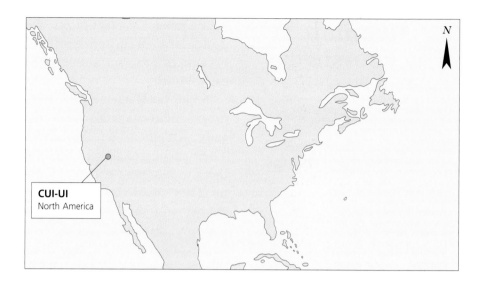

CUI-UI
North America

THE ONCE ABUNDANT cui-ui (pronounced kwee-wee) can claim one last stronghold on the North American continent: Pyramid Lake and its spawning grounds in the lower Truckee River of Nevada. There are many reasons for the decline of the cui-ui, including blockage of the Truckee River to spawning fish, poor water quality, and lack of water. Predation by birds, fish, and other aquatic animals take a big toll on cui-ui eggs and young.

In dry years upstream water use by city populations, as well as by farmers and ranchers, reduces stream flows for fish like the cui-ui. These factors, plus the lack of adequate numbers of adult fish, are the primary reasons for this fish's endangered status.

Adult cui-ui spawn in the Truckee River from April to July. Snowmelt from the Sierra Nevada mountain range apparently prompts their move from Pyramid Lake to the river. When the water temperature is at or below 57 degrees Fahrenheit (14 degrees Celsius), adults move to the head of gravel and sand bars in the river. Capable of producing as many as 40,000 eggs, a single female releases groups of sticky eggs at night in the presence of one or more males. She does this many times during a spawning sequence until her entire supply is distributed over a wide area. After the young hatch, they remain in the river for days and sometimes weeks before moving downstream to the lake. In the river cui-ui young congregate with other small fish such as Tahoe suckers to maximize their chances for survival.

Microscopic food

The cui-ui's preferred foods are microscopic water-dwelling animals called zooplankton, as well as some aquatic insects and algae. The cui-ui is considered a sucker and has the characteristic sucker body and mouth. However, the cui-ui is not a bottom-feeder like other suckers. Instead it follows its prey to areas in the lake that are 30 to 100 feet (9 to 30 meters) deep and near large algae-covered rocks. Many fish prefer the southeast of the lake near the mouth of the Truckee River, seeking water temperatures near 60 degrees Fahrenheit (15 degrees Celsius).

The cui-ui roughly resembles the common carp in body shape and ultimate adult size and carries large scales on the body and slightly forked tail. Normally black or brown on the back and sides, fading to white on the belly, the male is bright red and brassy in the breeding season. The female displays a blue gray color during most of the year.

This species is slow-growing but can live 40 years or more. Biologists use rings on fish scales, much like rings on a tree, to determine the age of a fish. Researchers are unclear about the age of some cui-ui, because after age six the scales are not a reliable aging tool. Unlike some fish, male and female cui-ui grow at about the same rate.

Efforts are under way to breed the cui-ui by using aquaculture techniques. Aquaculture has been used successfully to produce millions of juvenile fish. However, raising the fish to adult size and providing them with adequate natural spawning areas and conditions has proved to be more difficult.

William E. Manci

CURASSOWS

Class: Aves

Order: Galliformes

Family: Cracidae

Curassows probably got their English name from the island Curaçao, where the first specimens were captured. Although curassows were probably originally introduced to Curaçao by people, the Caribbean island lies just off the northwestern coast of Venezuela, not far from where curassows commonly occur.

The curassows belong to a family of 43 to 50 species which also includes guans and chachalacas. Fossils of related birds have been found in eastern North America and France, but living birds of the family are limited to Central and South America. However, the plain chachalaca (*Ortalis vetula*) lives as far north as the lower Rio Grande Valley of Texas. Most of the 13 or 14 curassow species inhabit northwestern South America, but one species lives as far south as northern Argentina, and another species can be found on the Yucatán peninsula of Mexico.

Blue-billed Curassow

(Crax alberti)

IUCN: Critically endangered

Length: 36 in. (91 cm)
Weight: Unknown
Clutch size: 2 eggs
Incubation: Unknown
Diet: Probably fruits, seeds, leaves, and flowers, plus insects
Habitat: Forests on valley floors, in foothills, and on lower mountain slopes
Range: Northern Colombia

To UNDERSTAND WHAT it means for a species like the blue-billed curassow to be in decline requires a general understanding of population differences among species. Any plant or animal species that occurs only in a small geographic area will have a small natural population. Species that occur over broader geographic areas will typically have larger natural populations. Since large animals need more space than small animals, more small animals can live in a given area. However, only so many individuals can live in a small space. This factor can determine how effective preservation efforts may be.

The blue-billed curassow has become endangered as Colombian forests have been cut. The more valuable trees are used for lumber products, and the less valuable trees are burned. The cleared land is then farmed either for crops or for grazing. The blue-billed curassow cannot adapt to agricultural land, and it shows no sign of accepting second growth forest. Because the species naturally occurs only in a small area of Colombia, no hope exists that it can survive in undisturbed habitat somewhere else.

Forest protection

The only way to protect the blue-billed curassow is to protect the primary forest in which it lives. When, or if, habitat is set aside for birds such as the blue-billed curassow, it must be in large enough tracts to accommodate the greater territorial needs of the larger species. If the preserves are too small, they may not be able to hold enough individuals to keep the population healthy. Colombia

The male blue-billed currasow is mostly black overall, but the lower belly, thigh, undertail, and tail tip are white. The female is black overall as well but has narrow white lines on the crest, the back, and parts of the wings, tail, and breast.

has established some national parks and other preserves, but the market for lumber and farmland makes it difficult to set aside enough land for all the people that need it. Enforcing the laws that protect the national parks and preserves has become very difficult. The economic benefits of raising coca plants for cocaine and poppies for opium have far exceeded the rewards for saving habitat for endangered species. Thus people willingly cut protected forest to cultivate crops that bring them cash. Those who profit enormously from the international drug trade have shown that they are willing to use extreme violence to continue their drug industry. The blue-billed curassow may eventually become a victim of the human appetite for cocaine.

Razor-billed Curassow
(Mitu mitu)

ESA: Endangered

IUCN: Extinct in the wild

Length: 35 in. (89 cm)
Weight: Unknown
Clutch size: Probably 2 eggs
Incubation: Unknown
Diet: Unknown
Habitat: Wet areas such as stream banks and marshes within dense forests
Range: Pernambuco, Alagoas, and northeastern Bahia, Brazil

OVER THE YEARS a small group of curassows, including the razor-billed curassow, has been

N

BLUE-BILLED CURASSOW
Colombia

RAZOR-BILLED CURASSOW
Brazil
Former range

RED-BILLED CURASSOW
Brazil
Former range
Present Range

classified differently by various ornithologists. Some have considered these birds part of the *Crax* genus, while others have argued that they are distinct and have placed them in the genus *Mitu*. Most ornithologists now accept the *Mitu* designation as the most appropriate.

The razor-billed curassow was once considered a broadly distributed species that ranged from southeastern Colombia, eastern Peru, and northern Bolivia eastward across Brazil south of the Amazon. However, further study

of specimens has prompted ornithologists to recognize the *Mitu* curassows in this area as two distinct species instead of one. The group that occupies the central and western portion of this vast range is now known as the greater razor-billed curassow (*Mitu tuberosa*). The group which once inhabited the wet areas of dense forests in eastern Brazil represents the now endangerd razor-billed curassow.

The razor-billed curassow may be extinct in the wild. A few birds survive in captivity, but captive breeding may not save the bird. Before releasing captive-bred birds into the wild, suitable habitat must be available and the conditions that caused the disappearance of the wild birds must be controlled or eliminated. It is possible that no habitat remains to receive and sustain razor-billed curassows.

Very little is known about the razor-billed curassow. Its preferred habitat of wet forests makes casual observation very difficult, so information that usually comes from sightings is very sparse. The habitat also complicates more formal studies. What is known about the razor-billed curassow suggests that it is much like other curassows.

Ground dwellers

Razor-billed curassows usually stay together in pairs. Groups of four or five probably indicate a family group with grown chicks that have not yet been forced out of their parents' territories. Razor-billed curassows spend considerable time on the ground, where they probably find much of their food. Their enlarged beaks may be adapted for a specialized diet. When alarmed or flushed from cover, these birds quickly fly into trees and hide in thick tangles. Males call in the mornings, evenings, and through the night but not during the hotter hours of the day.

To preserve any species, information about survival needs is necessary. This is true of the razor-billed curassow, for which more knowledge of its natural history must be acquired. However, because it may be extinct in the wild, collecting that information is probably impossible. One

alternative may be to study the related greater razor-billed curassow. Its habits and behaviors may be similar enough to those of the razor-billed curassow for the information to prove useful.

Red-billed Curassow
(Crax blumenbachii)

ESA: Endangered

IUCN: Critically endangered

Length: 31 in. (79 cm)
Weight: Unknown
Clutch size: 2 eggs (reported from just one nest)
Incubation: Unknown
Diet: Insects, fruits, seeds, and leaves
Habitat: Humid forests
Range: Sooretama Biological Reserve in Espirito Santo and possibly Monte Pascoal National Park, both in Brazil

FOR MANY YEARS only 12 specimens in museum collections proved that the red-billed curassow ever existed. First described in 1825, this bird of the dense forest slowly disappeared until ornithologists believed it had become extinct. The red-billed curassow was found still surviving in the Sooretama Biological Reserve in Espirito Santo, Brazil, where a few individuals came into a small settlement to feed with domestic fowl each evening.

Large expanses of primary forest still existed in northeastern Espirito Santo in 1939. By the 1970s all the forest had been cut

except for the 60,000 acres (24,300 hectares) within Sooretama. Cleared lands then became more valuable to agriculture. Cultivated fields now completely surround the reserve.

Forest canopy

The red-billed curassow apparently prefers forests with some canopy. It does much of its feeding on the ground, where it finds insects and fallen fruits. The bird also picks fruits from plants and eats leaves. When frightened, it flies into the lower branches of trees, then hops from branch to branch until it disappears into the canopy. This species also nests in trees, although very few nests have been reported.

Red-billed curassows are usually seen in pairs, although grown chicks may remain with the parents for some time. Some people described the birds as quite tame, but others reported them to be somewhat shy and difficult to approach except in cases where they fed with domestic birds and had grown used to people. When the bird is calm, its crest lies flat against its head; when alarmed, the bird causes the crest to stand erect and pumps it up and down.

Protection

In the past red-billed curassows have been hunted, but Brazilian law now prohibits this. Historically wildlife protection laws were poorly enforced, and poaching was a problem. Sooretama, however, is patrolled by wildlife officials, and visitors must obtain permits to gain entry. Population estimates for the red-billed curassow now run as high as a few hundred birds.

Kevin Cook

Eskimo Curlew

(Numenius borealis)

ESA: Endangered

IUCN: Critically endangered

Class: Aves
Order: Charadriiformes
Family: Scolopacidae
Subfamily: Tringinae
Tribe: Numeniini
Length: 12–14 in. (30–36 cm)
Weight: 8–16 oz. (227–454 g)
Clutch size: 4 eggs
Incubation: Unknown
Diet: Insects, snails, small fruits
Habitat: Arctic tundra, coastal plains, Great Plains prairies, and Argentine pampas
Range: Upper North America; winters in southern South America

THE ESKIMO CURLEW remains a mysterious bird. Despite all that is known and has been written about this species, very little is genuinely understood. The one conclusion no one disputes is that a once common bird suddenly became very rare.

The smallest of four North American curlew species, the Eskimo curlew is a medium-sized sandpiper. The overall color of the bird is brown to buff. The back, nape, and wings are patterned with brown and tan, and the throat and breast are dark buff, with brown streaks fading to a dingy belly and undertail. The underwing is cinnamon. There is a white or pale buff eye line. The crown is dark brown, either solid or with a lighter central stripe. The dark beak is shorter and less decurved than other curlews' beaks.

When abundant, the Eskimo curlew bred on the Arctic tundra, primarily in the MacKenzie District of Canada's Northwest Territories. During its breeding season the species was seen in northern Alaska and extreme northeastern Siberia, but nesting was never confirmed in these areas. The birds reached the tundra in mid-May and laid their four eggs by early June. Only 39 nests were ever found but all were shallow scrapes in the tundra soil and were lined with grasses and small leaves. The tundra offers the advantage of long daylight periods during the warm months, so plant and animal life experiences a quick, explosive growth. This growth provides ample food for chicks that must grow up in a hurry.

By late July the Eskimo curlews, which nested as solitary pairs and not in colonies, gathered in flocks in the same way as many sandpipers and other shorebirds. After flocking, the curlews flew eastward, probably along the Arctic coast to Quebec and Newfoundland on Canada's Labrador Peninsula.

The birds stopped along the Atlantic coast to feed. Gorging themselves on snails and crowberries (*Empetrum nigrum*), they rested until they regained the body fat lost while flying from their breeding grounds. Once at full weight, the curlews headed to sea for a 3,000-mile (4,830-kilometer) nonstop flight to South America. They used their body fat to sustain them.

No one knows where the curlews landed in South America or what course they took next,

The long-billed curlew (*Numenius americanus*) is a member of the same genus as the rarer Eskimo curlew, a species that was once much more common throughout its range.

but the birds ended their southern flight on the prairies of Uruguay and Argentina. There they rested and fed in the summer warmth of the Southern Hemisphere. By February the Eskimo curlews were flying north along an unknown route through South and Central America. They crossed the Gulf of Mexico and settled in great flocks along the Texas coast, where they once again recovered before moving farther northward. The birds then crossed the Great Plains on the spring journey that took them back to the tundra for another breeding season.

The curlew declines

The Eskimo curlew was mentioned in some bird literature of the early 1700s but it was not described as a species until 1772. The bird was generally regarded as abundant; observers wrote

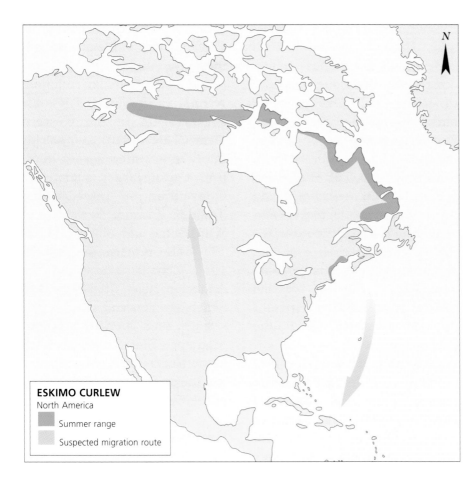

ESKIMO CURLEW
North America

Summer range

Suspected migration route

about seeing "immense numbers" and "huge flocks." By the mid-1800s the Eskimo curlew had become commercially valuable. Its pleasant flavor was apparently well liked, and the bird became increasingly available on the food market. As the once abundant passenger pigeon (*Ectopistes migratorius*) dwindled, hunters for the food market looked for other easily harvested game. Their eye settled on the Eskimo curlew.

Spring hunters in the Midwest and on the Great Plains found fewer birds during the 1870s. Autumn hunters in New England and Labrador found fewer birds by the 1880s. The Eskimo curlew had vanished from Labrador by the early 1890s.

Ornithologists believed the Eskimo curlew had slipped into extinction soon after the turn of the century. A single bird sighted in 1962 on Galveston Island, Texas, startled experts. Several Eskimo curlews were reported during the 1970s, but then in May 1981, a flock of 23 birds was discovered in Galveston Bay. Between 1982 and 1987 another 18 sightings were reported, including some from sites in Texas, Nebraska, and Maine. Despite the species' survival, the optimism is not complete. Ornithologists believe as few as 50 Eskimo curlews may be alive.

Imperfect data

Compared to so many other endangered birds, the Eskimo curlew seems to be well known. However, that knowledge is very superficial. Almost nothing is known for certain about the bird's life in South America. Details of the Eskimo curlew's

breeding habits, such as its incubation period, chick development, chick survival rate, age at first breeding, and life span are still unknown. The bulk of information on the bird comes from its migration stopover sites in Labrador, Texas, and the Great Plains, and most of that information only tells how many birds were killed for market.

No accurate figures

Descriptions of population size are interesting but offer very little insight. A term such as "immense flock" means different things to different readers a hundred years after the fact. No one actually counted the number of birds seen at a given site during a specific period. While such basic information remains lacking, one cannot meaningfully estimate the Eskimo curlew's population size before its decline. An accurate estimate might be useful in explaining the species decline.

ESKIMO CURLEW
South America

Winter range

Suspected migration route

There are many suspected causes. They include habitat loss, excessive shooting, poisoning, crop failure, drought, volcanic eruptions, and global warming. The global warming suspected of influencing the Eskimo curlew was a natural phenomenon following the so-called Little Ice Age that lasted from the 13th century into the 19th century. This warming period changed climate patterns, particularly the winds. If the winds shifted enough, they could have caused the Eskimo curlew to miss South America and perish in the southern Atlantic Ocean. However, no factual data has been found to support this idea.

Poisoning is doubtful as a cause of decline, because the curlews were not known to eat the kinds of bait that were used to poison nuisance species. An 1891 failure of the Russian wheat crop forced Argentina to improve its own wheat production rather than count on imported grain. Argentina turned to its own grasslands, where the curlews spent their winters, to grow more wheat. Did wheat farmers poison the birds as a result? Probably not: the Russian crop failure occurred in 1891, ten years after severe curlew declines were already being reported.

More theories

Volcanoes are a suspected cause of the Eskimo curlew's demise because of the ash they pump into the air. When thick enough, such ash layers can prevent sunlight from reaching the earth, resulting in a temperature drop. A mere one-degree drop can delay snowmelt in the Arctic, which could prevent the Eskimo

curlew from breeding successfully. However, if the Eskimo curlew could not produce young, other Arctic birds ought to have suffered as well. Likewise other birds migrate over the Atlantic Ocean to South America, and they should have suffered from wind shifts, too. The Hudsonian godwit (*Limosa haemastica*) and the American golden plover (*Pluvialis dominica*) both breed in the Arctic and migrate over the Atlantic. They suffered some population decline in the late 1800s, but neither species declined as drastically as did the Eskimo curlew.

Shooting remains another possibility. Although accurate records of the total number of Eskimo curlews shot are not available, general descriptions of the way people shot the birds offer some idea of the total loss. Eskimo curlews were often described as occurring in large flocks, even though population numbers were never recorded. Ornithologists now know that many sandpipers form large flocks that can represent nearly all of a given species. A large curlew flock may not have represented a huge population so much as it represented nearly all of the entire species.

Probably the real reason for the Eskimo curlew's decline was a combination of these events. Year by year on two continents, the bird found less habitat available, while continuous shooting reduced its numbers.

Possible recovery

Although dramatically reduced in number, the Eskimo curlew survives. It now receives some protection. For example, the bird

cannot be hunted in Canada, the United States, or Mexico according to the Migratory Bird Treaty Act of 1916. The Convention on Natural Protection and Wildlife Preservation in the Western Hemisphere (1940) also shields the Eskimo curlew against hunting. On a larger scale, the Convention on International Trade in Endangered Species of Wild Fauna and Flora (CITES. 1974) also protects the bird. In 1961 Canada established the Anderson River Migratory Bird Sanctuary. This and another preserve, the Kendall Island Migratory Bird Sanctuary, both in the Northwest Territories, protect the essential breeding habitat of the Eskimo curlew.

Recovery plans

In 1990 representatives of the Canadian Wildlife Service and the U.S. Fish and Wildlife Service agreed to begin recovering the Eskimo curlew. So far plans include public education to alert people that the bird is still alive, together with monitoring of traditional habitat in Texas and Nebraska. In addition there will be studies conducted on the little curlew (*Numenius minutus*) of Asia and Australia. Some experts believe that the little curlew and Eskimo curlew are a single species that merely live on different continents. Whether this is true or not, the little curlew is related closely enough to the Eskimo curlew to be useful. By studying the biology of the little curlew, ornithologists may find a way to breed Eskimo curlews in captivity. The young captives could then be released into flocks to increase the wild population.

Kevin Cook

Black-spotted Cuscus

(Spilocuscus rufoniger)

IUCN: Endangered

Order: Diprotodontia
Family: Phalangeridae
Weight: Female: 13–15 lb.
(6–7 kg); male weighs slightly
less than female
Diet: Fruit, flowers, and leaves
Gestation period: Unknown
Longevity: Unknown
Habitat: Arboreal in tropical
rain forests
Range: Rain forests of north
and east Papua New Guinea

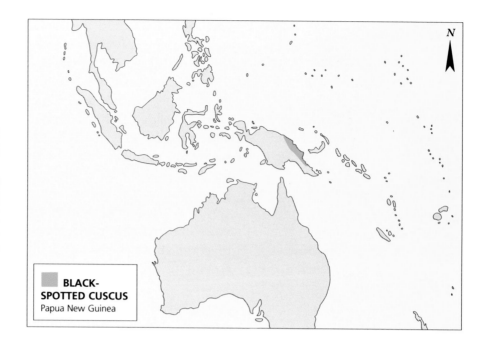

BLACK-
SPOTTED CUSCUS
Papua New Guinea

THE BLACK-SPOTTED cuscus and its close relative the spotted cuscus (*Spilocuscus maculatus*) are both members of the family Phalangeridae, but some disagreement remains as to whether they should be included along with eight other species in the genus *Phalanger* or form a separate genus, *Spilocuscus*.

Physical characteristics

The black-spotted cuscus is similar to a sloth in form but much more energetic and active in spirit. It possesses pink-rimmed eyes that protrude from its circular furry head. Only eighteen specimens of the black-spotted cuscus have been identified, and little is known about the ecology of the species. It has dense woolly fur that shows a pattern of black spots. It has a rounded head with a snout that is short and ears that are barely visible. This marsupial is found in the humid tropical rain forests of north and east Papua New Guinea.

The black-spotted cuscus is arboreal and navigates its way among the dense vegetation of the rain forest using a series of slow, deliberate movements. When moving about a tree, it maintains a strong grip with its feet at all times and achieves stability by using curved, sharply pointed foreclaws and clawless but opposable first hind toes. Despite its leisurely maneuverability amongst the trees, the animal is able to lope at speeds comparable to a fast human walk when on the ground.

The black-spotted cuscus gathers a variety of forest food such as fruit, flowers, and leaves and subsequently consumes them using its simple low-crowned teeth. It is primarily a nocturnal animal; very little is known about the social habits of the black-spotted cuscus. According to anecdotal evidence, the black-spotted cuscus, like other cuscuses, feeds and nests alone, and interactions between individuals are often aggressive. A well-developed forward-opening pouch accommodates its

maturing offspring, which suckle from the female's four mammae.

The black-spotted cuscus has been categorized as endangered by IUCN–The World Conservation Union. Despite the fact that this timid species represents no harm or economic value to humans, its numbers are declining. According to IUCN, the population is suspected to have declined by approximately 50 percent in the last decade. This decline is thought to be linked to the fact that the black-spotted cuscus is one of the larger species of cuscus and thus is particularly conspicuous to, and favored by, hunters for its coat and meat.

Bleak future

The black-spotted cuscus is subject to the effects of habitat destruction and is at the mercy of loggers and those who clear the rain forest for agricultural expansion. Because of the handicap of its physique and its restricted range in a deteriorating habitat, the outlook for this elusive arboreal marsupial appears bleak.

Adrian Seymour

Woodlark Island Cuscus

(Phalanger lullulae)

IUCN: Lower risk

Order: Diprotodontia
Family: Phalangeridae
Head-body length: Unknown
Weight: Unknown
Diet: Probably omnivorous
Gestation period: Unknown
Habitat: Probably in rain forests
Range: Woodlark Island, east of Papua New Guinea

WOODLARK ISLAND CUSCUS
Papua New Guinea

ENDEMIC TO WOODLARK Island, the Woodlark Island cuscus is known from only eight specimens. Four were collected in 1896, and a second four in 1953. It is uncertain whether this species has been seen since.

Although body measurements of this cuscus are unavailable, other members of the genus *Phalanger* have a head-and-body length of 12¾ to 23½ inches (32 to 60 centimeters) and weigh 2¼ to 4 pounds (1 to 1.8 kilograms). The fur on most cuscuses has a thick, woolly texture and comes in many shades, from white, red, and buff to gray and black. Although cuscuses may seem fragile as tree-dwellers, they are actually very strong animals. Cuscuses have a prehensile tail, much like a monkey's, that is able to grasp an object by wrapping around it.

Research needed

Next to nothing is known of the ecology or life history of the Woodlark Island species, and virtually all that has been written about it consists primarily of statements of its assumed similarity to other kinds of cuscuses. As of the late 1970s the species was believed to be at great risk due to the potential for commercial logging and agriculture on Woodlark Island. It is vital that surveys be done to determine if any cuscuses have endured and to establish the size of the remaining population. If possible, forest habitat should be set aside for reserves with this species' needs in mind. If the remaining population of Woodlark Island cuscuses is large enough, a captive-breeding program that is designed to generate individuals for relocation to other suitable islands or to safe habitat on Woodlark Island may be warranted.

Terry Tompkins

This male spotted cuscus (*Phalanger maculatus goldiei*) is a relative of the Woodlark Island cuscus, a species about which very little is known.

CYCADS

Class: Cycadopsida

Order: Cycadales

Cycads are a fascinating group of cone-bearing plants related to the conifers. They have a long history, revealed in the fossil record from the Triassic period onward (245 to 208 million years ago), and with their primitive appearance they are sometimes known as the dinosaurs of the plant world. Three families of cycad are recognized: Stangeriaceae, Cycadaceae, and Zamiaceae. Cycads, as a group, have been in decline since the Jurassic period (208 to 144 million years ago), and the species remaining today have a relict distribution mainly in the tropics.

The largest family, Zamiaceae, has 144 species in eight genera distributed in Africa, Australia, and, in the Americas, from Florida through the Caribbean and Central America to Colombia and Ecuador. Nearly 90 percent of the species in this ancient family are considered to be threatened with extinction on a global scale. The Cuban endemic *Microcycas calocoma* is a member of this family.

The Cycadaceae family consists of one genus, *Cycas,* of 35 species occurring in Madagascar, Asia, Oceania, and the Pacific islands. Several species of *Cycas* yield sago; others are sources of traditional medicines. Twenty *Cycas* species are now considered to be globally threatened and two endangered *Cycas* species are described below.

The Stangeriaceae family has just one species, the rare *Stangeria eriopus,* which grows in South Africa and Swaziland.

The fascination of cycads has been one of the reasons for their rapid decline over recent years, coupled with the effects of habitat modification and destruction in all the countries where they occur.

Collectors will pay very high prices for these often naturally rare and slow-growing plants. This has led to poaching from the wild and international smuggling. *Zamia purpurea*, a Mexican species, known only since 1983, has nearly been eradicated from the wild by collectors. *Encephalartos cerinus*, described in 1989 from KwaZulu-Natal, South Africa, has suffered in a similar way. All the plants have been removed from one of its two locations and the majority of mature plants and seedlings have been plundered from the other.

Cycads can be grown from seed, and several species are widely available as attractive pot plants. The best place to look at these unusual plants is generally in botanic gardens, which often have good cycad collections.

One species, *Encephalartos woodii*, can be seen only in botanic gardens. This South African plant was known from a single clump in the wild when botanists discovered it in 1895. By 1907 the species was extinct in the wild. Fortunately, some plants collected a century ago still survive in botanic gardens. Botanic gardens and nurseries are now helping to conserve wild populations of cycads, as well as maintaining genetic material in cultivation.

To help combat the impact of trade on rare wild species, all cycads are protected by CITES (Convention on International Trade in Endangered Species of Fauna and Flora). Under this convention, international trade in nursery-produced cycad plants is allowed, but international trade in wild plants of some of the rarest species is banned. Many cycads are protected by national legislation in their native countries. A wider appreciation of cycads may help to protect these rare species.

Cuban Tree Cycad

(Microcycas calocoma)

IUCN: Vulnerable

Family: Zamiaceae

Life form: Palmlike

Height: To 33 ft. (10 m)

Leaves: Glossy, from 6 to 40 leaves, 3 ft. (1 m) in length

Cones and seeds: Cones borne on stalks at the top of the trunk

Flowering season: Cone production irregular

Pollinator: Unknown, perhaps a weevil or beetle

Habitat: Open grassland or lightly shaded deciduous and evergreen forests on both limestone and siliceous clay soils

Range: Western Cuba

THIS IS ONE OF the most ornamental, and through its great rarity, also one of the most prized of cycads. Its Latin name is something of a misnomer; when it was originally described, the sole specimen available was of a few small leaves that resembled a small version of the Sago Palm (*Cycas revoluta*). *Microcycas* would be more appropriately called *Macrocycas* because it is the third tallest of all the cycads. It grows to 33 feet (10 meters) tall with a trunk of up to 24 inches (61 centimeters) across.

Restricted range

Perhaps as few as 400 and certainly not more than 600 individuals of this species survive in the wild. It is restricted to a very small area in the Órganos Mountains of western Cuba at an altitude of 160–650 feet (50–200

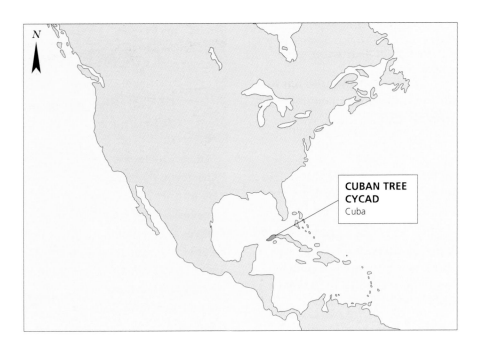

Dating agency
A recent census established that 16 mature plants exist in public collections, while a further seven are in private hands. Coning is irregular and few, if any, institutes will have both sexes simultaneously mature and coning. A network of enthusiasts run what is essentially a cycad dating service, ensuring that when precious male sperm is available somewhere in the world, it finds a mate, so that vital seed of critically endangered and vulnerable species can be produced.

Fred Rumsey

meters). Within this region it is known in four small distinct areas, with occasional isolated individuals elsewhere.

Male and female

Cuban tree cycads are dioecious, which means that male and female sex organs are borne on different individuals. The remaining populations are particularly vulnerable in that the numbers of male and female plants in each are very unbalanced. This results in a poor seed set, hence few new plants. It also takes many years for a cuban tree cycad to reach maturity and commence coning. The cones are almost always borne singly.

Habitat destruction may have played a role in reducing numbers of this species and fragmenting the populations. Its restriction to such a small area cannot be explained in terms of specialized climate or soil requirements. The Cuban tree cycad appears to have a broad ecological tolerance and grows readily in tropical and subtropical regions.

Protected and monitored

Plants are very sensitive to damage from cold weather. Specimens have been taken in the past for cultivation and for local uses of the plant parts (the roots have apparently been used to kill rats). This may have had a limited impact on plant numbers. The plants are now completely protected, and the populations are monitored on a regular basis.

The Fairchild Tropical Garden in Florida has had great success in breeding this cycad. Hundreds of seedlings have been produced by hand pollinating cones of the few mature specimens in this collection. These have been distributed worldwide to botanic gardens and collectors, while the Fairchild has retained enough to establish a breeding colony. Unfortunately the mature plants, which produced enough seed to double the world population, were killed by a lightning strike in 1991.

The Cuban tree cycad has 6 to 40 glossy, bright green leaves spreading from a rounded crown.

Cycas Wadei

IUCN: Endangered

Family: Cycadaceae
Height: Stem to a height of 3 ft. (1m)
Leaves: Palmlike, with narrow, rigid leaflets
Habitat: Lowland grassland
Range: Palawan, Philippines

THIS IS A MEDIUM-SIZED cycad with tall branched trunks growing to a height of 3 feet (1 meter). The young leaves of the plant are covered with cinnamon brown hairs. The leaves have narrow rigid leaflets displaying prominent pale midribs.

Cycas wadei is endemic to the Philippines, where it is restricted to the island of Palawan, in the vicinity of Culion.

This cycad, *Encephalartos altensteinii*, found in Cape Province, South Africa, is classified by IUCN as rare.

The plant grows in open lowland grasslands where the hot tropical climate has humid summers and mild moist winters. The area where Cycas wadei occurs was formerly used as a leper colony. Only a few plants now remain in the wild. The population has been estimated at 50 mature individuals. Palawan is one of the most botanically important islands of the Philippines. The whole island has been declared a biosphere reserve.

Cycas wadei can be grown from seeds, and a few plants are known to be in cultivation in botanic gardens and private collections. The species is included in Appendix II of CITES, which means that international trade in the species is controlled by the issue of licences.

Natal Grass Cycad

(Stangeria eriopus)

IUCN: Rare

Family: Stangeriaceae
Stem: Underground, up to 8 in. (20 cm) in diameter, sometimes branching
Leaves: Either compact, with smooth margined leaflets, or longer, with fringed leaflets
Cones: Covered with silvery hair, turning brown with age
Habitat: Coastal grassland and evergreen forests
Range: Swaziland; Cape Province and Natal, South Africa

THE NATAL GRASS CYCAD, (*Stangeria eriopus*), also known as Hottentot's bread, is the only species in its family. When it was discovered in 1853 it was thought to be a fern. Its importance to local people in South Africa is as

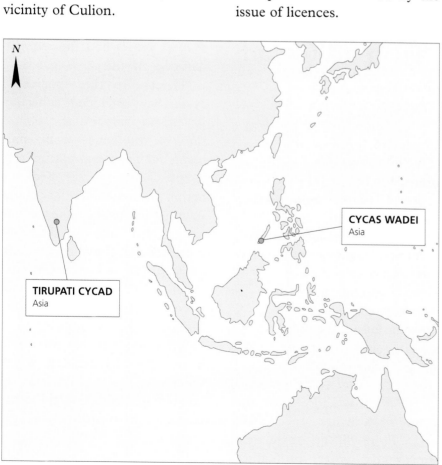

N

CYCAS WADEI
Asia

TIRUPATI CYCAD
Asia

a magical and medicinal plant. An infusion known as *intelezi* is believed to protect the home from lightning and evil spirits. The tuber is used to treat headaches, congestion, and high blood pressure. Tubers and seeds can induce vomiting if something poisonous is eaten.

This plant has a large tuberous root that is continuous with the underground stem. Up to four leaves grow from the top of each stem. The leaves vary in shape and size according to habitat. Plants of open grassland have compact erect leaves up to 12 inches (30 centimeters) long, whereas in forests the plants develop leaves of up to 6½ feet (2 meters). Each stem produces a cone. Male and female cones are on separate plants.

The Natal grass cycad grows only in eastern coastal areas of South Africa, from the Eastern Cape northwards through Natal to the border with Mozambique. It is found both in coastal grassland, growing in full sun, and in evergreen forests up to 30 miles (50 kilometers) from the sea. The plants in grassland areas are regularly subject to fire, which may be why they produce multiheaded plants when the stem-growing tip is destroyed by burning.

Over-collected

The Natal grass cycad is declining in the wild despite protection. It is collected as an ornamental plant, and around 50,000 plants are gathered each year for the medicinal trade. Conservation measures for the species include the development of large-scale cultivation for the medicinal trade, and protection for the species on Appendix I of CITES.

NATAL GRASS CYCAD
Africa

Tirupati Cycad

Cycas beddomei

IUCN: Endangered

Family: Cycadaceae
Stem: Up to 6 in. (15 cm)
Leaves: Feather shaped leaves up to 3 ft. (1 m)
Cones: Male and female cones born on separate plants
Habitat: Skeletal soils on exposed rocky slopes in dry deciduous forests
Range: India, Tirupati Hills

THE TIRUPATI CYCAD IS a small cycad with a short stem that grows to 6 inches (15 centimeters). From the tip of the stem emerges a cluster of feather-shaped leaves with long narrow leaflets. New foliage sprouts early each summer. Each plant has clusters of up to eight stems. Male and female cones occur on separate plants.

The Tirupati cycad grows only in the Tirupati Hills of the southern Eastern Ghats mountain range in India. The number of mature plants in the wild has been estimated at 500 specimens. The species was first discovered in the Cuddapah Hills over a hundred years ago, but is no longer found in this area.

The Tirupati cycad grows on skeletal soils on exposed rocky slopes in dry deciduous forest at an altitude of 985–2,950 feet (300–900 meters). It is a drought-tolerant species, adapted to survive the relatively long dry periods which occur in the Tirupati Hills. The Tirupati cycad grows with other drought-resistant plants such as the palm *Phoenix pusilla* and the red sandalwood *Pterocarpus santalinus*.

Threats to this species of cycad have included collection for private gardens, and collection of the cones from male plants for medicinal use by local people. The cones are used as a major ingredient in supposed rejuvenating tonics. Forest clearance and the spread of urbanization have also been major problems for this species.

The Tirupati cycad is the only *Cycas* species currently to be included in Appendix I of CITES, which means that trade in the species is banned. A few specimens are in cultivation in botanic gardens, but no other conservation measures are currently known.

Sara Oldfield

Kuznetzov's Cyclamen

(Cyclamen kusnetzovii)

IUCN: Endangered

Order: Primulales
Family: Primulaceae
Tribe: Cyclamineae
Size: About 4 in. (10 cm) high
Leaves: 1–1½ in. (3–3.5 cm) across
Flowers: Purple, pink, or white
Fruit: Spherical capsule
Seed dispersal: Carried by ants
Habitat: Oak and ash woodland
Range: Crimea, Black Sea

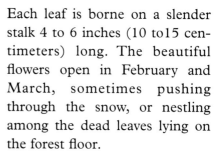

KUZNETZOV'S CYCLAMEN
Europe

KUZNETZOV'S CYCLAMEN is a small but highly attractive flowering perennial plant. It was discovered in 1955 and is known only from a very restricted area in the Belogorsk district, in the Biyuk Karasu river valley, in the Crimean Mountains, southern Ukraine, on the northern side of the Black Sea. It grows in humus-rich soil under a forest of oak (*Quercus* sp.) and ash (*Fraxinus* sp.), where maybe about 5 million plants exist altogether. With numbers in the millions, it may sound as if the plant is actually rather common, but the total area of forest in which it grows is estimated at a mere 120 acres (50 hectares). The plant is abundant in only a few places, whereas at most sites just a few individual plants occur. Kuznetzov's cyclamen is highly vulnerable because people dig up large numbers of the tubers to sell. They are in demand both as ornamental plants for cultivation in gardens and for medicinal purposes. In addition to this, because of their highly restricted natural range, any habitat damage could have catastrophic results.

Growing through snow

Kuznetzov's cyclamen grows in rich, humus soil from a disklike, underground tuber 1 to 1¼ inches (2.5 to 3 centimeters) across. From the tuber arise several broadly oval leaves 1¼ to 1⅓ inches (3 to 3.4 centimeters) across and deeply indented at the base. The upper leaf surface is dark green with a white, mottled pattern, while the underside is often deeply flushed with violet. Each leaf is borne on a slender stalk 4 to 6 inches (10 to 15 centimeters) long. The beautiful flowers open in February and March, sometimes pushing through the snow, or nestling among the dead leaves lying on the forest floor.

They are slightly fragrant, varying in color from purple to pale pink to white. Each flower has five oval petal lobes, ½ inch (1 centimeter) long, which are turned sharply upward from a downward-pointing mouth. The area near the mouth is spotted with dark lilac, with three stripes inside the throat. The seed capsule is globular and about ½ inch (1 centimeter) in diameter.

Easy to grow

Kuznetzov's cyclamen is easily raised from seed, and conservationists recommend that it is mass-propagated in nurseries to satisfy the horticultural and medicinal demand.

Digging or selling of wild plants should be forbidden. The areas in which it still occurs should be protected from damage and monitored to check the numbers of plants from year to year. Kuznetzov's cyclamen is already cultivated at the Nikita Botanical Garden in Crimea, and by cyclamen enthusiasts elsewhere. The plant is included on the Berne Convention Appendix I of Strictly Protected Flora Species. The Convention on the Conservation of European Wildlife and Natural Habitats, popularly known as the Berne Convention, was adopted in

The showy blossoms of *Cyclamen persicum* are cultivated as ornamental plants. Crossing this species with wild species results in exciting new hybrids.

1979 in Berne, Switzerland, and came into force in 1982.

Kuznetzov's cyclamen is similar to another, more common species, known as *Cyclamen coum*, which is widely cultivated in Europe and elsewhere as an ornamental plant. However, *Cyclamen coum* too is sufficiently rare, in Europe at least, to be protected under the Berne Convention, and it is included on Appendix I. The natural distribution of *Cyclamen coum* is continuous around the western, southern, and northeastern shores of the Black Sea, extending into the Caucasus mountains, with outlying areas in northern Iran on the shore of the Caspian Sea, and from northern Israel up through Lebanon and Syria into Turkey. Kuznetzov's cyclamen grows on the northern edge of this range. It differs from *Cyclamen coum* because its flowers are larger and fragrant. However, some botanists think they are one species.

Showy plant

Grown in cultivation by cyclamen enthusiasts, the small genus *Cyclamen* has fascinated gardeners because of the exquisite forms and colors of the flowers and leaves. So-called florists' cyclamen (large, showy hybrids based on the eastern Mediterranean species called *Cyclamen persicum*) have been developed over the last few centuries and are important to the horticultural industry. Genetic diversity of wild cyclamen should be conserved, not least because back-crossing (hybridization) of florists' cyclamen with wild species has had promising results in producing attractive new dwarf varieties.

Cyclamen are threatened because of their popularity as ornamental plants. Local people in the areas where the plants grow wild can supplement their income by digging up tubers to meet the demand from plant nurseries and importers. Legislation is in place to outlaw such trade. The gardeners who buy cyclamen tubers are usually unaware of the illegal origins of the plants and do not realize that their purchases are indirectly endangering wild populations.

More and more nurseries propagate cyclamens to satisfy the increasing commercial demand. This practice also maintains a valuable source of income for the local people.

Nick Turland

Gowen Cypress

(Cupressus goveniana)

ESA: Threatened

IUCN: Endangered

Family: Cupressaceae
Description: Small- to medium-sized cone-bearing, evergreen tree
Range: California

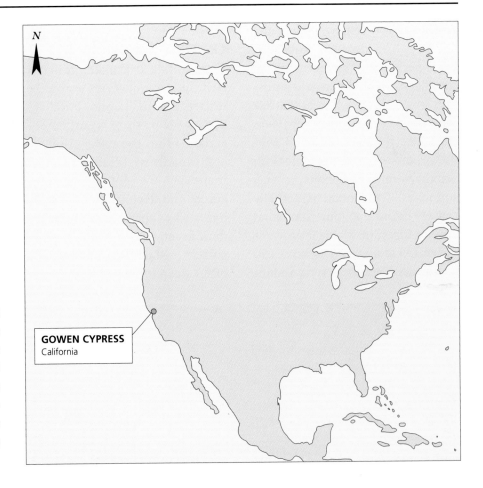

GOWEN CYPRESS
California

CUPRESSUS GOVENIANA is a conifer that occurs only in the state of California. California has a rich variety of conifers, with 53 native species, 12 of which are confined to the state. Two varieties of Gowen cypress are generally accepted and both are rare in the wild.

Five populations

Cupressus goveniana var. *goveniana* is the true Gowen cypress. This is a small to medium-sized tree of conical or broadly columnar appearance. The loosely arranged ascending branches have long, drooping, irregularly-divided branchlets and dark green foliage.

Five populations of the Gowen cypress are thought to exist, with fewer than 1,000 individuals. Two populations are protected in S.F.B. Morse Botanical Reserve and Point Lobos Reserve.

The other populations grow along the coast at altitudes of 98–985 feet (30–300 meters) in Mendocino and northwest Sonoma Counties. There are some pressures on these populations from local development, altered fire regimes, and possibly from invasive non-native plants.

Santa Cruz cypress

Cupressus goveniana var. *abramsiana* is commonly known as Santa Cruz cypress. It has previously been treated as a full species, *Cupressus abramsiana*. Santa Cruz cypress is a fast-growing symmetrical tree of dense columnar appearance. It is confined to fewer than ten groves in the Santa Cruz Mountains, growing at altitudes of 1,000–2,600 feet (300–800 meters). Pines such as *Pinus ponderosa* and *P. attenuata* commonly grow in association with this

A view of the coastline from Point Lobos, California, where the Point Lobos Reserve provides a protected habitat for the Gowen cypress. Other cypresses grow along the coast in Mendocino and Sonoma Counties.

variety. Each population of the Santa Cruz cypress is thought to have fewer than 100 individuals. This cypress is considered endangered by IUCN–The World Conservation Union.

Gowen cypress was listed as threatened under the U.S. Endangered Species Act in August 1998; the same act has listed the Santa Cruz cypress as endangered since 1987 (as *Cupressus abramsiana*).

Sara Oldfield

393

DACE

Class: Actinopterygi

Order: Cypriniformes

Family: Cyprinidae

The small and unassuming dace, while found primarily in the United States, can be found from the northern reaches of Canada to northern Mexico. Dace are cyprinids, like chubs, carps, shiners, minnows, and others. Of the 17 species and several subspecies of dace in North America, seven are in danger of extinction. Pollution and loss of vital habitat are the primary reasons for their decline.

Demands on water and land by thoughtless people and businesses for agricultural, urban, and recreational uses, together with the pollution and physical destruction that usually follow, contribute to the dace's peril.

Dace, like all species of fish, are important because they strengthen the biological diversity of the areas they inhabit. That is reason enough to protect them. In addition, because of their small size, many other fish and animals count on their strong numbers for food. Dace are part of the natural food chain that could disintegrate if too many species are lost.

What dace lack in size, they make up for with a unique variety of body patterns and colors. Far from merely being attractive, these colorations help dace survive in the wild. Dace are diverse and adaptable fish that can deal with a variety of habitats and environmental conditions. From the frozen Yukon of Canada to the desert of Sonora, Mexico, dace occupy important niches and positions in their environment.

All dace have an organ called the Weberian apparatus. This curious internal body part comprises bones that connect the fish's gas bladder to its inner ear and is probably responsible for their keen sense of hearing. Its main function, however, is to regulate buoyancy.

Blackside Dace

(Phoxinus cumberlandensis)

ESA: Threatened

IUCN: Vulnerable

Length: 2½ in. (6 cm)
Reproduction: Egg layer
Habitat: Covered river pools
Range: Kentucky and Tennessee

DISCOVERED AS A new species only recently, the blackside dace was mistakenly identified as another type of minnow before 1975. The range of this dace is very small and probably helps to explain why its identification came so late.

Today the blackside dace lives in the upper reaches of the Cumberland River in Kentucky and Tennessee. Natural waterfalls prevent its movement down the river or the movement of other fish up into its range, but it occupies this habitat with a handful of other fish species.

How the blackside dace entered this isolated area is still a mystery, but fisheries scientists believe that a geologic process called stream capture opened the area to this species. Stream capture involves the slow and steady movement by erosion of the stream source, or headwaters, into another river system. After a stream is captured, fish from the captured stream are free to move into the new area. The headwaters of the Cumberland River may have captured another stream, opening a new area for fish of the captured stream. In this case, the fish were the ancestors of the blackside dace.

This small, brightly colored dace probably lives to an age of three or four years. As the common name suggests, this fish displays a broad, dark, horizontal stripe down each side. Thinner matching dark stripes across the snout, cheeks, and gill covers meet the body stripes just behind the gills. The fish has a lighter, yellow-green back and head and a brilliant red belly and underside, which makes this fish stand out in a crowd. The red color of the mouth, throat, breast, and lower gill covers equals the brilliance of the belly. The fins are yellow and clear, and the tail fin is deeply forked for life in a river. The base of the dorsal fin on the back is red like the belly.

Sand eater

Despite its bold colors, the blackside dace is shy and prefers to spend most of its time in shaded or covered areas of the river over sand, rock, and rubble. The blackside dace searches in these areas for algae, small roots, and some insects and consumes large amounts of sand. Why the dace eats sand is not clear. It may help grind food or provide bacteria that grow on the sand grains.

The upper Cumberland River Basin is a very valuable area, as large deposits of coal are present.

Instead of digging mine shafts, miners expose the underground coal by stripping the surface area of overlaying rock. This strip-mining process causes soil erosion and siltation in the river and creates acid-runoff pollution.

Both siltation and chemical pollution threaten the continued survival of the blackside dace. Of the more than 20 populations of this fish in the upper Cumberland River, many have been threatened by past unregulated coal strip mining operations. An estimated 50 other populations have been eliminated by mining and other human activities.

Fewer trees, more roads

However, current mining activities are not believed to pose a threat when conducted in accordance with state and federal regulations. Deforestation and road building, both of which lead to siltation and the removal of shade, also are blamed for the decline of the blackside dace. The presence of the southern redbelly dace (*Phoxinus erythrogaster*) may also have contributed to the decline of the blackside dace in some areas.

Fortunately the kind of habitat destruction that could eradicate this fish does not have to occur. Through changes in mining and logging techniques, damage to the blackside dace and other fish populations could be minimized. Some protection is afforded by the Daniel Boone National Forest. Several of the larger populations of blackside dace live within the forest boundary. Hopefully the U.S. Forest Service will take steps to protect the blackside dace and attempt to reintroduce it to its former range.

Desert Dace
(Eremichthys acros)

ESA: Threatened

IUCN: Vulnerable

Length: 2½ in. (6 cm)
Reproduction: Egg layer
Habitat: Springs and creeks
Range: Soldier Meadows, Nevada

THIS NATIVE DESERT fish is confined to a very small area in northwestern Nevada called Soldier Meadows. In this 5,000-foot (1,525-meter) semi-mountainous basin the desert dace makes its home. Invasion by competing non-native fish and degradation of habitat by people threaten the desert dace's existence. The total population is estimated at several thousand, although this number may fluctuate seasonally. At present most of the fish's habitat is either under federal ownership or protected by a conservation easement. Conservation plans are also under way to protect the desert dace as well as the area's other endemic species.

When they think of mountains, most people imagine snow and cold. Soldier Meadows receives its share of both, but the desert dace is immune to their effects. The springs and creeks of Soldier Meadows can carry water as hot as 100 degrees Fahrenheit (38 degrees Celsius). The desert dace is one of the few fish that can tolerate hot water. This dace breeds in the summer and, like most fish, does not guard its eggs. It feeds on insects and algae and occasionally eats other fish.

Moapa Dace
(Moapa coriacea)

ESA: Endangered

IUCN: Critically endangered

Length: 2¾ in. (7 cm)
Reproduction: Egg layer
Habitat: Warm springs
Range: Moapa River, Nevada

UNDER THREAT FROM foreign invaders and from destruction of its habitat, the Moapa dace faces extinction if not protected. The spring-fed Moapa River in southern Nevada is home for this fish. The river begins at several hot springs that join and travel 26 miles (42 kilometers) south to Lake Mead, the reservoir created by the construction of the Hoover Dam on the main stem of the Colorado River.

Before 1950 the Moapa dace was abundant, but the Moapa River has changed dramatically since then. Invaders like the exotic mosquitofish and shortfin molly moved in on dace territory, claiming the limited space for

The Moapa dace faces stiff competition from exotic fish introduced into its habitat over the past century.

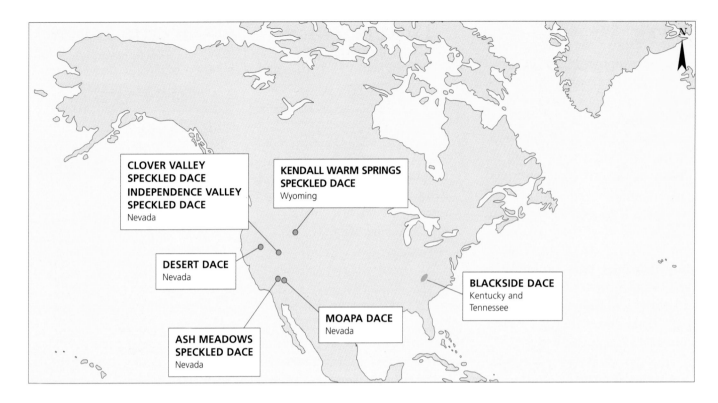

CLOVER VALLEY
SPECKLED DACE
INDEPENDENCE VALLEY
SPECKLED DACE
Nevada

KENDALL WARM SPRINGS
SPECKLED DACE
Wyoming

DESERT DACE
Nevada

BLACKSIDE DACE
Kentucky and
Tennessee

MOAPA DACE
Nevada

ASH MEADOWS
SPECKLED DACE
Nevada

themselves and bringing with them parasites that ravaged the native dace. Compounding the problems caused by these fish, people cleared protective bank vegetation, lined the channel with gravel and cement, and diverted water for drinking and crop irrigation. By the mid-1960s the total population of Moapa dace had fallen drastically, and by 1977 only a few hundred fish remained.

Stable environment

Because the Moapa River is spring fed, it is very stable both chemically and physically. Temperatures near the springs vary only slightly—between 82 and 90 degrees Fahrenheit (28 and 32 degrees Celsius)—and the Moapa dace has adapted to these stable surroundings. The river tends to become muddy as it winds its way to Lake Mead. This trait earned it the name *moapa,* which means "muddy" in the language of Native Americans of

the Paiute tribe. The remaining Moapa dace populations tend to congregate among algae mats in the clear waters of the river's source springs, but some can be found in the cloudier reaches below. Moapa dace seek gentle currents over small gravel and sand, hugging the banks that contain overhanging vegetation. Four other fish species are native to the Moapa River, but vigorous competition for habitat began only after non-native fish were introduced—a battle that the dace have failed to win.

The Moapa dace has a unique pattern of coloration and is the only member of the genus *Moapa.* Similar fish like the roundtail chub and the Moapa speckled dace lack the Moapa dace's dark stripe down the middle of the back and the spot at the base of the tail. The stripe covers an olive-green background. This glossy fish's sides are also striped and patched with a golden brown that overlays lighter colors. The

skin has scales that create a leathery look, hence the species name *coriacea,* or "leathery."

Insect eater

The Moapa dace is an insect eater and is often found among insect-filled mats of algae. Because of its stable spring-water environment, this species is unhindered by cold winter air temperatures and can spawn at any time of the year. However, spawning activity peaks in spring and summer.

Realizing in 1979 that private landowners were not going to aid this fish, the U.S. Fish and Wildlife Service bought 12 acres (4.9 hectares) of land along the Moapa River and some headspring water rights and formed the Moapa National Wildlife Refuge. By revitalizing stream segments that pass through the refuge and by reintroducing the fish to areas it once occupied, federal officials hope to aid the recovery of the Moapa dace.

Ash Meadows Speckled Dace

(Rhinichthys osculus nevadensis)

ESA: Endangered

Length: 2½ in. (6 cm)
Reproduction: Egg layer
Habitat: Desert spring streams
Range: Ash Meadows, Nevada

ASH MEADOWS IS a unique area in southern Nevada that is home to a number of endangered fish. This desert oasis provides sustenance for fish that depend on it for their survival and boasts more native plants and animals than any area in the United States. Here live the Devils Hole pupfish, Warm Springs pupfish, Ash Meadows Amargosa pupfish, and Ash Meadows speckled dace, all of which are listed as endangered or threatened.

Water is a valuable commodity in the Ash Meadows area.

Unfortunately the majority of water and property rights are currently owned by private companies that hope to develop the area by pumping out large quantities of groundwater. Pumping groundwater would almost certainly devastate springs in the Ash Meadows area and spell disaster for all the fish that inhabit the springs.

The Ash Meadows speckled dace is a subspecies of the speckled dace (*Rhinichthys osculus*) and, as its name implies, displays a spotted back and sides. The underside of this small dace is light yellow or creamy white.

Biannual spawner

The speckled dace usually spawns twice a year, a luxury made possible by the stable temperature of the springwater in which it lives. In unusually dry years water flow from the groundwater supply is reduced, and breeding adults defer their late summer spawning until the

following spring. Of the hundreds of eggs laid, fertilized, and hatched by a breeding pair, only a few survive to adulthood.

Unique habitat

The unique nature of Ash Meadows may be the key to the survival of its inhabitants. Under federal protection, land and water occupied by threatened and endangered species becomes less attractive to powerful developers. Moves have been made to transfer ownership of the area to the federal government or into the hands of conservation organizations. The success or failure of these attempts will seal the fate of the Ash Meadows speckled dace.

There are many subspecies of speckled dace (*Rhinichthys osculus*), a fish that, as its name implies, is covered with spots on its back and sides. Although the species itself is one of the most widespread fish on the North American continent, a number of the subspecies are endangered, including those found in the Ash Meadows, Clover, and Independence Valleys of Nevada and in Kendall Warm Springs in Wyoming.

Clover Valley Speckled Dace

(Rhinichthys osculus oligoporus)

ESA: Endangered

Length: 2 in. (5 cm)
Reproduction: Egg layer
Habitat: Warm springs
Range: Clover Valley, Nevada

HIGHLY RESTRICTED IN its range, the Clover Valley speckled dace is found at only a handful of sites in Clover Valley in northeastern Nevada. Ironically this fish is a subspecies of the speckled dace (*Rhinichthys osculus*), one of the most successful and widespread fish on the North American continent. However, over time, isolation under different local conditions created subspecies of speckled dace.

The Clover Valley speckled dace is restricted to warm springs outfalls and cool, small pools on some private lands where the landowners have made collecting specimens extremely difficult. One landowner introduced rainbow trout for recreational purposes, creating a dangerous situation for the Clover Valley speckled dace. This step, together with the local abundance of bullfrogs, has caused the Clover Valley speckled dace to become extremely endangered, since trout and bullfrogs are both aggressive predators.

The Clover Valley has a bright olive or golden green back and silvery sides that bear a poorly defined horizontal stripe from the base of the head to the base of the tail fin. The belly of the Clover Valley speckled dace is light and creamy. The entire body carries dark speckles that vary in pattern and size. Males display some red in the pectoral fins just behind the gills, the pelvic fins, and at the base of the anal fin.

The overall shape of this fish is fairly stubby. It has a rounded snout and a blunt tail fin. The body fins are generally triangular and not particularly large.

Breeding signs

Clover Valley speckled dace feed on insects and other invertebrates that inhabit their springs and pools. During the summer, vegetation tends to grow and clog these waters, and the dace search for food items among this vegetation. Little is known about this fish's breeding habits, but due to the fairly constant water temperatures in and near the springs, year-round spawning can be expected. Clover Valley speckled dace develop nodulelike tubercles on their body and fins as a sign of their readiness to spawn.

Independence Valley Speckled Dace

(Rhinichthys osculus lethoporus)

ESA: Endangered

Length: 1½ in. (4 cm)
Reproduction: Egg layer
Habitat: Warm springs
Range: Independence Valley, Nevada

THE INDEPENDENCE Valley speckled dace is the next-door neighbor of another endangered dace, the Clover Valley speckled dace *Rhinichthys osculus oligoporus*. The Independence Valley subspecies is in a more precarious position than its close relative and depends on only one water source—Warm Springs—for its continued well-being. Ironically, like the Clover Valley speckled dace and the Kendall Warm Springs speckled dace *R. osculus thermalis*, this fish is a subspecies of the speckled dace (*Rhinichthys osculus*), a widespread fish on the North American continent.

Threatening situation

The Independence Valley subspecies of the speckled dace shares its surroundings with several other fish and amphibians —the common carp and two voracious predators, the largemouth bass and the bullfrog. Without predators the outlook for this dace would, at best, be considered gloomy. However, these predators make the situation even more threatening. A positive note for the future of the Independence Valley speckled dace is that Warm Springs produces plenty of water—about 250 gallons (946 liters) per minute—and is in no immediate danger of failing. However, depletion of natural habitat has been the primary cause of the decline of this fish.

Tiniest speckled dace

At under 2 inches (5 centimeters) long, the Independence Valley speckled dace is the smallest of the speckled dace in the Nevada region and is considered a dwarf by fisheries biologists. Adults are not much larger than juveniles of only one year in age. The fish's coloration is very similar to that of the Clover Valley subspecies, with a bright olive or golden-green back and silvery sides. The sides are marked by a poorly defined horizontal stripe from the base of the head that extends and sharpens as it reaches the base of the tail fin. A second stripe below the first is visible on many specimens. The belly of this dace is light and creamy. The entire body carries dark speckles.

Dwarf fish

The overall shape of the Independence Valley subspecies is fairly stubby. It has a rounded snout and a blunt tail fin. The body fins are generally triangular and very large in proportion to the body, indicating a true dwarf population. The body fin size is one feature that makes the subspecies a distinct form from other speckled dace, which don't have particularly large body fins. The Independence Valley subspecies lacks the red fin coloration that is present in some Clover Valley speckled dace.

Breeding habits unknown

The breeding habits of the Independence Valley speckled dace are unclear. Specimens collected in the month of August showed no breeding colors to indicate their readiness to spawn.

The feeding habits of the Independence Valley subspecies are similar to those of the Clover Valley speckled dace. Insects and other invertebrates that inhabit the springs and pools are the fish's primary source of food. During the summer, vegetation tends to grow and clog these waters, and the dace search for food among this vegetation.

Kendall Warm Springs Speckled Dace
(Rhinichthys osculus thermalis)

ESA: Endangered

Length: 2 in. (5 cm)
Reproduction: Egg layer
Habitat: Pools in creek formed by springs
Range: Kendall Warm Springs, Wyoming

ONCE A POPULAR bathing area for local residents and tourists, the Kendall Warm Springs are now off-limits to humans. Cattle were excluded in the 1960s when it was discovered that grazing, trampling, and pollution were destroying the spring's only fish inhabitant, the Kendall Warm Springs speckled dace. Before 1975 people could wade, bathe with soaps, and launder their clothes in the springs. However, as the dace population in the springs dwindled, something had to be done. To protect this environment from further damage the springs were made off-limits to the general public.

Animals under stress

Studies done before and after the springs were closed showed some pollution related stress to all animals in the springs, not just the dace. The importance of this location to the Kendall Warm Springs speckled dace, a subspecies of the speckled dace (*Rhinichthys osculus*), is clear: the springs are the only remaining habitable site for this highly endangered fish.

A stable home

When not disrupted by the presence of people or cattle, the springs and creek are highly stable. Regardless of the time of year, water temperature is a relatively constant 79 to 85 degrees Fahrenheit (26 to 29 degrees Celsius). This "hot tub" fish prefers to stay in the creek itself, away from the spring's origin. Lack of oxygen and high levels of carbon dioxide are probably the reason for avoiding the origin. Water in the creek picks up oxygen from the atmosphere and gives up some of its carbon dioxide as it heads for the Green River, a short distance away.

Not a picky feeder

The density of food items tends to be higher in the lower reaches of the creek, farther away from the springs. Like the speckled dace, the Kendall Warm Springs speckled dace subspecies is not picky when it comes to diet and is known to eat algae, small insects, and other invertebrates. The Kendall Warm Springs subspecies is smaller than the speckled dace but retains many of the same physical features, such as a dark and spotted back, silvery sides, forked tail, streamlined shape, and clear fins.

The Kendall Warm Springs speckled dace uses vegetation not only for food but also as cover from predators. Clumps of plants in the creek offer safe havens for adults and small dace. Youngsters are found in the creek at all times of the year, indicating that spawning goes on more or less continuously. This adaptation is made possible by the steady water temperature.

William E. Manci

DAISIES (MAGUIRE DAISY AND PARISH'S DAISY)

Order: Asterales

Family: Asteraceae (Compositae)

There are about 150 species of the genus *Erigeron*, to which the Maguire daisy and Parish's daisy belong. They are spread all over the world, especially in the Western Hemisphere, with the western United States as the center of distribution. Some species are considered weeds and may even be serious pests to crops and gardens, but others

are much less vigorous and are sometimes restricted to a few tiny populations barely clinging to existence. The two species discussed here grow in the American West, in rocky places in canyons and mountain country. They are threatened by various human activities, especially mining and trampling, but the smallness and isolation of their few populations also make them vulnerable to inbreeding, which may in the long run be a natural cause of their decline.

Maguire Daisy

(Erigeron maguirei)

ESA: Threatened

IUCN: Vulnerable

Size: Perennial herb with sprawling or upright, hairy stems 2¾–7 in. (7–18 cm) tall

Leaves: Hairy leaves found at the base of the plant and on stems, basal leaves spoon- or spear-shaped, ¾–2 in. (2-5 cm) long

Flowers: 1 to 3 flower heads borne at the tip of each stem, each head with 15 to 20 white or pinkish white ray florets surrounding orange disk florets

Fruit: Small, dry, and nutlike; 1 seeded

Habitat: Sandstone canyons and mesas, often in wash bottoms of canyons

Range: San Rafael Swell in Emery County and Capitol Reef in Wayne County, Utah

MAGUIRE DAISY is a small, attractive plant known from only a few canyons and mesas in the state of Utah. It often grows in the wash areas (dry, gravelly streambeds) at the bottoms of canyons, but may also be found on the adjacent sandstone cliffs.

There are serious threats to the long-term survival of this species, but through careful land protection and good management it should be possible to secure its continued existence.

Maguire daisy was first described for science by the American botanist Arthur Cronquist in 1947 from a specimen collected in 1940 from the San Rafael Swell of Emery County, Utah. A supposedly different form of the plant was later described as *Erigeron maguirei* var. *harrisonii* by Stanley Welsh in 1983. This variety was first discovered in 1936 in the Capitol Reef of Wayne County, Utah. However, in 1989 both varieties were reported to be growing together at Capitol Reef, and it

was then suspected that var. *harrisonii* might be no more than a shade-growing form of the Maguire daisy. In other words, the supposed differences are actually caused by the habitat conditions (such as shade or sun) rather than by any in-built genetic difference. The United States Fish and Wildlife Service (U.S.F.W.S.) funded genetic studies as part of its recovery plan for the Maguire daisy in order to prove conclusively whether or not there is any genetic difference between the two varieties. By DNA analysis, it was discovered that there is in fact no genetic difference. Therefore, U.S.F.W.S. now recognizes Maguire daisy as a single undivided species, *Erigeron maguirei*.

Wider distribution

Maguire daisy was listed as endangered by the U.S.F.W.S. in 1985. When the plants at Capitol Reef (so-called var. *harrisonii*) could be included with those from San Rafael Swell (the original Maguire daisy, var. *maguirei*), it was seen that a larger number of individual plants were growing over a wider area than had previously been known. This expansion in range, and also the recent discovery of several additional populations of Maguire daisy, were reasons for the U.S.F.W.S decision to reclassify the species from endangered to threatened in 1996. The long-term survival of Maguire daisy is still considered far from certain, however, and there is now an officially approved recovery plan. There are several serious problems facing the plant: a large part of its habitat is threatened by mineral and energy exploration

Maguire daisy is found in sandstone canyons and mesas in Utah. This habitat is threatened by mining for minerals such as uranium.

1,000 to 2,000 plants over a range of some 31 miles (50 kilometers). There are now 12 known sites for Maguire daisy altogether, including the plants from the Capitol Reef region, bringing the world total to no more than 3,000 individual plants. Approximately 2,000 of these grow on land managed by the Bureau of Land Management, while the rest are located in the Capitol Reef National Park. Some plants grow in the Sid's Mountain Wilderness Study Area, where they face very few current threats, owing to the area's very difficult access. However, even here, the long-term protection is in doubt because the area has not been officially designated as a Federal Wilderness Area under the Wilderness Act. This would protect the land forever from mining, building, and logging. However, without such a designation, the area could legally be opened up to various ecologically damaging uses that could destroy the Maguire daisy's habitat.

Nick Turland

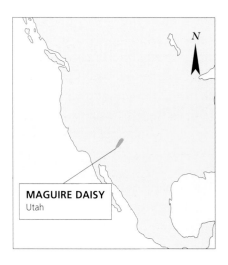

MAGUIRE DAISY
Utah

and development, such as uranium mining. There are also recreational activities in the areas, especially the careless use of off-road vehicles that damage both plants and habitat. Trampling of plants by humans and cattle, particularly in the wash bottoms of canyons, results in the species being restricted to less suitable habitat of sandstone crevices in canyon walls.

Inbreeding risk

Maguire daisy grows in small, geographically isolated populations that have become prone to inbreeding, with a consequent decline in genetic viability. This may be caused by a gradual buildup of lethal genes. A further concern is that the small populations, and also the specialized habitat, make the plant vulnerable to natural or human-induced catastrophes.

More plants discovered

Recent detailed surveys have increased the known distribution of Maguire daisy in the San Rafael Swell region from one to ten populations and from less than ten individual plants to

Parish's Daisy

(Erigeron parishii)

ESA: Threatened

IUCN: Vulnerable

Size: Small, clump-forming perennial herb, upright stems 4–12 in. (10-30 cm) tall, covered with soft silvery white hairs
Leaves: Narrow, strap shaped, covered in silvery hairs
Flowers: Up to 10 solitary, very showy flower heads borne at the stem tips, with deep rose to lavender ray florets surrounding a central disk
Fruit: The central disk sheds small, dry, nutlike, 1-seeded fruits
Habitat: Usually on limestone or dolomite substrates in pure or mixed woodlands of pinyon pine and juniper; sometimes also in blackbrush scrub
Range: San Bernardino Mountains, San Bernardino County, southern California

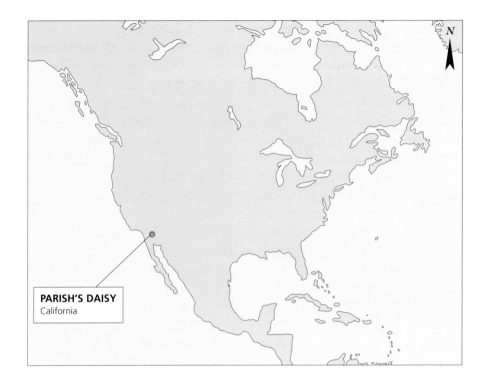

PARISH'S DAISY
California

THE SAN BERNARDINO Mountains in southern California are famous for their great diversity of natural habitats. This results from their geographical location between the southwestern deserts and the Pacific coast, their varied altitudinal zones, and certain unusual geological features such as limestone outcrops. The San Bernardino National Forest includes most of the San Bernardino Mountains. Even though this forest makes up less than 1 percent of the land area of the state of California, it contains over 25 percent of all the plant species known to grow wild in this state. This is a remarkable statistic that well illustrates the tremendous biological importance of the forest.

Confusion of species

Parish's daisy was first described for science by the American botanist Asa Gray in 1884. It has sometimes been confused with another species, Utah fleabane (*Erigeron utahensis*), which grows in the mountains of the Mojave Desert of southern California as well as in Arizona, Colorado, and Utah. Parish's daisy differs from Utah fleabane in its silvery white rather than gray-green stem and also in the structure of the pappus (the hairs and bristles attached to the fruit).

Rocky habitat

In the San Bernardino Mountains, calcium and magnesium carbonate (limestone and dolomite) rock outcrops are found in a number of bands oriented from east to west on the slopes facing the desert. A few isolated areas of carbonate also occur away from these slopes. These carbonate outcrops, or soils derived from them, are the principal home for Parish's daisy, which is currently known from fewer than 25 sites. In the entire world, there are estimated to be about 16,000 individual plants, and fewer than a third of the populations contain more than 1,000. Parish's daisy is normally associated with dry, rocky slopes, outwash plains, and shallow drainages on limestone or dolomite. They are found in pure or mixed woodlands of single-leaf pinyon pine *Pinus monophylla*, and junipers, mainly Utah juniper, *Juniperus osteosperma*, more rarely California juniper, *Juniperus californica*, or western juniper, *Juniperus occidentalis*, from 4,000–6,400 feet (1,220-1,950 meters) in altitude. It may also grow in scrub of blackbrush *Coleogyne ramosissima* on desert-facing slopes at lower altitudes.

The United States Fish and Wildlife Service (U.S.F.W.S.)

listed Parish's daisy as a threatened species in 1994. The plant is endemic (grows nowhere else) to the San Bernardino Mountains in southern California. Most of the carbonate deposits in this mountain range are within currently active mining claims or mining claims that are being maintained for their resources of minerals. Limestone, rather than dolomite, is being mined in the area at present, and this varies from low-grade cement quality to high-grade pharmaceutical quality. The open-cast or terraced mining method that is used, as well as the dumping of overburden and construction of roads, result in total habitat destruction for Parish's daisy. Additional threats to the plant include energy development projects, urban development, expansion of a skiing resort, and the careless use of off-road vehicles.

As with the Maguire's daisy in Utah, the small number of iso-lated populations, and often small numbers of individual plants within populations, leads to inbreeding and a consequent decline in genetic viability. This may eventually lead to the extinction of some populations.

Other habitats

The plant's tendency to grow on carbonate substrates is not universal. A few populations are found on an area of adjoining granite and limestone, while others at the eastern limit of the range of the species are on a quartz substrate. A tendency to grow on limestone makes Parish's daisy vulnerable to the activities of the mining industry, so it is fortunate there are a few sites away from limestone.

This vulnerability to mining practices can be illustrated by the following example. The most

The flowers of Parish's daisy display a ring of rose to lavender ray florets surrounding central disk florets.

westerly known populations of Parish's daisy are near a place called White Mountain, an outcrop rising to 6,890 feet (2,100 meters) in altitude. The third largest limestone mine in the San Bernardino Mountains is here, and it currently produces some 550,000 tons (500,000 tonnes) of limestone each year. The fact that the Parish's daisy grows in this area means that it almost certainly once also grew on the site now occupied by the mine. Unfortunately, the remaining westernmost populations will soon become extinct themselves because of a recently approved plan for further mining operations in the area. However, as part of a compensation package, San Bernardino County has instructed the mining company to sponsor horticultural studies and to experiment in reseeding Parish's daisy onto reclaimed areas of the mine site.

Nick Turland

DAMAS

Class: Actinopterygii

Order: Ophidiiformes

Family: Ophidiidae

The damas, or cusk eels, occupy just a few locations in underground waterways on the Yucatán Peninsula. One species of dama, dama blanca ciega (*Typhliasina pearsei*), is currently listed by IUCN–The World Conservation Union as vulnerable. This is because of its limited range and threats to its remaining habitat. Since scientific information is scanty, the nature of these threats is unclear.

Another species, nueva dama ciega (*Typhliasina* sp.), was formerly listed by IUCN but is no longer evaluated.

In many ways the physical form of these fish is quite different to that of other fish. They have a large head relative to the rest of their body, a bulbous belly, and a muscular tail that ends in a point. Both the dorsal fin on the back and the anal fin behind the belly extend the length of the tail and meet at the tip.

William E. Manci

DAMSELFLIES AND DRAGONFLIES

Class: Insecta

Order: Odonata

Dragonflies and damselflies are rather large, beautifully colored aquatic insects that belong to the order Odonata. This name is derived from the Greek word *odon*, meaning "tooth", and refers to the strong and sharp-toothed jaws, or mandibles, that damselflies and dragonflies use to prey on other insects. Adults may be readily observed on sunny, warm days near almost any body of fresh water. They are remarkably agile fliers that can hover in midair, glide lazily, or dip, dart, and dash about at speeds of nearly 60 miles (97 kilometers) per hour.

As wetlands throughout the world have been drained, dammed, and polluted, populations of several Odonata species have declined. The loss of clear, unobstructed streams is probably the greatest threat to most Odonata. Industrial pollution of both flowing and still-water habitats has also adversely affected many species.

Even though they are harmless to humans, Odonata species, or odonates, were probably first called dragonflies because of superstitious fear of them. Their appearance and behavior certainly can seem threatening. The faces of dragonflies and damselflies are characterized by a brutish appearance because of their greatly enlarged and glowing eyes and seemingly oversized chewing mouthparts.

Damselflies and dragonflies are enormous compared with most insects. Although they are graceful and elusive in flight, they will often sweep through the air near one's head while noisily rustling their wings. It is probably because of these habits that such common names as "devil's darning needles," "horse stingers," "clubtails," "snake feeders," and "snake doctors" have been used to describe them. Ironically odonates are incapable of biting or stinging. Another common name, "mosquito hawks," is based on the preference of some dragonflies to feed on mosquitoes, gnats, and other small flying insects. Even so, these features and names have made damselflies and dragonflies favorite subjects of poets, artists, naturalists, and collectors.

Odonata anatomy

Like all insects, damselflies and dragonflies have three main body regions: head, thorax, and abdomen. Three pairs of legs and two pairs of wings attach to the thorax. The four wings are elongated, veined, and membranous. The patterns of these wing veins are used to identify genera, families, and the two suborders Anisoptera (dragonflies) and Zygoptera (damselflies). At rest dragonflies and damselflies are unable to fold their wings over their abdomen. Damselflies hold their wings together above their bodies, while dragonflies hold their wings horizontally at rest. The thorax is relatively small and compact, while the abdomen is long and slender.

Today Odonata vary in length from about ¾ inch to over 5 inches (2 to 13 centimeters). Unlike other insects, damselflies and dragonflies have an ancient lineage, and numerous fossilized species have been found. The largest dragonflies lived about 250 to 300 million years ago and had a wingspan of 27 inches (69 centimeters). About 25 extinct families of Odonata are known only from fossils.

More than 5,000 species of odonates have been described and there may be more than 9,000, as many as there are bird species. The vast majority of odonate species are found in tropical regions. Among aquatic insects, the Odonata has the greatest number of species.

Breeding

Immature stages of Odonata live in a variety of aquatic environments but are most commonly found in ponds, marshes, lake margins, shallow areas of streams, and slower portions of rivers and creeks. The immatures are called nymphs or naiads because they live in water and use gill-like structures to breathe.

Anatomical differences in the gills are important for telling dragonfly and damselfly naiads apart. Gills of damselfly naiads form three leaflike structures at the end of the abdomen, and the naiads swim with undulating body motions, their gills functioning like the tail of a fish. The gills of dragonfly naiads form ridges in the rectum. When the dragonfly naiad breathes, it draws water into the anus and moves by expelling it—a primitive form of jet propulsion.

Opportunistic predators

Naiads are opportunistic predators that feed on other aquatic insects and invertebrates, even on small fish or tadpoles. Some immatures actively search for their prey while others lie and wait to ambush it. However, most young odonates are visually attracted to moving prey. Fish and amphibians are common predators of the naiads.

The time it takes for immature damselflies and dragonflies to mature and the numbers of generations produced per year vary dramatically, depending on the species. If water temperatures are favorable and food is readily available, some species will breed continuously and generations will overlap. Most species breed once a year, although a few are known to breed once every two, three, or four years.

Adult damselflies and dragonflies may live from a few weeks to a few months. Flight activity, which is mostly diurnal (that is, during the day time), is related to feeding and reproductive behavior. Adults are voracious predators. Males of some species establish territories for feeding and finding mates and aggressively defend their territories from a perch or by patrolling flights. Mating often involves specialized courtship behavior.

Damselflies and some dragonflies lay their eggs in floating vegetation or debris by puncturing the plant tissue with a well-developed ovipositor (egg-laying organ). In other kinds of dragonflies, the female lays her eggs by repeatedly striking the end of her abdomen on the water in a rhythmic pattern.

There are approximately 5,000 species of the order Odonata known worldwide, and 25 extinct species have been identified through fossils. Many of these insects are unusually colored, like the civil bluet.

Odonata in peril

The small hemiphlebia damselfly (*Hemiphlebia mirabilis*) is a bright metallic green species of the family Hemiphlebiidae. It was once thought to be extinct from its three original locations in Victoria, Australia, because of the damming of the Yarra and Goulburn rivers, which eliminated the seasonal lagoon flooding favored by this damselfly.

Since then, populations have been confirmed at other sites in Victoria, as well as in Tasmania and on the islands of the Bass Strait. At least three of the new populations are situated inside protected areas or national parks

The time it takes for immatures to mature varies between species of Odonata, as does the number of generations that are produced in a single year. Most species breed only once a year.

and are abundant. The small hemiphlebia damselfly is still considered rare, however.

In the United States, a rare snaketail dragonfly (*Ophiogomphus edmundo*) of the family Gomphidae was last seen in 1892. Its range included North Carolina, Tennessee, and Pennsylvania. Like related members of its genus, this species probably preferred open, grassy streams. However, the reasons for its decline and extinction are unknown. The Ohio emerald dragonfly (*Somatochlora hineana*) of the family Corduliidae was once found in bog habitats of northern Indiana and Ohio. Only 29 specimens were ever collected. Despite intensive searches, the Ohio emerald has not been observed there since 1953 and the species was thought to be extinct. A population was discovered recently at a site in Wisconsin, but its future is not secure because of plans for construction near its habitat.

Several other damselflies and dragonflies are near extinction. For example, *Coenagrion hylas freyi*, or Freya's damselfly, (family Coenagrionidae) is known from only a handful of small alpine lakes in the Austrian and Swiss Alps. This species breeds in stagnant waters, favoring beds of rushes (*Equisetum*) in shallow offshore areas. Little is known about the biology or ecological needs of this species, and this lack of information complicates efforts to conserve it. Threats include development and eutrophication (a high buildup of nutrients such as phosphates) of the few lakes that occur within its known geographic range.

In the United States the San Francisco forktail damselfly (*Ischnura gemina*) is known only from the San Francisco Bay area of California. Although it was described early in the twentieth century from specimens collected near San Jose, this species remained largely unknown and was feared to be extinct until 1978, when it was rediscovered north of San Francisco along the Point Reyes coast in Marin County. Subsequent surveys found the species associated with several urbanized bodies of water, including concrete-lined drainage and flood-control channels. Although the damselfly was found in 37 new locations, 11 have already been eliminated, 21 persist in highly altered or polluted wetlands, and only five are considered reasonably protected. Loss and alteration of these areas of habitat continue through the

This odonate's compound eyes may not give a very sharp image but they are excellent at detecting the movement of both predators and prey.

cleaning of flood-control channels, installation of underground culverts, channeling of streams, pollution, and drought.

To make matters worse, a more widespread species of damselfly may be interbreeding with the San Francisco forktail at some remaining locations, leading to hybridization and the forktail's eventual decline. For these reasons, the San Francisco forktail damselfly is now listed as endangered by IUCN–The World Conservation Union.

Although it was formerly found in Georgia, Florida, and possibly other parts of eastern North America, the Florida spiketail dragonfly (*Zoraena sayi*) is now restricted to just two small populations in northern Florida. One population, located near Gainesville, is threatened by development. The Florida spiketail requires three types of habitat in close proximity to successfully maintain its population: shallow, woodland streams for egg laying; silt deposits in the streams and seepages in which developing naiads can find cover; and open fields for mating. It is believed that Florida spiketail naiads need three to four years to mature.

Protected areas have rarely been set up to cater to odonates, although in Japan no less than 24 have been established for these insects and three or four have been set up in Britain. The following list names several species of Odonata that are considered endangered. In general, loss or alteration of habitat is behind

their endangered status. Remaining habitat needs to be protected so these species can be studied. Information about their natural history and habitat requirements is needed to devise appropriate conservation actions, particularly in light of the rapid destruction of rain forests.

Richard A. Arnold

Other endangered damselflies and dragonflies of the world

Family Calopterygidae

(no common name)	*Calopteryx syriaca*	Middle East

Family Chlorolestidae

(no common name)	*Ecchlorolestes nylephtha*	South Africa
(no common name)	*Ecchlorolestes perengueyi*	South Africa

Family Coenagrionidae

(no common name)	*Argiocnemis solitaria*	Mauritius
Southern Damselfly	*Coenagrion mercuriale*	Europe
Barren's Bluet Damselfly	*Enallagma recurvatum*	United States
(no common name)	*Megalagrion* (9 species)	Hawaiian Is.
(no common name)	*Mortonagrion hirosei*	Japan

Family Cordulegasteridae

(no common name)	*Cordulegaster mzymtae*	Asia

Family Libellulidae

(no common name)	*Brachythemis fuscopalliata*	Middle East

Family Megapodagrionidae

(no common name)	*Amanipodagrion gilliesi*	Tanzania

Family Platycnemididae

(no common name)	*Platycnemis mauriciana*	Mauritius

DARTERS

Class: Actinopterygii

Order: Perciformes

Family: Percidae

This highly diverse group of freshwater fish contains a total of about 150 species, of which 24 are considered threatened or endangered. Their diversity in North America is second only to that of the family Cyprinidae, which includes minnows and chubs. Despite their differences, the darters share many common physical and behavioral characteristics, and only three genera are used to name all darters: *Ammocrypta*, *Percina*, and *Etheostoma*. The majority of these brightly colored fish fall within the last-mentioned genus.

Dispersed across the Mississippi River system and rivers of the Great Lakes, Hudson Bay, Atlantic Coast, Gulf of Mexico, and Pacific coast of Mexico, darters truly have achieved a continental distribution. As a group, darters are distinctive in shape and size and are small relative to more commonly known fish such as trout or bass. Darters reach a maximum length of 8 inches (20 centimeters). Their slender, torpedo-like bodies include two prominent dorsal fins on their backs as well as pronounced pectoral fins on their sides for steering and maneuvring. The first, or spiny, dorsal fin contains spines for protection against predators. The second, or soft, dorsal fin has no spines.

Despite their small size, darters are closely related to some of North America's most popular game fish: the yellow perch, sauger, and walleye. They are all in the family Percidae. Unlike their relatives, the darters have small teeth and no gas bladder for buoyancy (or they have a gas bladder that is undersized relative to its body). This trait creates a tendency to sink and allows them to maintain their position within a stream.

The darter's preferred environments are the fast-moving, shallow "rapids" areas of streams. This preference may have several advantages over deeper pool areas. Larger fish that are potential predators tend to congregate in stream pools. Clearly, predator-free areas offer the best chance for survival. Additionally, stream riffles generally hold abundant supplies of food, such as insects, that are missed by competing fish until the organisms move downstream into pool areas.

Despite the advantages of river life, darters comprise the largest group of threatened or endangered fish in the world. Darters are no match for the potentially destructive power of reservoirs and flood-control projects, pollution, and stream bank and watershed deforestation that can harm their habitat. Dam and reservoir construction programs are doubly damaging to darter populations because such projects flood shallow river rapids and prevent the downstream movement of populations. Removal of water from streams for urban and agricultural use is also a cause for the decline of many darter species. Recovery for the darters will only be achieved by maintaining the springs and streams that are its preferred habitat.

Amber Darter

(Percina antesella)

ESA: Endangered

IUCN: Vulnerable

Length: 2¾ in. (7 cm)
Reproduction: Egg layer
Habitat: River currents
Range: Tennessee and Georgia

THE AMBER DARTER'S range is extremely small. The species is present only in extreme northwestern Georgia and extreme southeastern Tennessee in approximately 33 miles (53 kilometers) of the Conasauga River. One amber darter was taken in 1980 from a site on the Etowah River in Georgia, but subsequent surveys failed to yield additional specimens. Historically amber darters were found in Shoal Creek, a tributary of the Etowah River, but water projects flooded much of this habitat, and surveys indicate amber darters are no longer present. No current population estimates are available.

A saddled fish

The amber darter is among the smallest of the entire darter group. Its species name, *antesella*, means "anterior (forward) saddle" and refers to the shape of the back and the unusual position of the forwardmost, saddlelike coloration. The amber darter has four saddles along the length of its back. It has no scales on its belly and has eyes that are high on the head and closely set.

Coloration is tan to reddish brown on the back and pale hues on the belly. The name *amber* comes from the golden hues on the body and some of the fins.

During the spawning season males usually sport small nodules called tubercles on the fins and body. Some females also display these nodules when they reach breeding condition. The amber darter prefers moderate to swift river currents over shallow gravel or sand. It feeds on insects and other small aquatic animals in cool, clear water.

Decline

Loss of habitat and the burden of pollution are the primary reasons for the amber darter's highly endangered status. It is unclear what efforts have been made to rescue the species to date. However, increasing public awareness about the effects of pollution and dams on river-dwelling fish could make a difference for the future of this darter.

Bayou Darter
(Etheostoma rubrum)

ESA: Threatened

IUCN: Lower risk

Length: 2 in. (5 cm)
Reproduction: Egg layer
Habitat: River rapids over rocks
Range: Bayou Pierre and tributaries, Mississippi

THE ONLY KNOWN population of the bayou darter is located in Bayou Pierre and its tributaries in southwestern Mississippi. The fish prefers gravel rapids in water less than 12 inches (30 centimeters) deep. As degradation of habitat continues, numbers probably will continue to decline. Gravel mining in the Bayou Pierre drainage, flood-control dams, road construction and maintenance, and clear-cut logging near shorelines are causes of the decline of the bayou darter. Like other river fish, this species is sensitive to changes in water quality and flow rate and cannot tolerate floating silt, mud, weak currents, or deep pools.

Even smaller than the amber darter, the bayou darter displays dark coloration and the male has pronounced horizontal bands on its sides. In the female the bands are weak, presenting a checkered-flag appearance, or they are absent. Eight saddlelike patches on its back, with the eighth prominently displayed, help distinguish the bayou darter from its relatives. In addition the body sports nine to twelve vertical blotches that blend into the horizontal bands.

Colorful spawning

While little is known about the bayou darter's breeding habits, as a part of courtship the breeding male displays bright pink-red bands on all fins, unlike the less spectacular female. This fin coloration is believed to be the basis for the species name, *rubrum*.

Despite the advantages of river life, darters comprise the largest group of threatened and endangered fish in the world. Darters are no match for the massive destructive power of reservoirs and flood-control projects, pollution, and stream bank and watershed deforestation. Dam and reservoir construction is doubly damaging because it floods shallow river rapids and prevents the downstream movement of populations to more suitable river areas.

Given the small size of the remaining bayou darter population, this species is considered, at best, threatened. The mainte-nance of stable and silt-free gravel bottoms within the Bayou Pierre system and adjacent watersheds may reverse the current trend toward endangerment.

Coldwater Darter
(Etheostoma ditrema)

IUCN: Vulnerable

Length: 2 in. (5 cm)
Reproduction: Egg layer
Habitat: River pools and springs
Range: Coosa basin of Georgia, Alabama, and Tennessee

SMALL LIKE ITS cousin the bayou darter, the robust coldwater darter is considered a threatened species in its home range. Limited to a few small springs and pools in the Coosa Basin of Georgia, Alabama, and Tennessee, the coldwater darter is susceptible to habitat degradation at these few remaining sites. Recovery for this species will depend on the management of its preferred habitat—springs and headwaters of streams.

The male coldwater darter is particularly distinguishable during the spring and summer breeding season, displaying bright red coloration on its belly, red spots on its sides, and red bands on its fins. The female acquires some coloration during this period and lays her eggs on vegetation. Both sexes wield spines on the anal fin.

The scientific name *ditrema* means "two pores." Originally it was thought that all members of the species exhibited two pores on the top of the head. However, some specimens have only one pore, which is a trait in other darter species.

Unlike many darters, the coldwater darter prefers to live among aquatic plants or other submerged material in about three feet (91 centimeters) of water or less. Like all darters, they favor insects and their larvae as a food source.

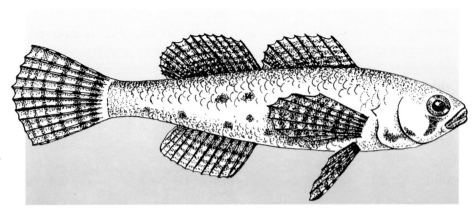

Conchos Darter (Dardo de Conchos)

(Etheostoma australe)

IUCN: Vulnerable

Length: 2½ in. (6 cm)
Reproduction: Egg layer
Habitat: Swift currents over sand
Range: Rio Conchos in Chihuahua and Durango, Mexico

FOUND ONLY IN the northern Mexican states of Chihuahua and Durango, the Conchos darter survives in the upper reaches of the Rio Conchos. The great need for agricultural water in this developing region leaves serious doubt about this species' ability to maintain its numbers. While the Conchos darter is common in some locations, continued demand for river water and the resulting decline in suitable habitat could mark the end for this fish.

Like many darters, the Conchos darter prefers fast-flowing stream water over sand and gravel and consumes insects. Despite its desert environment, this fish demands cool and clear water for spawning and must spawn very early in the year (from February to June). This rigid requirement could prove to be the Conchos darter's downfall, given the diminishing numbers of suitable natural streams. Prospects for recovery of this species are poor.

This darter is moderately sized and bears distinctive patterning. It has six to nine dark brown, saddlelike colorations on the back that blend into similarly colored vertical bars over a lighter brown-green background on the sides. These disappear into a light green belly in the female but continue down to meet at the middle of the green belly in the male. In most Conchos darters, a vertical row of three dark spots highlights the base of the tail. The spiny dorsal fin on the back is edged in black, which accents an adjacent red band. With the exception of the more deeply hued spiny dorsal fin, all fins are predominantly yellow orange and may display some spotting. The base of the anal fin tends toward a greenish coloration at the base and this coloration is more pronounced in the male than in the generally less spectac-

The coldwater darter is considered threatened because its range is particularly small. Any habitat loss seriously affects this fish.

ular female. The anal fin contains a thick spine. The belly of both sexes is nearly fully scaled, but the cheeks, gill covers, and breast are devoid of scales.

The breeding male, in addition to his bright colors, displays nodulelike tubercles on the belly. Females lack breeding tubercles and bright coloration.

Coppercheek Darter

(Etheostoma aquali)

IUCN: Vulnerable

Length: 2¾ in. (7 cm)
Reproduction: Egg layer
Habitat: Swift currents over gravel and rock
Range: Tennessee

LOCATED ONLY IN THE Duck and Buffalo Rivers in west-central Tennessee, this darter is in trouble because of threats to its habitat. Flood-control and water-supply construction projects are the primary threats. The coppercheek darter prefers shallow stream water over gravel or stones, but curiously it does poorly in waters below dams. The species name *aquali* is derived from the Cherokee word *agaquali*, which means "cheek."

The brightly patterned coppercheek darter stands out because of its numerous red spots that overlie narrow horizontal stripes. As the common name implies, the light cheek coloration of this fish stands out from the darker surrounding color pattern of olive brown.

Like some other darters, there is a considerable difference between the male and female of the species. In the male the spiny dorsal fin on the back has a black spot at its base, and its other fins are generally dark at the base. The dorsal fin spot is absent in the female. Some red fin spots and bands are also highlighted in the male. Unlike the male's, all the female's fins appear speckled, but their overall coloration is paler and much less spectacular.

Fountain Darter

(Etheostoma fonticola)

ESA: Endangered

IUCN: Vulnerable

Length: 1⅛ in. (4 cm)
Reproduction: Egg layer
Habitat: Warm and quiet springs
Range: San Marcos River and Comal Springs, Texas

ONLY TWO POPULATIONS of the fountain darter exist. One inhabits the headwaters of the San Marcos River (or nearby) in east-central Texas. The second is a reintroduced population at Comal River Springs, which is located several miles southwest of the San Marcos site. A captive population existed at New Mexico's Dexter National Fish Hatchery, but this program has since ceased. Recovery prospects for the fountain darter are poor.

Named for the fountainlike spring in which it was first found, the fountain darter is the smallest darter and is one of the smallest of all freshwater fish. The male is smaller than the female and rarely exceeds 1½ inches (3.8 centimeters).

The fountain darter has a small, blunt head and snout and a small mouth. The forward end of the white belly is unscaled, but there are some scales toward the tail. The fish's olive body is marked with seven or eight dark saddlelike patches down the back and numerous dark blotches on the sides.

Fin coloration and patterning varies between the sexes in the fountain darter. In the male the spiny dorsal fin on the back is lightly spotted at the edge and the spines are clear. Black and red bands on the spiny dorsal fin intensify during the spawning season. The female displays a spiny dorsal fin with alternating clear and darkened spines. The soft dorsal fin of the female is boldly banded; the male's is lightly banded. The tail fin in both sexes is mildly banded.

The fountain darter seeks dense beds of rooted vegetation and floating algae as its habitat. No bottom gravel or sand is present at the sites, only mud. This darter feeds on immature insects and microscopic crustaceans that live among the vegetation.

Additionally, given the lack of a suitable bottom-spawning medium, spawning among fountain darters must also take place on the vegetation. In the male, breeding nodules called tubercles develop on the fins surrounding the anus and genitals. Unless there is great success with the reintroduced population at Comal River Springs, the prospects for this fish are poor.

Freckled Darter

(Percina lenticula)

IUCN: Vulnerable

Length: 7½ in. (19 cm)
Reproduction: Egg layer
Habitat: Deep and fast rapids over rocks
Range: Georgia, Alabama, and Mississippi

THE RANGE OF the freckled darter includes northwestern Georgia, central Alabama, eastern and southern Mississippi, and extends into eastern Louisiana. The Etowah and Cahaba Rivers of Georgia and Alabama and the Pearl and Pascagoula Rivers of Mississippi and Louisiana are home to this gentle giant.

In stark contrast to the fountain darter, the freckled darter is the largest of all the darter species. It is also the most primitive. This distinctively patterned fish presents a vaguely giraffelike skin design as an adult. Brown blotches on the back and sides, sometimes outlined by a yellow-

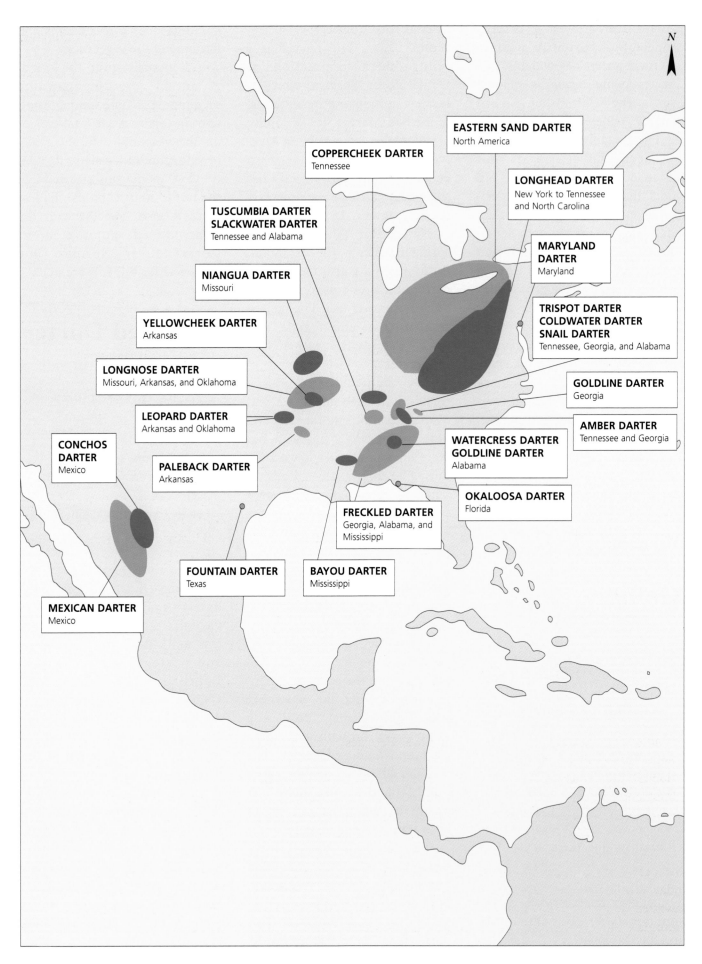

EASTERN SAND DARTER
North America

COPPERCHEEK DARTER
Tennessee

LONGHEAD DARTER
New York to Tennessee
and North Carolina

TUSCUMBIA DARTER
SLACKWATER DARTER
Tennessee and Alabama

MARYLAND
DARTER
Maryland

NIANGUA DARTER
Missouri

TRISPOT DARTER
COLDWATER DARTER
SNAIL DARTER
Tennessee, Georgia, and Alabama

YELLOWCHEEK DARTER
Arkansas

GOLDLINE DARTER
Georgia

LONGNOSE DARTER
Missouri, Arkansas, and Oklahoma

AMBER DARTER
Tennessee and Georgia

LEOPARD DARTER
Arkansas and Oklahoma

WATERCRESS DARTER
GOLDLINE DARTER
Alabama

CONCHOS
DARTER
Mexico

PALEBACK DARTER
Arkansas

OKALOOSA DARTER
Florida

FRECKLED DARTER
Georgia, Alabama, and
Mississippi

FOUNTAIN DARTER
Texas

BAYOU DARTER
Mississippi

MEXICAN DARTER
Mexico

tan background, produce this effect. In large females this background color can be completely obscured by the darker blotches. Side blotches tend to join up, forming a horizontal line on both sides in both sexes.

This pattern continues onto the base of the tail. The belly may have a stripe along its length as well. All fins show at least some brown banding, particularly in larger female specimens. The species name *lenticula* means "freckled" and refers to the spots at the base of the pectoral fins just behind the gills.

In addition to its unusual size, the freckled darter displays at least one other unique physical feature. The gas bladder, an internal organ that helps regulate buoyancy, is highly developed in this species. This adaptation suggests that the freckled darter prefers the water column (open water) to the bottom, which is favored by most darters.

Goldline Darter

(Percina aurolineata)

ESA: Threatened

IUCN: Vulnerable

Length: 2⅔ in. (7 cm)
Reproduction: Egg layer
Habitat: Deep rapids over boulders
Range: Georgia and Alabama

GOLDLINE DARTER populations today are confined to the Coosawattee River of northwestern Georgia and the Cahaba River in central Alabama. Only rarely

seen, goldline darters tend to congregate in vegetation over bedrock, boulder, and gravel rapids. Carters Reservoir inundated much of their suitable habitat in the Coosawattee River.

Unique pattern

This little darter has a distinctive pattern of coloration. On a tan background, two dark brown bands run from the head to the end of the soft dorsal fin on both sides of the back, hence the common name of goldline darter. Toward the belly a second set of dark brown bands of varying width extends from each eye to the base of the tail.

Unique characteristics of the goldline darter and its close relatives are three vertically aligned spots at the base of the tail; a lack of breeding nodules, or tubercles; and a row of scales along the center of the belly from the head to the base of the tail. Both dorsal fins on the back, the anal fin, and the tail fin of both sexes of the goldline darter have alternating dark brown and white bands.

During breeding, male goldline darters develop more orange and yellow on the upper body areas and the bands on the back become amber. The belly takes on a bluish green hue, and the chin, throat, and cheeks become all blue. Females develop some yellow on the lips and tail fin.

Water quality degradation has reduced the goldline darter's range within the Cahaba River system. Populations have also been extirpated by urbanization, sewage pollution, and strip-mining activities. In addition reservoir construction has fragmented and isolated some populations. The problem facing

this darter is all too common: it is trapped in a shrinking, degraded habitat with no escape. Recovery efforts are planned to focus on habitat protection and improving water quality.

Leopard Darter

(Percina pantherina)

ESA: Threatened

IUCN: Vulnerable

Length: 3¼ in. (8 cm)
Reproduction: Egg layer
Habitat: River rapids over gravel
Range: Arkansas and Oklahoma

FOUND ONLY IN the upper reaches of the Little River of southeastern Oklahoma and southwestern Arkansas, the leopard darter prefers gravel and rubble and shares space with other darters that are much more abundant. Construction of reservoirs on the Little River and other river systems has destroyed much of the leopard darter's habitat and restricted its movement to other suitable areas. Given this situation, prospects for recovery and expansion of this darter's range are not good.

The adult leopard darter is moderately sized. Its species name *pantherina* ("panther") is derived from the distinct dark blotches on its sides and back, resembling those of a leopard. The prominent blotches on the sides are connected by a lighter horizontal band that ends in a dark spot at the base of the tail. A

light-colored background behind the dark patterning continues around the fish to a pale belly. The lower jaw, throat, and breast are pale. The spiny and soft dorsal fins on the back tend to be darker at the base, but all fins are generally pale. The tail fin usually carries three distinct vertical bands. The gill covers are well scaled, but the neck is nearly naked with only a few scales near the spiny dorsal fin. A distinguishing characteristic is the large single scale on the breast.

Breeding leopard darter males do not develop colors as bright as those of their relatives. However, some yellow or orange can develop on the dorsal fins and the body can produce a greenish hue. Female coloration changes little if at all during breeding.

Longhead Darter

(Percina macrocephala)

IUCN: Lower risk

Length: 4¾ in. (12 cm)
Reproduction: Egg layer
Habitat: River pools and rapids
Range: Ohio River Basin

RANGING FROM WESTERN New York to southern Tennessee and western North Carolina, long-

The leopard darter gets its name from the distinctive dark blotches on its sides and back that resemble those of a leopard. Like other species of darters, this fish is threatened by the construction of reservoirs that have destroyed its habitat. Prospects for its recovery are bleak.

head darters can be found in the Ohio River and its tributaries, the Green River Basin, the Allegheny Basin, the Tennessee River Basin, and the Barren River.

The range of this darter is fairly wide, and some physical differences between populations do occur. Specimens from the Ohio River Basin are more robust in appearance and have the most well-defined side blotches. The

Green River inhabitants have the longest snouts, and the Tennessee River Basin populations have the smallest bodies, with a side stripe that obscures the side blotches.

While longhead darters can be captured fairly routinely in the upper Allegheny system, the species' total numbers and overall range appear to be decreasing. Reservoir construction is probably the biggest obstacle to the recovery of this darter.

Big head

At nearly 5 inches (13 centimeters) long, the longhead darter is one of the largest in its group. As its common name implies, the head and snout of this darter are unusually elongated. The species name *macrocephala* means "big head." The longhead darter and its close kin are easily distinguished by the large dark blotches on the sides, which are connected by a wide stripe nearly as dark in color. The middle of the back sometimes carries a much narrower dark stripe from the back of the head to just past the end of the soft dorsal fin.

However, the background is somewhat lighter and has a greenish cast. The belly and flanks are decidedly pale, creating a wide contrast in overall coloration. Unlike other male darters that become brightly colored during the breeding season, the longhead darter male usually darkens, almost obscuring its markings. Females follow suit but to a more limited degree.

The longhead darter is a river pool fish that seeks the fringes of rapids and faster water. It is not particularly choosy and can be found among either clean vegetation or over bedrock.

Longnose Darter
(Percina nasuta)

IUCN: Lower risk

Length: 3½ in. (9 cm)
Reproduction: Egg layer
Habitat: Rivers and lakes among vegetation
Range: Missouri, Arkansas, and Oklahoma

THE LONGNOSE DARTER inhabits southern Missouri, Arkansas, and eastern Oklahoma. It populates the St. Francis River, the White River, the Ouachita River Basin, and the Arkansas River in Oklahoma. The longnose darter is not as finicky as other darters with regard to habitat and has been found in both shallow rapids and deeper pools among aquatic vegetation. Some specimens also have been collected in lakes. This tolerance for different habitats could be the key to its continued survival in the wild.

Elongated snout

This darter has a similar appearance in shape to the longhead darter. The elongated head and snout (*nasuta* means "long nose") are like those of its cousin, but the coloration pattern is very different. A number of dark marks and blotches line the back and sides. Many of its spots are vertically elongated, and a faint horizontal stripe connects the 10 to 14 blotches on the sides.

The background color from back to belly is a vivid yellow brown. A narrow, dark bar extends from the tip of the snout to each eye. The cheek and jaw below the bar are very pale. The spiny dorsal fin on the back is lightly banded with black and orange red. This orange-red band is slightly more prominent in the male. The soft dorsal fin and tail also are mildly banded, with dark brown over pale yellow. The cheeks and gill covers have some scales, but the belly toward the throat is naked. Both sexes have a row of scales that cover the middle of the belly from behind the throat to the anus and the genitals. While not numerous within its home range, the longnose darter is more plentiful than originally feared, which offers additional hope that it will recover successfully.

Maryland Darter
(Etheostoma sellare)

ESA: Endangered

IUCN: Extinct

Length: 2¾ in. (7 cm)
Reproduction: Egg layer
Habitat: River riffles and shallow rapids
Range: Deer Creek, Maryland

THE MARYLAND DARTER holds the title as the rarest of all the darters and is listed by IUCN–The World Conservation Union as extinct. If this fish still exists it will be found in only one small rapids section of Deer Creek in Hartford County, Maryland, near the head of Chesapeake Bay. Salt water blocks the downstream movement of the last remaining fish, and the Conowingo Dam blocks expansion of the population

The Maryland darter is the rarest of all the darters. If it still exists it will be found in one section of Deer Creek in Maryland, near the head of Chesapeake Bay. Salt water blocks the movement of remaining fish downstream, and the Conowingo Dam blocks expansion to safer areas. For these reasons the fish is in extreme danger of extinction.

upstream to safer areas. Clearly if the Maryland darter is still alive its future is in extreme jeopardy.

The Maryland is a small darter. It displays four prominent saddlelike patches on its back, hence the species name *sellare*, which means "saddled." Some of the saddles may join with blotches on the sides and back, or the blotches may be separate from the saddles. The dark brown saddles and blotches contrast with the rusty or coppery background body color of both the male and female.

Maryland darters show a strong dark bar from the snout to each eye, as well as dark lines from the eyes to the throat. Most of the fins are darkened at the edges and are banded or spotted with dark brown color. The dor-

sal fins on the back are highly banded and colored. The cheeks and gill covers of the Maryland darter are heavily armored with scales. Most of the belly is scaled.

Color change

Breeding males can develop some slight additonal yellow coloration on the back and in the fins, but researchers disagree on this point. When breeding, the belly may also turn more white or golden. From the limited opportunities to study this animal, researchers have determined that this darter spawns in April and consumes snails and small insects. The maximum life span of this darter is about three years.

Government agencies have considered attempting artificial breeding and relocation of the Maryland darter. Normally this would be a radical and risky undertaking with such an endangered species. However, because of the current overwhelming odds against the fish's survival, extreme steps must be taken to bring it back from the brink of extinction. Unless drastic mea-

sures are taken to save the Maryland darter, any remaining population probably will be lost as a result of a pollution accident.

Mexican Darter (Dardo de Chihuahua)
(Etheostoma pottsi)

IUCN: Vulnerable

Length: 2 in. (5 cm)
Reproduction: Egg layer
Habitat: Shallow and cool rapids
Range: Chihuahua, Zacatecas, and Durango, Mexico

MEXICAN DARTERS OCCUR in limited areas of the Rio Conchos, Rio Nazas, Rio Aguanaval, and Rio Mezquital in the Mexican states of Chihuahua, Zacatecas, and Durango. Because of the Mexican darter's remote range, less is known about this darter than about others. However, researchers do know that recent volcanic activity and physical changes in the Rio Mezquital have made the Mexican darter the one and only darter species to gain access to a Pacific river drainage by natural means. Other darters may have established themselves in Pacific drainages but only as a result of artificial transplantation.

This fish's scientific name (*pottsi*) comes from the name of the man who collected the first preserved specimens, John Potts. It is also called the Chihuahua darter because part of its range extends into that Mexican state.

The Mexican darter has dark dorsal saddles on its back and several dark blotches on the sides like other darters. The side blotches are surrounded by a patchwork of smaller pigmented areas covering a lighter brownish background, creating a well-camouflaged look overall. The spiny dorsal fin on the back is banded near the outer edge and at the base, and the soft dorsal fin and tail fin are spotted to give a mildly banded appearance. Other fins are free of spots or banding but do become colored during the breeding season. The cheeks, breast, and gill covers carry no protective scales, but scales generally cover the rest of the fish.

Breeding male Mexican darters are extremely colorful, displaying bright red in the pelvic fins, the anal fin, and the belly. The rest of the body develops a reddish cast, and both dorsal fins on the back form red banding.

A prehistoric puzzle

Like the Conchos darter, a close relative with which it may share territory, the Mexican darter seeks out fast-flowing, shallow rapids in cool streams. The fish spawn in the spring and feed on insects. Biologists who study this darter have difficulty understanding how it originally expanded its range and moved from one river system to the next. However, they believe most movement occurred during prehistoric times when these rivers were linked by lakes. Today these lakes no longer exist. Encroachment by humans, in the form of continued urbanization and the spread of pesticides and other pollution threatens the survival of the Mexican darter.

Niangua Darter

(Etheostoma nianguae)

ESA: Threatened

IUCN: Vulnerable

Length: 3½ in. (9 cm)
Reproduction: Egg layer
Habitat: Shallow river pools over gravel
Range: Missouri

NIANGUA DARTERS ARE found only in southern tributaries of the Osage River in Missouri, including the Niangua and Little Niangua River basins. Both the common and species names are derived from these last two locations. Niangua darters are more commonly found in Big Tavern Creek and Maries River, also part of the Osage River system.

Colorful darter

Without a doubt the Niangua darter is the showiest of the endangered darters. This flamboyant fish is brightly colored during breeding and is distinctively shaped. It has a sleek body, a pointed snout, and an unusually large mouth for its size.

Like many other species of darter, the Niangua darter exhibits dark saddlelike patches on its back. These seven or eight patches join broad vertical bars down the sides of the fish. The base of the tail carries a vertical bar of equal width. The saddles and vertical bars below the soft dorsal fin extend their dark coloration up into the fin, resulting in attractive vertical bars from within the soft dorsal fin to the base of the anal fin.

Breeding colors

The Niangua darter's pectoral, pelvic, and anal fins are clear and usually display little or no color. Besides the chin and throat, the background color of both sexes is a brownish yellow with some areas of green.

During the breeding season the coloration of the male Niangua darter brightens dramatically to orange yellow, and red vertical stripes or spots separate most of the dark vertical bars on the body. The spiny dorsal fin on the back also develops a red band along its entire edge, and the soft dorsal fin may include a few red spots between the black vertical bars. The tail may develop red vertical bands or spots near its middle and tip. The male produces a row of nodulelike tubercles down the center of the belly from the throat to the tail as well. Female coloration during breeding is similar but less spectacular than the male's.

This insect-eating darter seeks the protection of vegetation near rapids or pools in smaller streams. While little is known about the courtship behavior of most darters, the courtship and spawning sequence of the Niangua darter has been observed. After a courtship in April that includes a head-bobbing display by the male, the female burrows into the bottom with only her head and tail exposed and releases some eggs. The male hovers over her and releases sperm. The female repeats her egg-laying procedure with other eager males.

The Niangua darter has never been observed in great numbers. The species is threatened because of its limited range, but

some researchers believe its situation is worse than ever and argue that it should be listed as endangered.

Okaloosa Darter
(Etheostoma okaloosae)

ESA: Endangered

IUCN: Endangered

Length: 2½ in. (6 cm)
Reproduction: Egg layer
Habitat: Small streams among vegetation
Range: Florida

THE OKALOOSA DARTER is not inclined to linger in fast-moving water and selects small to medium-sized streams among vegetation instead. This darter is restricted to six tributary systems of the lower Choctawhatchee Bay in Florida's Okaloosa and Walton Counties. The tributary systems drain two bayous, Boggy Bayou (Toms, Turkey, and Mill Creeks) and Rocky Bayou (Swift, Turkey, and Rocky Creeks). The darter's exact current population level is unknown, but estimates range from 1,500 to 10,000 fish.

Blotchy appearance
The small Okaloosa darter is recognized by a generally dark appearance created by the many overlapping dark blotches on the back and sides. In some individuals the blotches are connected by smaller and slightly lighter spots. The background is a lighter yellow-green color. Both dorsal fins on the back, the tail fin, and the anal fin are highly banded and

The Niangua darter is brightly colored during breeding and is distinctively shaped. It has a sleek body, a pointed snout, and an unusually large mouth for its size.

spotted with dark color, similar to the body blotches. The pectoral and pelvic fins just behind the gills and throat are much lighter and clear. The cheeks, gill covers, chin, throat, and breast also can be spotted. Like the pectoral and pelvic fins, the belly is light and clear of bands or dark spots, although some specimens carry light spots on the belly. The Okaloosa darter is highly scaled and grows to approximately 2½ inches (6 centimeters) in length. The breast and throat may have naked patches devoid of scales.

Lacking the bright colors and tubercles (breeding nodules) of other darters, the male Okaloosa darter is no showstopper. The female prefers to be inconspicuous as well. This darter spawns in sand or on vegetation and seeks areas near the shoreline for both breeding and everyday activity. Rather than spawning during a set period of time each spring like many other darters, the Okaloosa darter breeds when weather conditions and water temperatures are favorable.

Limited range

Because the Okaloosa darter only lives in small to medium-sized streams, it is found only in Turkey Creek, Rocky Creek, and in a few very small streams in Florida's Okaloosa and Walton counties. The range of the Okaloosa darter is very small and its numbers are depleted to the extent that it is considered endangered by both IUCN–The World Conservation Union and the ESA.

The Okaloosa darter has an overall dark appearance created by overlapping dark blotches on the back and sides. Some individuals display blotches connected by smaller and slightly lighter spots.

Population levels of the Okaloosa darter have declined since the introduction of the brown darter in the lower Rocky Bayou system. Another reason for this decline is most likely habitat degradation on Eglin Air Force Base, where some of the darter's range is found.

Paleback Darter
(Etheostoma palididorsum)

IUCN: Vulnerable

Length: 2 in. (5 cm)
Reproduction: Egg layer
Habitat: Quiet river pools
Range: Arkansas

THE PALEBACK DARTER can be found only in the Caddo and Ouachita Rivers of southwestern Arkansas. Because of its small range, the paleback darter is considered at risk of extinction. The construction of reservoirs that have flooded this darter's habitat and restricted its movement is

the primary reason for the fish's current status.

This small darter has fewer body markings than many of its relatives. It does display some saddlelike blotches on the back, which is decidedly pale down the middle and is the inspiration for both the common and scientific names (*palididorsum* means "pale back"). The red or orange belly of the male is quite different from the light brown and brown green of the female's, but both have a scaled belly from well behind the throat to the anus and genitals. The pale chin and cheeks are separated by a prominent dark, vertical bar, and the throat just behind the gills is dark as well. The spiny dorsal fin on the back of the male is dark at the edge and base and is horizontally banded with red at its center. The female's spiny dorsal fin is clear at the edge and base and banded with dark brown. The soft dorsal fin on the back and the tail fin in both sexes are spotted with brown and may give the appearance of banding. The pectoral and pelvic fins just behind the gills and throat are usually pale and clear. The cheeks, gill covers, and breast carry no scales.

Belly tubercles

In addition to its spectacular red and orange breeding coloration, the male paleback darter develops nodulelike tubercles on its belly. The females become somewhat brighter during breeding, but their color is weak compared to their suitors. The paleback darter spawns in February and March in shallow stream water. The slightly larger females generally outnumber males on the spawning grounds. Like other

The paleback darter can be found only in the Caddo and Ouachita Rivers of Arkansas. Reservoir construction is the primary reason for its decline.

darters, females spawn with more than one male. This species is found in shallow pools over rocks and mud and among vegetation. Little is known about the daily habits of the paleback darter, but the species tends to be found in the same place as the Arkansas darter, a species that is not threatened with extinction.

Slackwater Darter

(Etheostoma boschungi)

ESA: Threatened

IUCN: Endangered

Length: 2½ in. (6 cm)
Reproduction: Egg layer
Habitat: Slow streams
Range: Tennessee and Alabama

THE SCIENTIFIC NAME for the slackwater darter, *boschungi*, was given in honor of the fisheries scientist Herbert T. Boschung. As its common name implies, this species prefers slow-flowing streams and makes its home in the Buffalo River and Tennessee River Basin of southern Tennessee and northern Alabama. This darter has a saddlelike pattern of coloration on the back, and an expressive face with a strong vertical bar under the eye. The red cheeks are bare of scales as are the spotted breast and part of the neck. Dark side blotches run together and into the saddles to form a patchwork midway down the sides. Most of the underside is not patterned except for some spots.

Spiny fin
Adults out of breeding season are less colorful but display a brown background on the back and sides and reddish tones on the sides and belly. All fins are spotted or blotched. The spiny dorsal fin on the back is lightly banded and the tail fin may appear banded in some fish.

During the breeding season the male slackwater darter transforms to a bright coloration. When ready to attract females, the brown background becomes enlivened with stronger tones. In addition to the red and orange underside, the mouth and spiny dorsal fin on the back become strongly shaded with red.

The breeding ritual of this darter is very unusual. This spring spawner leaves its home in streams and creeks to find extremely small seepages, where groundwater comes to the surface, or even flooded fields in which to reproduce. Fertilized eggs hatch in these incubation areas (usually no more than puddles), which are lined with decaying vegetation and silt. The fry return to the stream. Many of these areas are dry during most of the year, and the survival of incubating eggs is precarious during unusually dry spring weather.

Degradation of habitat
Given the specialized breeding habits of the slackwater darter, it is not surprising that its numbers are decreasing. Urbanization, ditching to drain areas of shallow groundwater, and degradation of ground and surface water as a result of pesticides and waste are all serious threats. For example, the population in the Flint River drainage in Madison County, Alabama, is threatened by changing land-use patterns associated with the growth of the city of Huntsville, Alabama.

The slackwater darter is so named because of its preference for slow-running streams.

Snail Darter

(Percina tanasi)

ESA: Threatened

IUCN: Vulnerable

Length: 3½ in. (8 cm)
Reproduction: Egg layer
Habitat: Rivers over gravel
Range: Tennessee, Georgia, Alabama

The tiny snail darter (not much larger than a paper clip) became a symbol of the environmental movement in the late 1970s when it was used as an example of the damage that can be done to wildlife by dam construction.

NO OTHER DARTER is as famous as the snail darter. This fish became a symbol of the environmental movement in the late 1970s and literally made daily headlines in newspapers and on television. During that period the effect on the snail darter of the Tellico Dam in Tennessee was used as an example in the attempt to prevent the construction of the dam. However, the attempt failed. Nonetheless the debate over the wisdom of saving rare and endangered animals and plants intensified.

One positive consequence of this debate was that the federal officials with the Tennessee Valley Authority were forced to move about 200 snail darters to the Hiwassee River as a means of saving some individuals from an almost certain death.

Cherokee connection

The snail darter's scientific name, *tanasi*, comes from the name of a Cherokee Native American town on the Little Tennessee River. The state of Tennessee was also named for this riverside town.

The snail darter is an unassuming fish marked with four dark saddlelike blotches on the back. The saddles join with a line of dark, connected blotches on the sides, creating the appearance of four wide, diagonal bars. This species has a uniform yellowgreen background color, with the exception of the throat and belly, which are pale. The head and gill covers are dark, but the cheeks are lighter.

Big fins

All the snail darter's fins are large. The spiny and soft dorsal fins on the back and the tail fin all display significant spots. The remaining fins are clear or very lightly spotted. Snail darters differ from other darters in that the female tends to be more pigmented than the male. In most individuals the breast and belly lack scales, but the cheeks and gill covers are scaled.

Snail darters live over sand and gravel rapids and prefer deeper water than do most darters. As the fish's name implies, it feeds primarily on snails, but it also consumes insects. The snail darter grows to approximately 3¼ inches (8 centimeters) in about two years. Breeding occurs in February and March over a two-week period.

Trouble with dams

Today the snail darter has probably been lost from the Little Tennessee River, the site of the Tellico Dam. However, healthy populations still reside in the Chickamauga Creek, the Sequatchie River, the Sewee River, and the Hiwassee River. Despite efforts to save the snail darter, dams in the upper Tennessee River basin continue to threaten this fish and its future.

Trispot Darter

(Etheostoma trisella)

IUCN: Vulnerable

Length: 2 in. (5 cm)
Reproduction: Egg layer
Habitat: River pools near vegetation
Range: Tennessee, Georgia, and Alabama

THE TRISPOT DARTER can be found in the Coosa River Basin in Tennessee, Georgia, and Alabama. Sightings of this darter used to be so rare that the capture of a specimen used to merit a report in scientific literature. Information on the trispot darter's biology is only sketchy, but the species' preferred habitat seems to be vegetated pools.

Three dark patches

The top of the trispot darter's head and its back are mottled and blotchy over a background of light yellow brown. In common with many other darters, the trispot darter possesses saddlelike patches on its back. In this species there are three of these patches and this is the inspiration for the common name "trispot" and the scientific name *trisella*. The chin, throat, breast, and belly are lighter in color.

A dark bar from the fish's snout to the eye and from the eye to the end of the gill-cover marks a distinct boundary between the top and bottom of the head. The distinction is less pronounced in the body, as it is marked by a line of uneven blotches from the gills to the tail.

Dark fins

All the trispot darter's fins, except for the pectoral and pelvic fins just behind the gills and throat, are fairly dark and show some spots or banding. The pectoral and pelvic fins are pale. The fish's cheeks, neck, and gill covers are scaled, but the breast is naked. Like many other species of darter, the male takes on brighter coloration during the breeding season. The dark, pale colors on the head remain, but the body turns shades of red and orange. The lips become yellow and the side blotches may become dark green.

Backwater lounger

The trispot darter does not favor rapidly moving water. Instead it is content to lounge in vegetated backwaters of rivers. If a backwater is not available, this darter will hug the stream bank in slower water to minimize its need for swimming. It grows to a full length of approximately 2 inches (5 centimeters).

The trispot darter is the victim of dam construction and stream alteration, and the future of the few remaining populations is in serious doubt.

Tuscumbia Darter

(Etheostoma tuscumbia)

IUCN: Vulnerable

Length: 2 in. (5 cm)
Reproduction: Egg layer
Habitat: Springs among vegetation
Range: Alabama

THIS SPRING-DWELLING darter is found only in the great southern bend areas of the Tennessee River in northern Alabama. The Tuscumbia darter also used to inhabit the Tennessee River within the state of Tennessee but was lost after the construction of the Pickwick Reservoir. This darter was particularly abundant at the great spring at Tuscumbia, Alabama, but the spring has since been dammed and developed as a water supply for the city. Surveys to find survivors in the spring failed to locate fish of any species at all. Pesticide poisoning may explain the complete lack of fish. The lack of fish should warn consumers of unhealthy water.

The little Tuscumbia darter is heavily scaled from head to tail. The nose is blunt and the mouth is small. The back has five to seven dark saddlelike blotches over a background that is medium green. The entire underside is pale to yellow and spotted most heavily on the cheeks and tail. A dark vertical bar at the base of the tail is present in many but not all individuals. The eyes appear to rest at the center of a cross because of the vertical and horizontal bars that seem to pass through them. The spiny and soft dorsal fins on the back and the tail fin are dark and mottled or mildly banded. The pectoral and pelvic fins and the anal fin are much lighter and only mildly spotted. Breeding adults do not change color but do become brighter in the month of June. Little else is known about the reproductive habits of this darter.

A choosy fish

The Tuscumbia darter is quite choosy when it comes to acceptable areas in which to live. It prefers strong water flow through heavy vegetation in a spring or stream. These sites usually contain amphipods, snails, and insect larvae. Unfortunately many of these acceptable sites have been lost as a result of human development. Since other springs in the darter's range have been dammed or walled off for use as water supplies, recovery of this fish to its previous abundance is highly unlikely.

Watercress Darter

(Etheostoma nuchale)

ESA: Endangered

IUCN: Endangered

Length: 2 in. (5 cm)
Reproduction: Egg layer
Habitat: Among river watercress over mud and silt
Range: Bessemer, Alabama

FOUND ONLY IN a few springs near the town of Bessemer in northern Alabama, the watercress darter is in grave danger of extinction. Attempts have been made to save this fish by transplanting individuals to other springs, but those attempts have ended in failure.

Count the saddles

The watercress darter is similar to many other darters in having saddlelike dark patches on the back. Individuals may show as many as nine or as few as three saddles. The sides are blotchy, forming spots toward the front and vague vertical bars near the rear. The background color is a fairly uniform light brown green.

The watercress darter's pale head has strong vertical and horizontal bars through the eyes, with another vertical bar just behind the gills. A column of three vertical spots often is present at the base of the tail. The spiny and soft dorsal fins and the tail fin are strongly banded in the male and to a lesser extent in the female. All other fins basically are clear. The watercress darter is only moderately scaled; the breast is naked and the cheeks only are lightly scaled.

The breeding male exhibits spectacular color on the fins and belly. The dorsal fins on the back are banded in red and blue, the anal fin is blue, and the belly is orange red. The sides often show orange spotting.

A hump-backed fish

The scientific species name *nuchale* means "nape" or "neck" and refers to the small hump on the neck of male watercress darters. The common name *watercress* refers to this darter's preference for swimming amid the leaves and stems of the aquatic plant watercress. Mud and silt hold the watercress and other plants that this darter uses as cover. The watercress darter eats snails, insects, and other small aquatic animals and probably breeds sometime between March and July.

Deforestation and loss of other vegetation in the area is suspected of reducing the groundwater table that supplies springs. As the growth of Bessemer continues and the flow rate of the springs decreases, loss of the watercress darter populations at these sites is inevitable.

Yellowcheek Darter

(Etheostoma moorei)

IUCN: Vulnerable

Length: 2¾ in. (7 cm)
Reproduction: Egg layer
Habitat: Fast rapids over gravel
Range: Arkansas

THE YELLOWCHEEK darter's home range currently is confined to the south and middle forks of the Little Red River in northern Arkansas. Significant habitat was flooded by the creation of the Greer's Ferry Reservoir, and resort development threatens the yellowcheek darter's remaining stream habitat.

The yellowcheek was given its species name in honor of fisheries scientist George A. Moore. It is a short but stocky darter with a darkly colored body of blue and gray. The nine saddlelike blotches on the back are barely visible, as are the side blotches and vertical bar near the tail. The face and cheeks carry both vertical and horizontal bars. Contrary to its name, the yellowcheek's background cheek color is dark blue. The chin, throat, and breast are pale in females but dark in males.

The spiny and soft dorsal fins, the tail fin, and the anal fin in nonbreeding yellowcheek darter adults are all generally dark at the base and darkly banded or spotted. The pectoral and pelvic fins just behind the gills and throat are mostly clear, with some darkening at the base and edges. The cheeks, neck, and breast are scaleless, but the gill covers are fully armored with scales.

Rainbow fins

Breeding males produce vivid colors in the fins. The bases of the fins become dark green and extend out into tones of red and orange edged with white. In the female only the dorsal fins on the back show red-orange coloration. Unlike other darters' breeding colors, those of the yellowcheek darter tend to persist for the majority of the year, even after spawning has ended.

The yellowcheek darter likes clean gravel and boulder areas of deep, fast-flowing streams. It tolerates some vegetation in its preferred sites, but clean, silt-free water is a requirement. The species' numbers are so small that little is known about this darter. Some scientists suggest that adults should be captured and bred in aquariums to increase numbers for stocking in other sections of the Little Red River. Whether or not this would work is unclear, but without assistance the future of the yellowcheek darter is not bright.

William E. Manci

DEER

Class: Mammalia

Order: Artiodactyla

Family: Cervidae

Deer as a family are slender animals with long legs, and every genus except for two have antlers (the prominent horns on top of the skull). Antlers are found only on the male (except for the genus *Rangifer*) and are sometimes the only obvious trait that distinguishes one genus from another. Antlers play an important part in the deer's rutting or mating ritual because male deer use their antlers to establish dominance. Males literally lock horns with other males to protect their harems.

Deer live in many different habitats, from the tundra of the extreme Northern Hemisphere to deserts, grasslands, and swamps. Deer are noted for their running ability, but they can also swim well. Some species migrate; others prefer one habitat. On the whole deer are brownish, with some species bearing spots.

Argentine Pampas Deer

(Ozotoceros bezoarticus celer)

ESA: Endangered

IUCN: Endangered

Weight: 66–100 lb. (30–45 kg)
Shoulder height: 24–28 in. (61–71 cm)
Diet: Grasses, leaves, and twigs
Gestation period: 6–7 months
Longevity: 12–14 years
Habitat: Wooded and scrub grasslands, grasslands
Range: Argentina

THE PAMPAS DEER of South America is found in the pampas, or grassland area, that is drained by the Rio Plata and many of its tributaries. There are three different subspecies: the Brazilian pampas deer (*Ozotoceros bezoarticus bezoarticus*), which ranges in the north; the Chaco pampas deer (*O. bezoarticus leucogaster*) of the Chaco region of Paraguay, Brazil, and northwest Argentina; and the Argentine pampas deer (*O. bezoarticus celer*) of central Argentina near the Atlantic coast. The pampas deer has also been called the stinking deer because of the strong onionlike odor the males emit from glands located between their hooves.

Summer congregations

The Argentine pampas deer is a member of the subfamily Odocoilinae, or New World roe deer. The deer spends most of its time in wooded grasslands but often ranges into regular grasslands, or pampas, from which it derives it name. During winter

PAMPAS DEER
Argentina

Former Range

Present Range

the deer tend to live singly or in very small groups. In the summer they come together in congregations of 12 to 18 or so. The adult bucks live away from the does except during the rutting season.

The dangers

Humans and wild dogs are the Argentine pampas deer's biggest enemies. However, people by far are the most dangerous because of heavy poaching and the destruction of the deer's habitat. Once Argentine pampas deer were hunted commercially for their hides, and there must have been a very big population because nearly two million hides were exported toward the end of the 19th century and early in the 20th century.

Today, however, the Argentine pampas deer is banned from international commercial trade

under the Convention on International Trade in Endangered Species of Wild Fauna and Flora (CITES) and the subspecies is fully protected. Nonetheless, only two populations remain, with a total estimated population of 550 to 600 animals.

Captive population

An estimated 40 Argentine pampas deer are held in captivity in zoos in Argentina, and more than 70 live in other zoos around the world. This captive population is not large enough to act as a hedge against disaster in the wild. As a result, the Argentine pampas deer is seriously endangered. Of the other pampas deer subspecies, the Brazilian pampas deer is threatened because its population is so small. The Chaco pampas deer is probably in the best shape for survival.

Bactrian Deer
(Cervus elaphus bactrianus)

ESA: Endangered
IUCN: Vulnerable

Weight: 440–770 lb. (200–350 kg)
Shoulder height: 43–51 in. (109–130 cm)
Diet: Grass, leaves, and twigs
Gestation period: 230–240 days
Longevity: 18–20 years
Habitat: Riverine woodlands in arid regions
Range: Afghanistan, Kazakhstan, Tajikistan, Turkmenistan, Uzbekistan

THE BACTRIAN DEER belongs to a subfamily of deer called the Cervinae, or red deer. This large

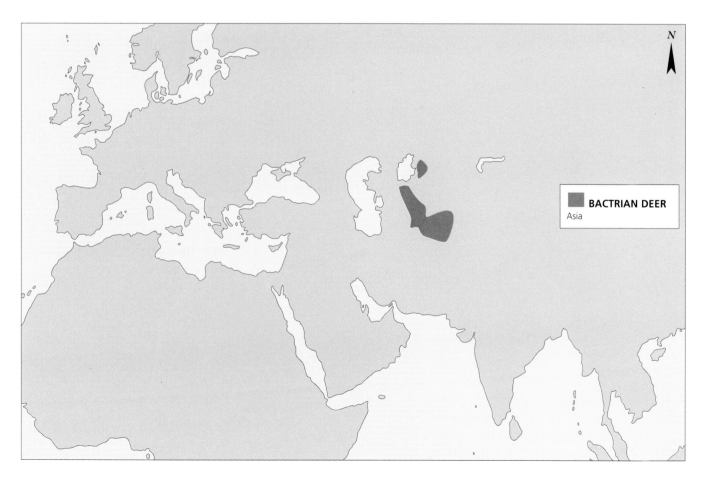

N

BACTRIAN DEER
Asia

group of deer is found extensively throughout Europe and Asia. Red deer go by a variety of different names, depending on the subspecies and the locale.

The Bactrian deer comes from a portion of northern Afghanistan and the adjacent border provinces of the former Soviet Union. The Bactrian deer is the only red deer that lives in the desert. It is found along river banks, in open grasslands, and in fringe areas. However, over a period of time encroachment and competition from the livestock of nomadic peoples, as well as severe poaching, have reduced its numbers.

Today most Bactrian deer are found in protected areas of the former Soviet Union, where populations have declined as a result of development of the Amu Darya River valley. The status of this subspecies in Afghanistan is unknown. However, hunting, settlement, stock grazing, and reed burning have reduced available habitat in both Afghanistan and other neighbouring countries. Estimates of Bactrian deer numbers suggest that fewer than 1,000 individuals exist. International trade in Bactrian deer is regulated under the Convention on International Trade in Endangered Species of Wild Fauna and Flora (CITES).

The Bactrian deer shares many traits with other red deer. It is found on grasslands and in low forests, grazing on whatever vegetation is available. Bactrian deer are most active at twilight and dusk. However, if undisturbed, they will also feed during the day. In the rutting season the females and males come together, and some prodigious battles take place between adult males intending to mate with females. The rut normally takes place in the fall between late August and early September, extending through October and early November. The fawns are born in the late spring.

Besides human beings, the Bactrian deer's natural predators are wolves, lynx, and tigers, but tigers have now vanished from the deer's range. There are reports that bears may sometimes prey on deer but this is probably uncommon.

The Barbary deer and the Bactrian deer (pictured here) are both members of the red deer subfamily Cervinae.

Bactrian deer are fairly social and are found in groups of 15 to 20. There are still small breeding groups in captivity in Russia and Europe. In recent years a small population has been nurtured in North America. However, the captive numbers of Bactrian deer are too small to restore the wild population. Therefore, the future of this deer is certainly in doubt.

Barbary Deer
(Cervus elaphus barbarus)

ESA: Endangered

IUCN: Lower risk

Weight: 330–485 lb. (150–220 kg)
Shoulder height: 43–45 in. (109–114 cm)
Diet: Grass, leaves, and twigs
Gestation period: 230–240 days
Longevity: 18–20 years
Habitat: Oak and pine forests
Range: Border between Tunisia and Algeria

THE BARBARY DEER is a member of the Cervinae, or red deer, subfamily. It is the only true deer that is found on the continent of Africa. Now extinct in Morocco, Barbary deer are still found in an area that straddles the border of Tunisia and Algeria. Here, however, their numbers have declined due to hunting, particularly during the Algerian War, and as a result of habitat degradation caused by fires.

The Barbary deer's habits are much the same as those of other red deer, although Barbary deer are among the smallest of the red

deer. The sexes live separately and only come together during the rutting season in the fall. The fawns are born in the spring.

Male Barbary deer grow a new set of antlers each year, beginning in the early spring. While the males are away from the females, their antlers continue to grow all summer. This growth is one of the most rapid in the animal kingdom—by fall, the males have developed a large, magnificent set of antlers. The skin that covers the antlers is called the velvet, and it supplies the blood that is essential to the antlers' growth.

Annual antlers
In fall the blood supply stops and the velvet drops off, leaving the hard antlers still attached to the

deer's skull. The antlers have no nerves or blood vessels. After the rutting season, which occurs around January, the old antlers drop off and new ones begin to grow. In the first year of a male Barbary deer's life, his antlers will consist of just a single spike. As he continues to age, the male will acquire more spikes.

Experts have tried to estimate the age of deer in this way, but it is not consistently accurate for every species.

Increasing numbers
In Algeria the Barbary deer is restricted to the Beni-Salah, ben Abed and El-Kala forests, with a population of about 2,000 animals. In Tunisia the population has increased to about 2,000, largely as a result of reintroduc-

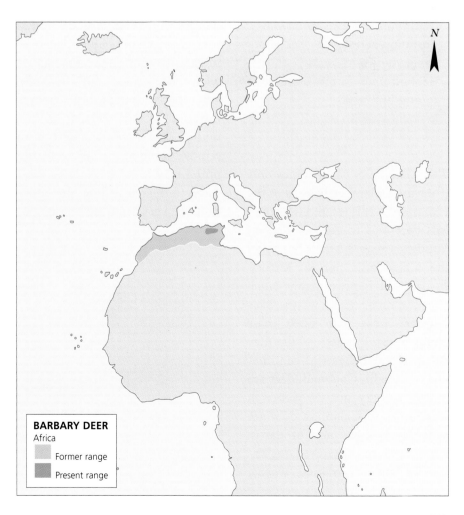

N

BARBARY DEER
Africa

Former range

Present range

tions of the deer in the El Feidja region. However, the Barbary deer, even though its numbers have increased, does not have a secure captive population as an insurance against disaster.

Also, the protected animals are concentrated in a small area, where disasters such as disease and forest fires could easily threaten their survival.

Calamian Deer
(Axis calamianensis)

ESA: Endangered

IUCN: Endangered

Weight: 88–110 lb. (40–50 kg)
Shoulder height: 30–36 in. (76–90 cm)
Diet: Grasses, leaves, and twigs
Gestation period: 210–225 days
Longevity: 10–12 years
Habitat: Open forests, swampy forests, and scrub
Range: Calamian Islands

THE CALAMIAN DEER comes only from the Calamian Islands of the Philippines. It is related to India's axis deer and to the hog deer of Southeast Asia. Little is known of the Calamian's natural history. In habits it is presumably much like the hog deer, which likes swampy areas with open grass plains and tall grass. Adults may be up to 36 inches (90 centimeters) in height. Calamian deer are mostly solitary but do gather in small groups. Calamian deer are active at twilight and at dawn. They feed on whatever vegetation is handy—grasses, weeds, shoots, and twigs.

Excellent swimmers
Because they prefer to live by water, it is not surprising that Calamian deer are excellent swimmers. They often rely on their ability to swim to escape danger, and their primary predators are humans. Calamian deer must also compete for habitat with hundreds of African antelopes, giraffes, and zebras introduced to the area in the mid-1970s, although efforts to remove some of the antelopes are under way.

As a result of the introductions, a very limited number of

The Calamian deer is found only on a single island group in the Philippine archipelago. Because its range is limited to these islands, the Calamian is extremely vulnerable to poaching and human encroachment on its habitat.

Calamian deer remain, with the largest population of about 550 animals found on Calauit Island. Because their range is limited to the Calamian Islands, the deer are extremely vulnerable to poaching and the cultivation of habitat. The largest captive population is found at San Diego Zoo, which held 20 animals in 1997.

Warren D. Thomas

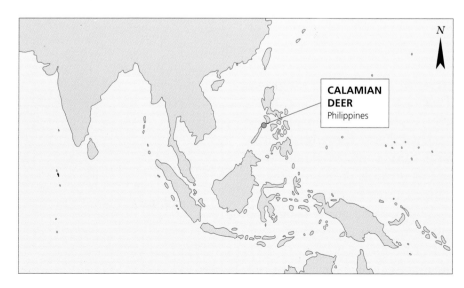

CALAMIAN DEER
Philippines

GLOSSARY

actinopterygii: the scientific name for bony fish

albino: any organism lacking color in the skin or fur; albino species have pink eyes, while albino fish often have no functioning eyes

amphibia: the Latin scientific name for amphibians

apically: relating to, or situated at the apex

arboreal: living in or adapted for living in trees; arboreal animals seldom, if ever, descend to the ground (see terrestrial)

arthropoda: the Latin scientific name for crustaceans and spiders

aves: the Latin scientific name for birds

barbels: a slender growth on the mouths or nostrils of certain fishes, used as a sensory organ for touch

bipedal: any organism that walks on two feet

bract: a leaf at the base of a flower stalk in plants

buff: in bird species, a yellow-white color used to describe the plumage

calyx: the green outer whorl of a flower made up of sepals

captive breeding: any method of bringing several animals of the same species into a zoo or other closed environment for the purpose of mating; if successful, these methods can increase the population of

that species

carnivore: any flesh-eating animal

carnivorous: flesh eating

carrion: the decaying flesh of a dead organism

class: a biological ranking of animals who share a common set of traits, below the rank of phylum and above the rank of order

classification: how a species is ranked biologically in relation to other species (see taxonomy)

clear cutting: a method of harvesting lumber that eliminates all the trees in a specific area rather than just selected trees

clutch, clutch size: the number of eggs laid during one nesting cycle

contiguous: touching, meeting, joining at a surface or border; the home of an animal is contiguous if it is uninterrupted by natural or artificial boundaries

corolla: the separate petals, or the fused petals of a flower

cotyledon: the first leaf developed by the embryo of a seed plant

deciduous: dropping off, falling off during a certain season or at a regular stage of growth; deciduous trees shed their leaves annually

decurved: curving downward; a bird's beak is

decurved if it points toward the ground

defoliate: to strip trees and bushes of their leaves

deforestation: the process of removing trees from a particular area

dioecious: male and female sex organs borne on separate plants

diurnal: active during the day; some animals are diurnal, while others are active at night (see nocturnal)

dominance: the ability to overpower the behavior of other individuals; an animal is dominant if it affects others of its own species in a way that benefits itself; also, the trait of abundance that determines the character of a plant community: grasses dominate a prairie, and trees dominate a forest

dorsal: pertaining to or situated on the back of an organism; a dorsal fin is on the back of a fish

ecology: the study of the interrelationship between a living organism and its environment

ecosystem: a community of animals, plants, and bacteria and its interrelated physical and chemical environment

endemic: native to a particular geographic region

erose: slightly uneven

estrous: the time period when female mammals can become pregnant

exotic species: a plant or animal species that is not native to its habitat

feral: a wild animal that is descended from tame or domesticated species

fishery, fisheries: any system, body of water, or portion of a body of water that supports finfish or shellfish; can also be used as an adjective describing a person or thing (for example, a fisheries biologist)

flabellate: shaped like a fan

forest: a plant community in which trees grow closely enough together that their crowns interlock to form a continuous overhead canopy

fry: young fish

gestation: the period of active embryonic growth inside a mammal's body between the time the embryo attaches to the uterus and the time of birth; some mammals carry dormant embryos for several weeks or months before the embryo attaches to the uterus and begins to develop actively, and this dormancy period is not part of the gestation period; gestation period is the time length of a pregnancy

granivore: any seed-feeding animal

granivorous: seed feeding

guano: manure, especially of sea birds and bats

habitat: the environment

where a species is normally found; habitat degradation is the decline in quality of a species' home until it can no longer survive there

halophyte: salt lover

herbivore: any plant-eating animal

herbivorous: plant eating

hibernate: to spend the winter season in a dormant or inactive state; some species hibernate to save energy during months when food is scarce

home range: the area normally traveled by an individual species during its lifespan

hybrid: the offspring of two different species who mate; see interbreed

hybridization: the gradual decline of a species through continued breeding with another species; see interbreed

immature(s): a young bird that has not yet reached breeding maturity; it usually has plumage differing from an adult bird of the same species

in captivity: a species that exists in zoos, captive breeding programs, or in private collections, perhaps because the species can no longer be found in the wild

incubation: the period when an egg is kept warm until the embryo develops and hatches

indigenous species: any

species native to its habitat

inflorescence: a group of flowers that grow from one point

insecta: the Latin scientific name for insects

interbreed: when two separate species mate and produce offspring; see hybrid

invertebrate(s): any organism without a backbone (spinal column)

juvenal: a bird with an intermediate set of feathers after its youngdowny plumage molts and before growing hard, adult feathers

juvenile(s): a young bird or other animal not yet mature

lore(s): the irregularly shaped facial area of a bird between the eye and the base of the beak

migrate, migratory: to move from one range to another, particularly with the change of seasons; many species are migratory

milt: the reproductive glands of male fishes; also, the breeding behavior of male fishes

mollusca: the Latin scientific name for mussels, clams, and snails

monotypic: the only member of its genus

montane forest: a forest found in mountainous regions

nocturnal: active at night; some animals are nocturnal, while others are active by day (see diurnal)

omnivore: any species that eats both plants and animals

ornithologist(s): a scientist who studies birds

pelage: the hairy covering of a mammal

perennial: persisting for several years

plumage: the feathers that cover a bird

prairie: a plant community without trees and dominated by grasses; a grassland; often incorrectly used synonymously with plain or plains, which is a landform feature and not a plant community

predation: the act of one species hunting another

predator: a species that preys upon other species

primary forest: a forest of native trees that results from natural processes, often called virgin forest

primate(s): a biological ranking of species in the same order, including gorillas, chimpanzees, monkeys, and human beings (*Homo sapiens*)

range: the geographic area where a species roams

recovery plan(s): any document that outlines a public or private program for assisting an endangered

or threatened species

relict: an isolated habitat or population that was once widespread

reptilia: the Latin scientific name for reptiles

riffle(s): a shallow rapid stretch of water caused by a rocky outcropping or obstruction in a stream

riparian: relating to plants and animals close to and influenced by rivers

roe: fish eggs

rufous: in bird species, plumage that is orange-brown and pink

secondary forest: a forest that has grown back after cutting, forest fire, or other deforestation; secondary forests may or may not contain exotic tree species, but they almost always differ in character from primary forests

sedentary species: one that does not migrate

serpentine: mineral rock consisting of hydrous magnesium silicate. It is usually a dull green color, and looks mottled

siltation: the process of sediment clouding and obstructing a body of water

terrestrial: living in or adapted for living principally on the ground; some birds are terrestrial and seldom, if ever, ascend into trees (see arboreal)

territory: the area occupied by an organism or group, defended by aggressive displays and physical combat

tubercle: a prominent bump on a fish's body connected to a spine

tussock: a thick bunch of twigs and grass, often

found in swamps

veldt: a grassland region with some scattered bushes and virtually no trees; other terms are *steppe*, *pampas*, and *prairie*

ventral: on or near the belly; the ventral fin is located on the underside of a fish and corresponds

with the hind limbs of other vertebrates

vertebrates: any organism that has a backbone (spinal column)

watershed: the area of land that contributes water to a single stream or stream system, usually including the soil and

plants in the area because they can store water and affect water flow and water cycling in that landscape

woodland: a plant community in which trees grow abundantly but far enough apart that their crowns do not intermingle, so no overhead canopy is formed

INDEX

The scientific name of a plant or animal is entered in *italics*; its common name is in roman type. Page numbers in *italics* refer to picture captions.